Harassed

Harassed

GENDER, BODIES, AND
ETHNOGRAPHIC RESEARCH

Rebecca Hanson and Patricia Richards

UNIVERSITY OF CALIFORNIA PRESS

University of California Press, one of the most distinguished university presses in the United States, enriches lives around the world by advancing scholarship in the humanities, social sciences, and natural sciences. Its activities are supported by the UC Press Foundation and by philanthropic contributions from individuals and institutions. For more information, visit www.ucpress.edu.

University of California Press
Oakland, California

Library of Congress Cataloging-in-Publication Data

Names: Hanson, Rebecca, author. | Richards, Patricia, author.
Title: Harassed : gender, bodies, and ethnographic research / Rebecca Hanson and Patricia Richards.
Description: Oakland, California : University of California Press, [2019] | Includes bibliographical references and index. |
Identifiers: LCCN 2018049391 (print) | LCCN 2018055001 (ebook) | ISBN 9780520970953 () | ISBN 9780520299030 (cloth : alk. paper) | ISBN 9780520299047 (pbk. : alk. paper)
Subjects: LCSH: Sexual harassment of women. | Ethnographers— Social conditions.
Classification: LCC HD6060.3 (ebook) | LCC HD6060.3 .H36 2019 (print) | DDC 305.42—dc23
LC record available at https://lccn.loc.gov/2018049391Manufactured in the United States of America

26 25 24 23 22 21 20 19
10 9 8 7 6 5 4 3 2 1

CONTENTS

Acknowledgments vii

Introduction 1

1 · Ethnographic Fixations 25

2 · Gendered Bodies and Field Research 53

3 · Sexual Harassment in the Field 92

4 · The Costs 126

5 · Constructing Knowledge 154

6 · Moving Forward 175

Notes 195
References 215
Index 229

ACKNOWLEDGMENTS

When we started this project we intended to write an article based on our own experiences with sexual harassment and sexualization in the field. Then we decided to do a few interviews. A few interviews turned into almost sixty, and we realized that there were more things to be said on this issue than we could fit into one article; perhaps we would write two or three. But it was the encouragement we received over the course of developing this project that convinced us that this research could fill a book. All books are a collective endeavor, and here we would like to briefly acknowledge those who provided feedback and sustained us throughout the process.

Our heartfelt thanks to the women and men we interviewed for this project. Words of gratitude seemed to consistently fall short as we considered everything they contributed to this book. Our conversations with them were energizing and essential in generating the concepts and arguments contained herein. We are grateful for their time, enthusiasm for the project, and thoughtful reflections. We hope these chapters have done justice to the experiences they shared with us and that their experiences make fieldwork a bit less solitary for those who read about them.

We also thank Abbey Berghaus, Ashleigh McKinzie, Jeff Gardner, Britta Girtz, and Ashley Crooks-Allen for research assistance. Michelle Swagler, Chris Cuomo, and Liz Cherry provided valuable input at key moments early on in the project. We are grateful to Kirsten Dellinger, Patti Giuffre, Gloria González-López (special appreciation to Gloria for encouraging us to ask our participants about self-care), Ashleigh McKinzie, Pamela Neumann, Susan Paulson, Barbara Sutton, Justine Tinkler, and Christine Williams for reading and commenting on various parts of the manuscript. Thanks also to Laura Orrico, Corey Fields, and Elizabeth Hordge-Freeman for their valuable feedback at sessions we organized for the Sociologists for Women in Society (SWS) and American Sociological Association (ASA) meetings. The excitement these scholars and friends felt about this project continuously sustained us.

The questions and insights from attendees of various sessions at ASA and SWS conferences also helped us move this project forward. Special thanks to Katie Sobering and the Urban Ethnography Lab at the University of Texas at Austin; Natasha Borges Sugiyama at the Center for Latin American and Caribbean Studies and the Center for 21st Century Studies at the University of Wisconsin—Milwaukee; Christine Williams and the graduate student members of the Feminist Ethnography Project who organized the conference "Gender of Ethnography & the Ethnography of Gender" at the University of Texas at Austin; Menara Lube Guizardi and Karina Bidaseca at the Núcleo de Estudios de Género, Instituto de Altos Estudios Sociales, Universidad de San Martín in Buenos Aires; Christina Crespo and Samm Holder at the University of Georgia Department of Anthropology; and Shamus Khan at Columbia University. All of them hosted talks or organized workshops focusing on this project, and we greatly appreciate their efforts and the interest and perceptive reflections of people who attended these events.

At the University of California Press, we are grateful to Seth Dobrin for initially approaching us about this book, Naomi Schneider for her enthusiastic support from the beginning, and Benjy Malings for patiently answering all our inquiries. Gloria González-López and Junmin Wang provided valuable feedback as reviewers. And Sheila Berg was a truly stellar copy editor. Parts of the book appeared in initial form in an article in *Sociological Forum* in 2017.

Conceptualized together and entirely coauthored, this project has been perhaps the most satisfying either of us has ever worked on, both professionally and personally. Through talking with each other and to other researchers about the issues discussed in the book, we (hope to) have become more reflexive researchers and more supportive mentors ourselves. We are thankful for having had the opportunity to work on this together. Patricia also thanks Oscar, Menina, and Julio Chamosa for love, nourishment, and entertainment. Rebecca is indebted to Patricia but also to Veronica, Noida, Leo, and David, all of whom sustained her through the dissertation research that eventually catalyzed the writing of this book.

Introduction

IT SHOULD PERHAPS COME AS LITTLE SURPRISE that women researchers face sexual harassment and violence while conducting field research. Ethnographic research often entails traveling alone to new locations, taking an intense personal interest in the people there, and seeking to become a part of their daily lives. These very activities may later be used to explain, if not justify, the harassment and assault of women ethnographers. Some have even taken sexual harassment in the field as a "given," asking why women ethnographers would be treated differently than women in other social contexts. As Gary Alan Fine writes, "These obnoxious and brazen attempts at sexual acquaintanceship are part of the territory in a sexist world."[1]

Some researchers have reacted to unwanted attention and sexual advances in the field by publishing reflections on their experiences, in which they have proposed tips and strategies to help women prevent or at least negotiate sexual harassment in the field.[2] These reflections seek to give women tools to protect themselves but most often look to the worlds in which research is conducted to account for why women confront, and might acquiesce to, sexual harassment and advances, less often analyzing the field of academia in which researchers are embedded. Norms and practices within academia, which allow for and contribute to women's harassment and assault, have largely been ignored in discussions about violence against women and fieldwork. Assumptions that academia is a progressive safe haven—that violence is something that happens "out there," outside of the "civilized" spaces of academia—evidence the ongoing influence of colonialism within departments and disciplines. And although it is important to learn how to negotiate violence in the field, focusing on what happens "out there" structures conversations on sexual assault and harassment as a problem *women* must learn to deal with if they are to conduct research. The focus on sexism and gendered violence in our field sites ignores the fact that academia, too, is structured by patriarchy and obscures the legacies of sexism and other structures of inequality within it.

Because much of this literature focuses on individual fieldwork reflections, we lack a systematic analysis of the training, mentorship, and fieldwork narratives that construct sexual harassment in the field as a "given," just one more hardship worth navigating to gather good data.[3] In their review of methods books, Fran Markowitz and Michael Ashkenazi found that the few times that sex and sexuality were mentioned, "they were given short shrift or trivialized. Sexuality in the field was treated as a joke, brushed aside with funny anecdotes about how to avoid 'romantic encounters' or embarrassment."[4] Though there has been an increase in anthropological texts and courses on these issues, Markowitz and Ashkenazi acknowledge that including sex and sexuality in ethnography remains risky.

In this book, we use women's experiences with harassment in the field to interrogate the epistemological foundations of ethnographic methodology within sociology and related disciplines. Indeed, this methods book is novel in that it is based on empirical research conducted with qualitative researchers. Although we recognize that social norms and cultural codes in the social worlds we study inform experiences of harassment, our analysis situates the problem not in those worlds but rather in the academic community itself. We explore in detail the ethnographic standards that inform understandings of what "counts" as good research. Standards of solitude, danger and intimacy—which we refer to as "ethnographic fixations"—encourage researchers to endure various forms of violence in the field. As we show throughout this book, while women face sexual harassment and other forms of sexual violence more frequently, men also are encouraged to endure physical and emotional violence associated with expectations of hegemonic masculinity. These experiences are always mutually constituted by other structures of inequality as well, including race and heteronormativity. These standards shape ethnographic knowledge produced even by researchers who choose to transgress them, as they too seek to align their tales of the field with the standards by editing certain decisions, and the embodied interactions that informed them, out of vignettes and methods sections. As we discuss in chapter 6, many researchers edit embodied experiences out of their tales of the field, pushing them aside and into a category that Joan Fujimura has called "awkward surplus."[5] These experiences, which can be both difficult and risky to fit into our findings and theories, become superfluous stories, excess that must be cut to get at the "real" data.

This book intervenes at three levels. First, it fills a gap in the methodological literature on qualitative research. Experiences of sexual harassment in the field—and violence more broadly—and their implications for the construction of knowledge have not been sufficiently addressed in the methodological literature. This leaves students unprepared to confront these experiences while conducting research and to acknowledge their importance in the collection, analysis, and presentation of data. Rather than relegate these experiences to awkward surplus, we advocate for embodied reflexivity about these issues. Embodied reflexivity calls attention to aspects of our field sites and the people we study that are obscured by established procedures and dominant assumptions of ethnography. Second, this book comments on the current state of ethnography and delivers a call for changes in training, mentorship, writing, and recognition; in short, it demands a transformation of ethnography as a profession. We hope it will contribute to this transformation by challenging students and mentors to think about the principal tool of the qualitative researcher in the field—the body—and how it shapes research. While previous methods books have suggested that researchers relegate embodied experiences to "venting journals" or appendixes, this book calls on readers to incorporate embodiment throughout the research process, from proposal to research, analysis, and writing. Third, this book provides a case study on sexual harassment in academia at a time when sexual harassment charges are rapidly emerging in various occupations. These charges are being taken more seriously than they were in the past, resulting in resignations of men in positions of power, an outpouring of support for women's advocacy, and demands for change from Hollywood to the university. However, we argue that if efforts to reduce sexual violence are to succeed in academia, we must deconstruct the foundations of knowledge production in the social sciences and move beyond the restrictive categories and rules that limit how we conceptualize and understand the social world.[6] Our contributions, then, are a critique of the construction of ethnographic knowledge, a guide to conducting and writing embodied ethnography, and a demand for open recognition of the inequalities and oppression that continue to structure academic disciplines and universities.

In this introduction, we describe how we came to write the book and introduce the problem of embodiment and qualitative research. We explain how we use instances of unwanted sexual attention in the field to investigate this often-overlooked aspect of research. We contextualize fieldwork as an amorphous or dual workplace, shaped by the competing norms of academia and the ethnographic field, both of which can enforce conspicuous silences around sex and gender. We describe our interview method and discuss the variety of projects in which our participants were engaged, showing that embodiment is an important consideration for the production of all qualitative knowledge.

Our findings show that the ethnographic fixations on solitary, dangerous, and intimate research not only put researchers at risk but also have negative implications for the construction of ethnographic knowledge. They encourage researchers to edit gender and sexuality out of their fieldwork discussions and publications, thus contributing to a disembodied presentation of research, which is both ethically and epistemologically problematic.[7] We contribute to this body of work by arguing that writing the researcher out reproduces a concept of validity inherited from an androcentric, positivist, and colonial past that obscures the embodied nature of fieldwork. Furthermore, we show that although experiences are structured differently according to a researcher's positionality, these ethnographic fixations encourage researchers to adhere to a homogenized narrative of data collection. This narrative conceals the multiple paths ethnographers take to collect their data.

The silence surrounding sexual harassment is motivated by and reproduces norms that valorize certain types of fieldwork.[8] The internalization of these norms might explain why, despite evidence that sexual harassment of women researchers is common,[9] there is relatively little discussion of the topic in the profession outside of feminist circles. Our data show that few women realized they would face sexual harassment in the field and many were confused about what to do and how their mentors would respond to their reports. Most had not discussed these issues in their methods classes, and only a few had discussions with committee members about them before going into the field. If we assume, along with Fine, that sexual harassment in the field is just "part of the territory," then why do discussions about it remain marginal in methods classes? If sexual harassment is consistent and common among field researchers, then why is there such an absence in ethnographic narratives about this issue? We argue that this silence is indicative of a broader problem: the writing of researchers' embodied—and therefore raced and gendered—experiences out of qualitative research. By examining the experiences of women ethnographers, which have been marginalized in the dominant canon, we can identify and understand the underlying assumptions of ethnographic knowledge that obscure bodies in ethnographic narratives. Thus we do not focus on women's experiences because only knowledge produced by women is structured or negatively affected by these fixations. Rather, we analyze women's experiences to show how they are structured by gendered systems within academia.

It is because women's experiences are often excluded that they can operate as sites of transgression—in this case, of the ethnographic canon.[10] In her study of women's political practices in Northern Ireland, Begoña Aretxaga points out that women's bodies and experiences can constitute "irruptions[,] . . . disturbing presences that break the order of authorized historical narratives and in so doing raise questions about the nature of such order."[11] Though our study is not focused on the same political practices that Aretxaga examines, we use women's tales of the field in a similar way: to disrupt dominant field narratives and raise questions about the taken for granted assumptions that undergird ethnography. Following Barbara Sutton, we argue that women's embodied practices should be understood both as individual experience and as structured by underlying social relations of inequality.[12] Similarly, although Joan Scott warns against taking women's experiences as unquestioned evidence of social processes, she argues that analyzing these experiences can open up an inquiry into the production of subjectivities.[13] Examining how women are socialized into and reproduce hegemonic narratives and ideologies allows us to also analyze how domination and power operate in academia more broadly.

Rather than take experiences as evidence of difference or similarity, Scott argues, experience must be interrogated if we are to understand "how difference is established, how it operates, how and in what way it constitutes subjects who see and act in the world."[14] Thus we do not use women's experiences to suggest that there is a common thread that connects all women but to introduce difference into ethnographic research and writing. Methodologically, Dorothy Smith argues that a focus on "women's experience" is not an analytic homogenization but a means to challenge the "male" sociological gaze that preemptively writes women's existence out of its scientific narrative.[15]

At first glance, this book may appear more useful to researchers working in "dangerous" settings. However, only some of our participants did their research in what would be considered unsafe areas or on dangerous subjects. Others were working on topics such as music festivals, sports, and education that would not seem to be associated with threats to researchers. Some had spent years working in the field off and on, while others conducted shorter projects or ones that were interview based. The fact that researchers working on such distinct projects faced similar issues speaks to the need to discuss embodiment, danger, and sexual harassment with all students of qualitative research, regardless of their area of research or the amount of time they will spend in the field. We hope this book serves as a conversation starter for faculty and students, as well as a source of debate in sociology and other fields invested in the construction of ethnographic knowledge.

HOW WE CAME TO WRITE THE BOOK

This book has its roots in a conversation between the two authors, when Rebecca—on a break from her dissertation fieldwork—hesitantly admitted to Patricia that she had been experiencing near-constant sexual harassment throughout her time in the field. When she was conducting her research, Rebecca did not think about modifying her project or changing it altogether to lessen or avoid harassment. It did not occur to her that these options were available. Modifying or changing her project, she assumed, would reflect poorly on her as an ethnographer. Even talking to someone about the harassment would be professionally risky, she thought. In fact, it had taken more than six months for Rebecca to mention it to one of her committee members. When she did, she introduced it as a joke, laughing about the "awkward" situations she had experienced. However, when she discussed these experiences with Patricia, the conversation led the two to reflect on their experiences of harassment in the field and formulate the questions that provided the impetus for this study. This book is, in part, a response to these concerns.

We received overwhelming support from women who approached us after conference panels or contacted us after hearing about the project. These responses largely centered on one theme: sexual harassment was common and widespread, but few women felt comfortable talking about it publicly. Others acknowledged that it had never even occurred to them to talk about these experiences in relation to their fieldwork. The consistent outpouring of stories of sexual harassment in academia and in field sites sustained our belief throughout the writing process that there is a pressing need for this book.[16]

We seek to provide all ethnographers (regardless of gender) with alternative ways in which to think about their research and data, ways that evaluate modifications, changes, withdrawals, and boundaries as part and parcel of the research process. We want to reassure researchers that "falling short" of hegemonic ethnographic standards is as common as "falling short" of hegemonic standards of femininity and masculinity and to encourage our disciplines as a whole to rethink these standards and evaluate critically how we consciously and unconsciously reinforce them.

CRITIQUING ETHNOGRAPHIC METHODS

We recognize that there are multiple, competing, and mutually contesting ethnographic methodologies. As John Van Maanen notes in the second edition of his *Tales of the Field,* the literature on ethnography has expanded since the 1980s to such a degree that it is impossible to keep up with the "new theories, new problems, new topics, new concepts, and new critiques of older work."[17] Nevertheless, as Foucault argues, knowledge and its production occur within a dominant "episteme," his term for the conditions and prevailing beliefs that give power to certain forms of knowing and knowledge. Thus there are always dominant epistemological assumptions that "define the conditions of possibility of all knowledge, whether expressed in a theory or silently invested in a practice."[18] Similarly, Gramsci reminds us that hegemonic discourses, practices, and institutions, while contested, still allow dominant groups to shape society by claiming to represent "universal" or "neutral" interests.[19] This is why, despite the increasing diversity of ethnographic methods since the 1980s, the ethnographic fixations continue to give form to tales of the field. These fixations continue to be important in the minds of researchers because they "make sense" within the white, androcentric, and positivistic episteme that remains dominant. It is in this sense that we use the terms "dominant" and "hegemonic" throughout this book, keeping in mind that there are always alternative and subaltern forms of knowledge and knowledge production at play.

Nancy Scheper-Hughes has referred to the ethnographer mythologized since the nineteenth century as the "Victorian butler, always present and keenly observant, but invisible in his ministrations and empty of personal affect and passion."[20] To some extent, this myth continues to influence how sociologists think about conducting and evaluating the validity of ethnographic research. For instance, Michael Burawoy reminds us that Robert Park and the Chicago school championed the objective and detached character of ethnography.[21] As with other methodological approaches, the goal of ethnography was to understand human conduct through systematic scientific investigation, to reflect "without distortion the way the world is[,] . . .

corresponding to a reality that is 'out there' and unchanged by the human study of it."[22] As Norman Denzin has argued, even interpretivist schools like symbolic interactionism continue to struggle with this legacy.[23] Of course, these values were not the only ones, even during the heyday of the Chicago school. Jane Addams was integral to the founding of sociology in the United States, but she and those who worked with her were marginalized by the men of the Chicago school and conducted research and advocacy work at Hull House instead.[24] W. E. B. Du Bois began the Atlanta University Studies decades before the Chicago school emerged. In his research at Atlanta University, DuBois rejected the scientific objectivity that would be championed by the Chicago school, advocating instead for scholarship as activism.[25] Nevertheless, the values of the Chicago school became hegemonic. One need only look at the references to the Chicago school compared to the Atlanta school in undergraduate and graduate methods texts to confirm its eminence: between 1897—when the Atlanta University Studies began—and 1999, only three sociological analyses had been published on the school led by Du Bois.[26]

Over the past several decades, scholars influenced by postmodern and postcolonial thought, critical race theory, and feminism have critiqued the notion of the "objective" researcher. Their many contributions are too substantial to review in full, but we wish to draw attention to several key points, focusing in particular on feminist critiques.[27] Identifying a number of androcentric norms and masculinist biases that structure positivist social inquiry, feminist scholars have critiqued the concepts of objectivity and neutrality as first excluding and then marginalizing forms of knowledge that do not correspond with those of white elite men. They have highlighted the exclusion of certain spaces and actors from study,[28] the selection and definition of problems for inquiry,[29] and the delegitimization of the experiences of women and the validation of those of men as legitimate "knowledge" as evidence of androcentric norms that structure all aspects of the research process.[30]

Building on these critiques, Harding developed the notion of "strong objectivity."[31] Strong objectivity requires recognition of the situatedness of the researcher and a corresponding commitment to reflexivity, which demands that researchers "subject themselves to the same level of scrutiny they direct toward the subjects of their inquiry."[32] Recognizing multiple or partial truths, feminist scholars also have sought to dismantle the self/other and subject/object dichotomies. Other approaches, such as interpretivist and critical ones, have similarly challenged ethnography's positivist origins, drawing attention to how researchers' presuppositions shape the field of study,[33] as well as how dominant views of objectivity may reinforce power hierarchies.[34]

Some of these contributions are now broadly accepted as standard ethnographic practice, even as they are not always recognized as feminist contributions. (Certainly, they have multiple trajectories.) This is true in particular of the call for reflexivity about how multiple positionalities shape research processes, access, and outcomes. Nevertheless, our findings demonstrate that many women ethnographers, even those who are aware of these contributions, continue to evaluate their projects according to standards that obscure the gendered and sexual dynamics inherent in research. Furthermore, they anticipate that others will use these standards when evaluating their research projects. Indeed, it is important to keep in mind that most of our research participants were graduate students or assistant professors for whom, arguably, these standards should hold less weight given the proliferation of research methods and epistemologies. While we agree that there has been an overwhelming expansion in ethnographic approaches, we believe it is important to ask why certain standards continue to weigh on researchers *despite* the dizzying array of publications, presentations, blogs, and groups dedicated to the diversification and critiques of ethnography. Indeed, instead of holding less weight for those trained after methodological interventions made by feminist, critical race, poststructural, and postcolonial scholars, early career researchers are often most vulnerable to the pressure of abiding by hegemonic standards in the field even if, internally, they are critical of these standards.

To be clear, we are not advocating for approaches that turn research into an exposé of the ethnographer but for using embodied analysis and writing to explore and critique the production of gender, race, class, and so on within academia and our field sites. Embodied research and writing is not simply another call to include the self in research and writing. Practically, reflexive research that incorporates positionality does not require that researchers take center stage in their ethnographies. It does not require that we include positionality in all vignettes or analysis.[35] Rather, it is a call to think and write about how our bodies—the meanings, practices, and experiences that constitute them—are implicated in the research process. We are less focused on researchers writing their subjectivities into their research (though there is of course a place for this) and more concerned with using embodied experiences to "address the question of *how* these subject positionings affect knowledge construction."[36] Like Bourdieu, we call for a reflexivity that "focuses not on the individual sociologist as subject, but on the organizational and cognitive structures that shape sociologists' work."[37]

FIELDWORK AND INTERSECTIONALITY

This book is written from an intersectional perspective, and we encourage readers to think about how intersecting systems of power structure their academic and fieldwork experiences. Because we focus heavily on gender and how it intersects with other systems of domination, here we first provide a brief discussion of what we mean by "gender" and related terms and then address our understanding of intersectionality.

We start from the position that people are not born as women or men but instead become gendered persons. This "becoming" is made possible by both rigid gender structures and more flexible practices and meanings. Gender is both a social structure and a social construct, accomplished and performed through social interactions. Gender as social structure refers to a patterned social arrangement, a system that has been reproduced over time and is capable of giving form to "the individual, interactional, and institutional dimensions of our society."[38] Conceptualizing gender as structure does not mean denying the interactional dimensions of gender but recognizing how these come to be reinforced in ways that reproduce inequality. Indeed, as Leslie Salzinger points out, gender's defining characteristic is its dichotomous structure, which reproduces "two, unequal, othered categories" and the stratified distribution of resources and power.[39] These categories are intransigent and have changed relatively little over time; hence the classification as a structure.

Nevertheless, while gender categories have structural consequences, the content of these categories is variable, fluid, and constantly negotiated. Gender is produced, modified, and given meaning through discourse and performance. As Candace West and Don Zimmerman write in their formative article, gender is an accomplishment achieved through everyday performances in interaction.[40] According to Judith Butler, gender is "an identity tenuously constituted in time—an identity instituted through a stylized repetition of acts."[41] In this way, gender is "the appearance of substance[,] . . . a performative accomplishment which the mundane social audience, including the actors themselves, come to believe and perform in the mode of belief."[42]

Although we understand gender as performative—which allows for contestation and change—it is also performance, a performance that is assessed and for which actors are held accountable.[43] While individuals can contest and reinterpret gendered meanings, they are held accountable, and face repercussions, when they "do gender" in ways that rupture taken for granted scripts. These accountability mechanisms are, in turn, fundamental to understanding gender as structure, because they increase the probability that certain discourses and "stylized repetition of acts"[44] will be reproduced, generating patterns that maintain social structures. Doing gender in "appropriate" ways (which, of course, means different things in different contexts) is essential to conducting fieldwork, and this is a key component of the issues many of our participants faced in the field. In some cases, researchers may engage in performances that challenge gender essentialism, for example, if one wants to study drag culture. In other cases, the researcher might need to adhere to hegemonic femininity or masculinity, as would be the case if one were to research the Southern Baptist Church. Whether research means challenging or reproducing gendered meanings, ethnographers try to demonstrate that they are competent performers given the contexts in which they attempt to build relationships.

While expectations may vary in different academic fields (and depending on the location, history, and type of university and department), researchers must also perform gender in certain ways to get ahead in the academy. Thus, as we discuss in chapter 2, women may redact certain experiences with sexual harassment (in field sites and in academia) in order to avoid being labeled overly emotional and by extension, irrational and incompetent. These concerns suggest—unsurprisingly—that academic fields are structured by gendered inequality. Performing gender "appropriately" in some academic contexts can mean neutralizing signs that mark a body as feminine. Indeed, like the hegemonic ethnographic narrative that demands researchers present themselves as "passive vessels" in the field, rid of "enculturation, adult and gendered statuses, and desires, passions, comforts, and disgusts," similar narratives may hold true for women researchers when they return from the field to their academic departments.[45]

Like other scholars, we recognize gender and other aspects of embodiment as nuanced, complex, and fluid. Nevertheless, the fixations we discuss in this book and the broader systems of power in which they are embedded produce similarities across ethnographic narratives. Despite the fluidity and variability of gendered meanings, gendered categories are structured by inequality, an inequality that has historically worked to the advantage of those who identify and present themselves as white, straight, elite men. While we agree that gender can be unpredictable, inconsistent, contradictory, and fragmented, we argue that researchers receive signals (implicitly or explicitly) that they should produce a seamless narrative of fieldwork that is uninterrupted by researchers' bodies or by manifestations of inequality. By examining women's experiences in the field, we seek to undermine this "staying power," introducing ruptures and inconsistencies to hegemonic narratives.

In addition, gender is always also intersecting with race, class, heteronormativity, and other structures of inequality.[46] Our findings show that experiences of gender inequality in the ethnographic field (as well as the academic one) are mutually constituted by assumptions about race, nation, and sexuality in particular. Therefore, we cannot understand gender in the field without also understanding these other social structures and how they are reproduced in social interaction. The implications of intersectionality are various. It signals that a group of people (such as white women) might be oppressed on the basis of one category of domination but privileged, and thus capable of oppressing others, on the basis of other categories. It also signals that oppression on the basis of multiple categories (such as race, class, and gender) is not additive but rather a unique product of the ways those categories interact with, reinforce, or contradict one another. Moreover, as post- and decolonial feminists have indicated, feminist researchers are not exempt from the colonialist gaze. They also impose Western categories and skewed accounts of realities in the Global South.[47] Recent work by Maya Berry and colleagues and Bianca C. Williams shows how race, gender, and nation intersect in particular ways to shape the experiences of women of color in the field.[48] We are attentive to these intersectional experiences over the course of the book, highlighting how assumptions and expectations about whiteness, blackness, Latinas, Asians, and Muslims, as well as about LGBTQIA+ people, can lead to different gendered dynamics of harassment in the field.

In an attempt to avoid reifying gender categories, throughout this book we often use terms such as "gendered meanings" and "gendered practices" rather than "gender" alone, with the hope of reminding readers that gender does not exist outside of performance, discourse, and symbolic logics.[49] We refrain from using the biological and essentializing terms "male" and "female" except in a few cases, which are explained in context. Many of our research participants did use this terminology (unsurprising, given its ubiquity in everyday conversation), and in these cases we have left the phrasing unchanged.

We use Kloß's definition of sexual(ized) harassment as "coercive behavior, which may include gestures, actions, and other modes of verbal or nonverbal communication, with sexual connotations, which intimidate, humiliate, and exercise power over another person."[50] We define sexual assault as "any kind of sexual activity committed against another person without that person's consent—for example, vaginal, oral, or anal penetration, inappropriate touching, forced kissing, child sexual abuse, sexual harassment, or exhibitionism."[51] We do not use the term "attempted assault" because we do not see that this concept applies to actual experiences; it is a semantic sleight of hand. When victimizers are in the process of "attempting" to assault another person, they are assaulting them. "Attempt" here creates a false category that exists in no concrete place or time, as if the beginning stages of an assault do not count in the same way as what comes after. We use the term "rape" to refer to "penetration with the use of force and without the person's consent." Penetration may occur "in the vagina, anus, or mouth [and] can be committed with a body part or instruments such as bottles or sticks."[52]

Though we have agreed on precise definitions of these terms for the book, sexual harassment and sexualized interactions in the field involve a range of behaviors that elude simplistic definitions. And labeling of and subjective experiences with sexual harassment vary and are structured by race, class, gender, nationality, citizenship, age, and so forth.[53] Unsurprisingly, then, our participants often struggled with how to define harassment and other sexualized interactions in the field, noting that they left them feeling "uncomfortable." For example, a conversation that demeans or objectifies women might take place when the researcher is present, or body language might be sexual but not targeted directly at the researcher. We consider these covert forms of sexual harassment, even though participants were ambivalent about how to characterize them. In some cases, we use the term "sexualized interactions" to refer to experiences that do not necessarily reach the threshold for harassment; these might include unwelcome come-ons, compliments, or flirtation that the researcher was uncertain about how to handle in the field. In certain instances, we include kissing and touching in this category, rather than in the category of sexual harassment, because the research participant did not understand the experience as harassment. Likewise, some researchers enjoyed come-ons from some participants and saw flirtation as a pleasant interaction. In some cases, women rejected advances not because they were unwanted but out of ethical concern as researchers. Indeed, though not within the purview of this book, ethnography must recognize researchers as sexual beings, not only sexualized beings, an issue we briefly discuss in chapter 3.

FIELDWORK AS DUAL WORKPLACE

We conceptualize fieldwork as a dual or amorphous workplace. Fieldwork is constitutive of our academic careers, and what we do in the field is shaped by scholarly norms and expectations, as well as the norms and expectations that structure the social worlds we study. The norms and expectations of these overlapping fields can come into conflict. For example, many of our participants expected that they would be treated as professionals while they conducted fieldwork, that their credentials would garner respect and, thus, protect them. But this often was not the case. Fieldwork takes place at the interstices of the public and the private, opening up the possibility for violation of boundaries between the professional and the personal. Our participants reported being objectified, mistreated, and regarded as innocent, naive, and dumb and confronting the same sexual dynamics that many women do in their daily lives. Although there are mechanisms in place that women can use to report harassment and abuse in academia (however inadequate they may be), there are often no institutions through which to seek justice when they are harassed and abused in the field. Moreover, social rules about navigating and responding to violence and sexual harassment can be difficult to ascertain in an unfamiliar cultural context.

These experiences were often compounded by conflicting messages within academia. Students might be given sexual harassment training or required to sign a code of conduct that bars harassment and discrimination, but, as our data show, they are almost never provided with guidelines in their ethnography and other methods courses for how to handle these behaviors when they occur in the field. Students also may be told that being a "good ethnographer" means "sucking it up" and doing "whatever it takes" to get the data. In this context, many participants perceived that talking about harassment in the field could discredit the researcher and put her professional relationships and career at risk. Similarly, in academia, where "credentials are everything," women's credentials can be marred by public disclosures of harassment and abuse.[54] Indeed, some participants reported deciding to smile and go along with harassment from professors and mentors rather than report it. The underlying message is similar across academia and field sites: talking about harassment is neither welcome nor appropriate. This creates a workplace scenario in which it is very difficult to know how to deal with harassment and violence more generally.

Gender itself is produced in the workplace, and sexual harassment is often a central component of this process.[55] In academia, gender is produced through training, mentorship, and coursework—all of which can be thought of alongside guidelines or employee manuals—in ways that leave researchers unprepared to navigate and acknowledge sexualized harassment when it occurs in the field. Writing on the reproduction of white logic in academia, John Clausen observed that sociologists are socialized to "accept, internalize, and act as though the prevailing norms of the role to which [they are] aspiring 'has validity for [them].'"[56] Similarly, and like other workplaces, students are socialized to internalize norms that ignore gender. This is not to negate that the workplace is an important site of gender production. Rather, it is to say that the construction of gender in the workplace and the gendered performances that we engage in are not acknowledged as such. The denial that academia is a workplace like any other—where gender as structure divides bodies and assigns them to unequal categories—has been well captured by recent responses after sexual harassment accusations against (mostly) men academics began to trickle into and then flood news and social media.[57] Accounts from students and faculty members suggest that harassment is just as common in academia as in other workplaces. Nevertheless, our study shows that these "it doesn't happen here" mores filter into the training of graduate students, resulting in little guidance on how to deal with harassment in the ethnographic field and leading them to avoid talking about it openly for fear that they will be judged and their work considered invalid if they do.

EMBODIMENT AND QUALITATIVE RESEARCH

Ethnographic training and writing continues to be "disembodied." This, we argue, is because bodies (particularly those that look different from those of white men) present problems for neutrality, validity, and objectivity within the positivist tradition. In 1974 Dorothy Smith observed that it was precisely the association between women and the mundane particularities of daily existence (which often includes caring for others' bodies) that allowed men to exclude women from producing the objective and abstract knowledge revered in sociology.[58] Intersectional approaches that go beyond Smith's work show how not only sexism but also racism, classism, and colonialism exclude certain people from knowledge production on the basis of the meanings assigned to their embodiment.[59] While women of color inhabit social positions that allow them to better understand the interlocking nature of oppression,[60] these same scholars are often delegitimized as hypersensitive, overly emotional, and biased.[61] Negative associations between scholars' bodies and knowledge have undoubtedly been challenged over the past several decades. Nevertheless, as we show, researchers are still encouraged to leave out particularities of daily existence that bring bodies into our work.

To redress this absence, we call for embodied ethnography, ethnography that not only recognizes bodies as tools to get closer to the worlds of research participants but also takes seriously the presupposition that all data and knowledge emerge from experiences, conversations, and interactions shaped by the bodies that engage in them. Indeed, collapsing the mind-body duality and showing that all knowledge is embodied are principal aims of this book. In this section, we briefly summarize the literature that influences our concept of embodied ethnography.

First, we understand bodies as historically situated and constituted by power relations; there is no interior essence separate from the social that gives bodies meaning. According to Foucault, bodies are controlled, worked upon, and maintained by power and molded through daily practices in institutions.[62] The work done on bodies creates certain forms of identification and categorization but also forms of thinking, feeling, and expressing. Feminist theorists have also conceptualized the body as the product of power, more specifically, power that reproduces patriarchal, androcentric, racist, and heteronormative systems and institutions.[63]

While keeping in mind that bodies are constituted by systems of power, we are also interested in the gaps and contradictions created by the production of gendered bodies and the lived experiences of researchers as gendered, racialized subjects. Phenomenological and feminist traditions have both focused on lived experience, as a methodological and an epistemological approach. From phenomenological theory we adopt the concept "being-in-the-world," a "temporally / historically informed sensory presence and engagement."[64] These experiences of being-in-the-world cannot be retold or examined without including how our bodies experience being: our sensations, our emotions, our movements, and our viscerality. Bodies are energized, scarred, emboldened, mortified, repulsed, warmed, energized, and desensitized as we fumble into the social worlds that we study.[65] Including visceral descriptions of participants' social worlds cannot be limited to what these worlds feel like to them but must also include what being in these worlds does to us as researchers.

Finally, reflexive research must be grounded in an awareness of our bodies—what they mean to us as well as what they mean to others. Reflexive research can only exist where we consider the social relations—within the academy as well as the ethnographic field—that make possible social scientific inquiries and claims, the same social relations that structure who gets to make these inquiries and claims in the first place.[66] To move away from disembodied, colonialist, and androcentric research, ethnographers must reflect on how and why their bodies fit into (or disrupt) the places they study, situating their being-in-the-world within the power dynamics that constitute all social worlds.

Embodied ethnography, then, is not just about including embodied experience in our work, but grounding these experiences in the social conditions that allow them to occur. As Mary Steedly has noted, "Experience is that which is at once most necessary and most in need of examination."[67] Indeed, a main contention of this book is that paying attention to what happens to our bodies in the field is a form of data collection. How others respond to our bodies, where we are allowed to go and with whom we are allowed to associate, and the types of violence and dangers we experience while conducting research all tell us about the systems of power that structure our field sites. If bodies are tools of research, then we must consider how these tools structure daily experiences, which eventually become ethnographic data, facts, and knowledge. Embodied ethnography includes understanding our bodies as objects out in the world, objects to which meanings are assigned, objects that are perceived and treated differently according to these meanings, and objects that elicit distinct feelings and responses in others. Finally, as Nancy Naples has written:

> An embodied perspective (one that is tied to particular social locations and particular positions in a community) emphasizes how researchers' social positions (not limited to ones gender, race, ethnicity, class, culture, and place or region of residence) influence what questions we ask, whom we approach in the field, how we make sense of our fieldwork experience, and how we analyze and report our findings.[68]

In short, a fully embodied approach begins with research design and extends to analysis and writing.

Taking these steps can be unsettling, as they rupture the way in which scholars understand themselves as creators of knowledge. Even scholars who are women and/or people of color, who cannot lay claim to hegemonic knowledge creation in the way elite white men can, may struggle in adopting ethnographic practices and narratives that more closely map onto their experiences. This struggle is undoubtedly compounded by these scholars' structural locations in the university, where a precarious hold on academic legitimacy discourages them from speaking out against hegemonic narratives. Nevertheless, while bodies are the creation of multiple forms of domination, they are also, as feminist theorists have argued, the terrain upon which the subversion of domination can be carried out.[69] Incorporating our bodies into research and writing, we hope, will contribute to a questioning and, eventually, dislodging of hegemonic narratives that reproduce oppression and inequalities in academic departments and disciplines.

METHODS

We carried out fifty-six in-depth interviews for this study, which was approved by our university Institutional Review Board (IRB). These interviews are supplemented by our own conversations regarding these issues. Interviewees were recruited via calls for participants sent out to several listservs and also through snowball sampling. Most participants were graduate students or early assistant professors. A few were more seasoned associate professors. The majority were sociologists, although several anthropologists and some scholars from other disciplines were interviewed. All but one had conducted fieldwork within the past ten years. Most had done so much more recently, and a few were still in the field. Roughly half of our participants conducted research in the United States and half in other countries (mostly in the Global South). This was intentional. We wanted to avoid contributing to a stereotypical view that the extent to which sexual harassment occurs in the field depends on misunderstandings or clumsy encounters between "backward" men from the Global South and naive gringa researchers.

Forty-seven participants were cisgender women, including 29 white / anglo women and 18 women of color (5 Asian Americans, 8 Latinas, 2 black women, 1 Muslim American, and 2 women of mixed race / ethnicity).[70] Thirteen identified as lesbian, bisexual, or queer; 4 did not report their sexual orientation; and the remainder identified as heterosexual / straight (with a few of these identifying as fluid or "mostly" straight). After starting with a sample consisting entirely of women, we interviewed 9 men in order to help clarify some of our theoretical ideas and avoid essentialist traps. Of these, 6 were white / anglo, 2 were Latino / Latin American mestizo, and 1 was of mixed race / ethnicity. Six of the men were cisgender straight / heterosexual, and 3 identified as gay or queer. One individual was trans. We purposefully sought a diverse sample on the basis of race / ethnicity and sexual identity / gender expression because we anticipated that experiences of the sexualized fieldwork context would be shaped by these factors as well. Our experiences also informed the writing of this book, and in the spirit of embodied ethnography, we have included these as data. At the time that we began this project, Rebecca's experiences were those of a white, cisgender bisexual PhD sociology student just back from the field. Patricia is a straight, cisgender, white professor of sociology and women's studies. We did not ask participants to discuss all aspects of their positionalities; most glaringly, perhaps, we did not ask participants if they self-identified as able-bodied, an omission that speaks to how occupying privileged social locations (in this case, being able-bodied, a position that both authors share) can blind us to research questions and the lived experiences of those that diverge from our own. And although our sample does include LGBTQIA+ researchers, more systematic interviews with that community are important as scholars move forward with this and similar research. We did not conduct systematic interviews with men of color. While we interviewed two Latino / Latin American mestizo men and one man of mixed race / ethnicity, we did not interview any Asian American or black men. It must be acknowledged that men of color's embodiment carries distinct and more severe costs than the embodiment of white men: they are also an "other" to the hegemonic "neutral" ideal researcher, and their experiences and insights would have undoubtedly revealed implications and costs associated with ethnographic fixations that did not arise in interviews with women. We therefore want to note here the importance of recognizing that the "neutral" researcher is not only embodied as male but also as white, and we hope other researchers will pursue this line of inquiry in the future.

The types of objectification, sexualization, sexual harassment, and/or assault experienced by participants covered a wide spectrum, as did the degree. Some reported having to deal with these issues infrequently. Others faced them on a daily basis. Some navigated light flirtation, sexual banter, or frequent comments on their physical appearance. Many were asked out, propositioned, or touched without giving their permission. Others were physically assaulted, and one was raped. Most experienced various forms and degrees of these behaviors.

Each coauthor conducted roughly half of the interviews, which usually lasted between one and two hours. Most interviews took place via Skype, although whenever possible we conducted them in person. Interview questions focused on issues of trust, power, and building relationships in the field, experiences of unwanted sexual attention, and methodological training. Although all interviews were coded separately by both authors, we checked our interpretations and codes with each other in many conversations during the coding process. In these conversations we noted a high degree of overlap between our codes and were thus able to come to an agreement on salient themes and processes emerging from the interviews.

Interview excerpts included here have been edited for clarity (generally, fillers like "um," "like," and "you know" and repetitions have been removed). Participants are identified by pseudonym. We have tried to provide some contextualizing information while protecting anonymity. For most participants, we have included racial identification and location in their academic career. When race is not specified, it is to protect the participant's identity. Other identifying characteristics generally have been omitted, unless they are particularly important to understand the analysis at hand. Likewise, we have avoided referring to precise locations and overly specific topics of research. In some cases, participants specifically asked that particular identifying characteristics be withheld; Michelle asked that we not reveal any characteristics that could identify her. Although this may cloud clarity in a few cases, it was imperative to honor these requests for the security of our participants. Because of the sensitivity of some of the subject matter, we sent all excerpts and contextualizing details to participants prior to publication in order to ensure their comfort with the level of confidentiality provided.

We refer to our interviewees as men and women because this is how they identified. The vast majority of our sample is cisgender. Where we refer to women and men, however, we ask readers to keep in mind that these are socially constructed categories that ground our participants' identities and the meanings they and others attach to their bodies. Though gender is not natural or biological, it is taken for granted in everyday interactions and was sometimes discussed using essentialist language in our interviews.

Finally, many of our participants faced issues that have historically been problematic for ethnographers, particularly in regard to studying the other, representation, and the reproduction of colonialism. Our participants were sensitive to these issues and often found themselves confounded by worries about how they might reproduce stereotypes if they reported having experienced sexual harassment in the field.[71] This is perhaps one of the messier issues confronted by our participants, especially those whose work involved traveling from the Global North to the Global South. Participants in some (though not all) cases expected that they would be treated like professionals, somehow absolved from local power relations and gender norms. Although this did occur in some cases,[72] this expectation reflects the colonialist legacy of ethnography and the assumption that researchers can somehow stand above and beyond the community they study. Ethnographers are of course drawn into local power dynamics, including gendered ones. At the same time, many participants were trained to recognize and compensate for the power they would exert by their very presence over people in their field sites. This often worked against reporting or even resisting unwelcome sexualized behavior in the field. This training, however, does not necessarily encourage researchers to consider why we think we have the right to be in the field in the first place and why our bodies should be accepted there—both questions precluded by the colonialist assumptions that continue to be pervasive in academia.[73] Thus these competing forces—a sensitivity to power and the place of ethnography in a postcolonial world, ongoing expectations for the revered position of the ethnographer, the desire to be sensitive to local norms, and a desire to avoid harassment and assault—all combined to create various dilemmas for our participants.

PLAN OF THE BOOK

This book makes applied as well as theoretical interventions; the theory informs the methodological practices for which we advocate. In chapters 1 and 5 we present critiques of ethnographic epistemology and put forth a theory and practice of embodied ethnography as an alternative to this androcentric, positivistic epistemology. Chapters 2 through 4 can be considered the nuts and bolts sections, where we develop practical applications for researchers. In these chapters, we include illustrative vignettes and specific takeaways for students as well as advanced researchers. These chapters also include questions and discussion topics to inspire conversations about harassment (as well as other potential risks), embodiment, and research. These discussions will be useful in preparing new ethnographers for challenges they may face in the field, how to deal with them, and how to include them in their writing.

In chapter 1 we present and examine the standards of contemporary ethnography that inform ethnographers' reactions to interactions in the field. These standards are woven throughout and connect the subsequent chapters. We develop the concept of ethnographic fixations as a way to theorize about the silence surrounding sex, gender, and bodily production in the field. Drawing from women ethnographers' understandings of and reactions to harassment in the field, we identify three intersecting standards—solitude, danger, and intimacy—that our participants made recourse to when talking about disciplinary expectations for the "best" ethnographic research. Two interrelated institutional and structural explanations that we propose contribute to understanding why these fixations might have stuck with the women we interviewed, becoming particularly salient when negotiating problems in the field. We argue that the ongoing dominance of the positivist and androcentric perspective in academia has a silencing effect on researchers and that women ethnographers may interpret their own experiences as evidence of "polluted" research, worrying that the validity of their work will be called into question. Having demonstrated the need to move beyond these underpinnings, the following chapters challenge researchers to think about traditional concepts like access, power, and documentation from an embodied perspective.

Chapter 2 focuses on access, trust, and building relationships in the field from an embodied perspective. The goal of this chapter is to consider three issues. First, we look at how expectations in the academic field encourage researchers to adhere to "neutral," disembodied narratives of the ethnographic field. Second, we analyze how embodiment and stereotypes of different types of bodies result in distinct opportunities and drawbacks over the course of fieldwork for all researchers. And third, we engage with issues of flirtation and sex in the field, topics that tend to be overlooked in methods books and courses. At the end of the chapter, we discuss ways to present embodied ethnographic and interview data. Chapter 3 documents the spectrum of our participants' experiences with sexual harassment and sexualization in the field and describes the coping strategies they used, addressing which were successful and which were not. In this chapter, we encourage students to think about how the three ethnographic fixations contribute to and shape research. We provide examples of a range of behaviors confronted by our participants, from flirtation and come-ons to attempted assault and, in one case, rape. We examine the different resources researchers have to draw on in navigating danger due to these differences. Chapter 3 also addresses how participants ultimately dealt with their experiences, exploring three common approaches: abandoning the project, modifying it, and suffering through it. It includes discussion questions encouraging readers to consider how their own identities might shape the harassment and other forms of danger they could encounter in the field and the resources they have to address it.

While previous methods texts and articles have focused on the effects we can have on the field and our participants, we examine in chapter 4 the effects fieldwork can have on the researcher. We do so by analyzing the consequences of attempting to meet the three fixations for individual researchers. We address an often-overlooked issue: how participants' power and positionalities affect the researcher. Individual researchers report emotional and psychological costs (self-blame, feelings of inadequacy, emotional splits, etc.) as well as material and physical costs (ranging from the bodily effects of assault to the potential career consequences if they are open about their experiences of harassment and other unwelcome sexual advances in the field). We show that gendered expectations and fieldwork experiences often make women ethnographers complicit in the reproduction of gender hierarchies. At the end of the chapter we discuss strategies that could help researchers navigate these costs without suggesting that they can be avoided.

In chapter 5 we focus on the consequences of ignoring embodiment for the construction of ethnographic knowledge. We draw on Joan Fujimura's concept "awkward surplus" to suggest that interactions that bring sex, gender, and the body to the fore often become residual data or are ignored altogether. Furthermore, we argue that calls for reflexivity have paradoxically resulted in only a superficial acknowledgment of the effects embodiment has on fieldwork. We conclude by arguing that all ethnographic work is shaped by researchers' gender, sexuality, and corporality, and suggest that a more open discussion of how these dynamics contribute to the production of ethnographic knowledge would lead to better, more complex and nuanced ethnographies. We provide examples that will motivate students to discuss whether or not the three fixations we critique in the book remain valuable. We end by discussing how to integrate "surplus" data into analysis and writing.

The celebration of danger, solitude, and intimacy as the means by which ethnographers collect the most illuminating data communicated to many of our participants that there is only one path to a worthwhile ethnographic contribution. In chapter 6, we argue that there is a multiplicity of ways that high-quality fieldwork is carried out and that our narratives and evaluations of ethnography should support and reflect this diversity. We critically engage with the three fixations, proposing several approaches to rethinking their utility and reducing their influence in the academic field. We call for ethnographers to stop fixating on danger, the solitary researcher, and intimacy in order to provide more complex tales of the field as well as prioritize researchers' lives over the data they gather. Our bodies, we argue, should not be considered drawbacks or points of critique but should be incorporated into our analysis and writing in order to strengthen the validity of our work. All research is embodied and, in this final chapter, we suggest how mentors can teach research methods as such and how researchers can acknowledge this crucial aspect of knowledge production in their writing. We also situate our work as part of broader efforts to challenge the culture of silence and legitimation surrounding sexual and other forms of harassment in our disciplines.

ONE

Ethnographic Fixations

IN THIS CHAPTER WE USE WOMEN'S EXPERIENCES WITH harassment in the field to interrogate the epistemological foundations of ethnographic methodology, examining the standards of contemporary ethnography that inform ethnographers' reactions to interactions in the field. Although we recognize that social norms and cultural codes in the social worlds we study inform experiences of harassment, our analysis situates the problem not in those worlds but rather in the academic community itself. Our findings show that women who have experienced sexual harassment while conducting fieldwork call upon particular standards of ethnographic research to explain why they find it difficult to confront these experiences both in the field and in their disciplines, believing that doing so could be detrimental to their careers.

We develop the concept "ethnographic fixations" as a way to theorize why sex, gender, and the body are often left out of tales of the field. We use women ethnographers' understandings of and reactions to harassment in the field to identify three intersecting standards—solitude, danger, and intimacy—that our participants made recourse to when talking about disciplinary expectations for the "best" ethnographic research. We analyze these standards as "ideological forms," a term coined by Dorothy Smith, and argue that they should be understood as "fixations" because of the importance placed on them by the women we interviewed and their perception that they are fundamental in the larger sociological community.

We propose that the ongoing dominance of positivist, racist, and androcentric perspectives in academia has a silencing effect on women researchers, who worry that the validity of their work will be called into question if they discuss gendered and sexualized experiences. The internalization of norms predicated on homogenized field narratives might explain why, despite evidence that sexual harassment of women researchers is common,[1] there is little discussion of the topic in the profession outside of feminist circles.

IDEOLOGICAL FORMS AND THE
CONSTRUCTION OF KNOWLEDGE

It is somewhat ironic that in what might be described as the heyday of thinking about the body in ethnography, many women feel, for good reason, that what happens to their bodies and how they are perceived in the field are not appropriate topics to include in their ethnographies. This project has led us to question why—despite the diversification of ethnographic methods, the introduction of feminist ethnography, and multiple critiques of the historical roots of ethnography—discussions of gender, sexuality, and sexualization remain at the margins of ethnography. Why, despite the embracing of embodiment, are women reticent to discuss what happens to their own bodies while conducting research? We argue that the fixations we describe in this chapter remain dominant within ethnography, reproducing androcentric expectations about how fieldwork should be conducted, presented, and represented.

The standards used to evaluate ethnographic knowledge (and how that knowledge is created) are not natural or objective; they were constructed by groups with particular interests, positionalities, and experiences. Though formed by political, material, and symbolic interests and subjective experiences, once accepted as standards, they become "disinterested,"[2] "objective," and universally applied. And once taken as universal standards for knowledge production, they provide unitary and unifying narratives, covering over the diverse and multifaceted experiences of groups within academia.

Dorothy Smith used the term "ideological forms" to refer to the process by which the subjective experiences of a dominant group become the standard by which members of less powerful social groups navigate and evaluate their experiences and knowledge.[3] Smith draws from the Marxian concept of ideology to argue that ideas and images are imposed on and adopted by others whose perspectives, interests, and experiences are not represented by those ideas and images. According to Smith, ideological forms within academia are produced by educated middle- and upper-class men who occupy positions that allow them to construct and control ideas, images, and representations. Similar to Gramsci's concept of hegemony, Smith argues that these forms operate as a normative commonsensical guide, becoming taken-for-granted assumptions about how knowledge ought to be constructed, and by whom. The concept of ideological forms is useful for analyzing the three fixations we present throughout the book; indeed, these fixations can be understood as ideological forms that structure ethnographic methodology. These fixations emerged from white men's experiences of conducting ethnography—men who originally came and often still come from colonizing countries to study colonized places—and leave out alternative standards and forms of evaluation that do not make sense within these academic norms.

As in other communities, disciplinary norms and standards (i.e., ideological forms) shape individuals' behavior and understanding of their experiences. However, it need not be the case that researchers are explicitly told in methods classes and articles to leave sexuality and gender out of their fieldwork narratives. In other words, norms and standards do not have to be explicitly stated to influence behavior and understandings; one could argue that the most effective norms and standards are those that no longer need to be stated and explained. The fact that gender and sexuality are frequently left out of methods courses and ethnographies can also communicate that they do not belong in our tales of the field. Such silences may guide behavior without any direct signs from mentors or colleagues.[4] The lack of discussion about how gendered bodies shape research relationships, data collection, and fieldwork experiences reproduces the idea that these topics need not be discussed. This "vocal silence" can help us understand how experiences that appear so obvious are easily elided as we prepare for the field.[5]

Understanding fixations as ideological forms also helps us explain why gender, sex(uality), and the body continue to be largely ignored despite the fact that ethnographic methods have diversified and the number of women in the social sciences has increased dramatically since Dorothy Smith's time. Our data show that despite the development of feminist methodologies, women's experiences of harassment and sexualization in the field are shoved aside, marked as unimportant and irrelevant to the construction of knowledge. Scholars including Kimberly Kay Hoang, Mignon Moore, Aldon Morris, and Victor Rios have similarly shown how the fieldwork experiences of men and women of color are trivialized, ignored, and interrogated to a greater extent than those of white researchers and subordinated to the ingrained racism of hegemonic sociology.[6] As we show throughout this book, harassment faced by women of color in the field is shaped by the intersections of race and gender expectations and stereotypes.[7] And LGTBQIA+ researchers are likely to face forms of discrimination and marginalization related to gender as well as trans / homophobia and other structures of inequality. While feminist, critical race, and intersectional methodologies exist, we should not assume that these have the same power within academia as traditional methodologies. As Smith has written, "Authority is a form of power which is a distinctive capacity to get things done in words. What is said or written merely means what the words mean until and unless it is given force by the authority attributed to the author. When we speak of authority we are speaking of what makes what one person says count."[8] While there may be more room in academia now for voices from marginalized groups, this does not necessarily mean that what members of these groups say "counts." This is especially true when their voices critique knowledge and knowledge production based on the androcentric, racist, and heteronormative norms that have long structured the university. Furthermore, inequalities do not simply disappear with increased access to the academic workplace. To say that standards are taken for granted is to say that many practitioners consent to these standards and recognize them as important. In other words, women participate in the reproduction of and reverence for ideological forms and fixations.

THE THREE FIXATIONS

The multiplication of ethnographic methodologies has allowed for diversification of standards to evaluate good data and trustworthy fieldwork. Nevertheless, in explaining their experiences in the field and how they dealt with them, participants consistently returned, explicitly or implicitly, to three ideological forms that they understood as widely held by the larger ethnographic community. Although contested, these ethnographic fixations are deeply woven into the history of ethnographic methods. In this section, we examine these fixations—solitude, danger, and intimacy—arguing that they obscure the embodied character of fieldwork and take on particular importance as women ethnographers think about how their work will be evaluated by others.

Solitary Research

According to Lisa Wedeen, ethnography has historically been considered a practice of suffering, as the ethnographer weathers the hardships of another culture to exist as the "expert *in situ*."[9] Although we agree with Wedeen, we would add that there is another key assumption regarding this suffering—that the ethnographer will endure it alone. Many of our participants conceptualized ethnography as an individual endeavor, sometimes making reference to the ideal researcher as "a brave and solitary adventurer conjured up by Malinowski's descriptions of his fieldwork," reflecting a belief that to be a good ethnographer one must enter the field alone and cope with the dangers and emotional difficulties that may arise.[10] Elena, a Latina who is now an associate professor, described an occasion when, as a young graduate student carrying out fieldwork in Mexico, she turned down an invitation to dance at a party in the small community where she was working. Later that night, the man, accompanied by some others, came to the house where she lived alone. He attempted to enter, presumably intending to assault her. She managed to open a window and scream, and her neighbors came to help. Elena never told anyone except her husband about this experience. She reflected, "I think the idea at that time with anthropologists is that you have to be on your own, basically. And I felt that I needed to deal with it." This feeling was most likely informed by what Elena referred to as an assumption on her committee's part that because of her ethnicity she could deal with any problem that arose. Though she is not Mexican, Elena felt they assumed, "You are Latina, you should be fine in any other Latin context."

Elena's belief that she "needed to deal with it" suggests an understanding of ethnography as a process of "trial by fire" or a "Malinowskian . . . test of competence," as if withstanding the difficulties of conducting ethnographic research alone is what makes one a good qualitative scholar.[11] Others agreed. This position has consequences, however, for what kind of support ethnographers are able to seek. Brittany, a white woman conducting research on historical reenactments, saw reaching out to mentors while in the field as "weakness." While discussing challenges she faced following feminist methodology while in the field, she said, "That was the, that was just a, a very difficult thing for me. . . . Maybe when you're, especially at the student level, . . . these are things that you don't want to bring up with your mentors because you don't want to show that weakness. . . . So I think there's a little bit of loneliness out there when you're doing your ethnography." Rosie, a white PhD student studying gender expression at music festivals in the United States did seek support (though not from her adviser) when she was threatened. At the beginning of her research she would pitch her tent and stay alone at campgrounds. One night, she asked the men in a neighboring tent to quiet down so she could fall asleep. They verbally threatened her, and she relocated to her locked car for the night. After this interaction, she brought men friends along when she went into the field. However, Rosie was uneasy about this decision. She felt she was cheating. She explained, "I feel as if somehow I am creating this methodological flaw. . . . It feels as if I am tampering with the data or tampering with some sort of methodological process [by] having some other people around." Here we see how the fixation of solitude operates as an ideological form, a taken for granted assumption that informs Rosie's understanding of how to conduct good research but does not reflect her embodied experience of fieldwork.

As Maritza, a Latina urban ethnographer pointed out, the isolation of fieldwork can compound problems related to sex and gender in the field because there is almost no way of knowing if others are experiencing similar problems. Sofía, a Latina professor studying sexuality in Latin America, talked about the importance of not isolating yourself in the field, even though she recognized a tendency to do so. She explained:

> I think that, because I was so far, and this happens to some of our students as well, you tend to isolate yourself. And that's a big no-no. You need to talk to people, you need to process, you need to, you know? Because if you go to the field and then you're doing your work the problem is that you think that you're supposed to know what to do. And then you're so embarrassed to come and talk to someone who may not even have the answer. I mean, not even your mentors may know. They may even be in a state of shock when you tell them what's happening to you. I think that in retrospect I would definitely talk more to people. I would not isolate myself.

Sofía's reflection illuminates the cycle of isolation in which researchers can become trapped. When methods courses do not cover issues of gender, sex(uality), and embodiment, researchers will encounter things in the field for which they are unprepared. However, because many believe "you should know what to do anyway," as Sofía put it, they worry about reaching out to others, thinking they should know how to deal with the hand the field has dealt them. However, Sofía's and Maritza's reflections highlight the importance of talking to others, even if they cannot provide solutions to problems. By talking to others, ethnographers can fight back against the isolation that, as Maritza observed, individualizes challenges faced in the field.

Feminist researchers have advocated for collaborative research,[12] and group ethnographies are now more common.[13] However, our findings suggest that the image of the "intrepid ethnographer"—who enters *his* site alone to fully immerse *himself* in his surroundings, contaminating them as little as possible—remains indelibly imprinted on the ethnographic imaginary.[14] This myth remains influential despite the fact that early ethnographers, most of whom were men, are known to have been assisted in the field by their wives or "native" research assistants, both of which seem to have been understood as appendages of the ethnographer self (thus reinforcing the idea that the ethnographers did it alone).

The valorization of solitary fieldwork does not exist only in the minds of the researchers we interviewed. It was reinforced in their coursework and by the ethnographies commonly held up as exemplars in their disciplines. The doling out of material support for research and academic rewards and accolades also structures research this way. As Helen Sampson and Michelle Thomas have written, in many cases "the proliferation of contract research and current mechanisms for research funding militate against" the researcher's ability to remain connected to the outside world while in the field.[15] In the case of graduate students, most grants, fellowships, and stipends seek to fund an individual researcher, making collaborative research virtually impossible. And when students are encouraged to make contact with others working in the same location, an underlying apprehension about being scooped often informs those interactions.

The few participants who engaged in collaborative research (usually as part of an adviser's project) spoke about how this strategy could preemptively close down uncomfortable flirtation and harassment. Yet, although students may be assigned group projects in methods classes, collaborative research is not an option for dissertations, and students can rarely afford to hire research assistants. Cathy, a white researcher who conducted fieldwork for her dissertation in Mexico, reflected that having a research assistant would have made her work easier. However, she followed this thought with the real-life constraints she faced: she did not know how to find assistants, much less pay them. Perhaps more important, several participants voiced concern that there is something inauthentic, discrediting, or disingenuous about not conducting ethnographic research in isolation. This notion is reinforced when the participation of research assistants in the field is not mentioned in the final written product.

Danger

Participants felt being a good ethnographer meant doing anything for the data. Indeed, a belief that worthwhile ethnographic research requires facing danger is intimately connected to the fixation of solitary research. Cathy described how the allure of good data led her to do things she wouldn't normally do. When explaining how she found herself on a beach in a torrential rainstorm as night approached, accompanied by a man who was a potential participant with no one else in sight, she told us, "My wish for information for the research was so strong that it trumped my needs for safety.... You always want more, it's never enough.... I think that makes it hard to walk away from a situation where you could get some great data."

Cathy added that at times it was easier to think of herself as a researcher and not pay attention to how sex and gender dynamics were operating in her fieldwork, even though this could lead to potentially dangerous situations: "It feels better to think about myself as researcher than as a woman who needs to protect herself. [Because] that feels so defensive, [and] it's so exhausting. And, I think, maybe some of that plays into it too." The exhaustion caused by having to constantly consider her own safety led Cathy to "refuse to do it" at times: "'I'm just not gonna think about my safety right now,' I would say to myself. [Laughs.] But then that's how you do get into dangerous situations."

Some participants mentioned losing perspective in the field and engaging in behaviors that they would avoid in their everyday lives. Once, when Gina, a white graduate student, was conducting fieldwork for an adviser's project in a Latin American city, Doug (an expat and one of her participants) hit on her at a bar, touching and trying to kiss her. Later, when she went to the bathroom, a man she didn't know tried to assault her. She escaped and turned to Doug for support. Though he expressed anger at what had happened, he continued to try to touch and kiss her. Gina reflected:

> I think I definitely had moments where I was like, "Oh God [Doug]! Why are you putting your arms around me? Like I am here to do something and I need to get this thing before I leave. Like I need to make sure I have good data. I can't go home and tell [my adviser] I didn't get anything because I failed." So at some level I really was like, "I am here to get something, and I am going after it."

Gina went on to point out that often the awareness of danger many women develop as they are socialized is muted while conducting fieldwork, due to a desire to get "good" data or to concentrate so that they can get it all down.

Harriet, a sociologist studying organizations, also described finding herself in potentially unsafe settings that in her everyday life she would have avoided. On one occasion, when she attended a conference with research participants—all of whom were men in their forties and fifties—she went back to their hotel room. She recalled having a moment "where I was like, 'I'm in a faraway place, in a conference center, in a hotel room with three men. How does this look to others in the community?' But also, 'Am I gonna be in danger?' I don't know. Like I think I trust these people. . . . But as a woman you would never, as a normal person, do that, right? [Laughs] But as an ethnographer they're like, 'Hey, why don't you come here?' You're like, 'Wow, this is gonna lead to good stuff.'" Here Harriet identifies two forms of gendered danger: the risk to her reputation and her safety.

Ideological forms structure our ideas about what is expected of us while in the field. Gina, Harriet, and Cathy all spoke about putting themselves in potential danger—acting without reflection and doing things they normally would not—because they assumed this is what researchers do to get good data.

Some participants did not struggle with decisions to end relationships or avoid potentially uncomfortable or dangerous situations; for them, emotional stability and physical safety were not worth the data they might have obtained. For example, when we asked Frances, an Asian American who worked in Europe, how people reacted to her attempts to recruit them to her study, she told us, "Some of the men, I did feel like they said yes and they were excited because they were, you know, potentially interested in getting to hit on me or something. And for some of those, . . . I didn't follow up with them, because my antenna was kind of up already, you know?" Frances clarified that her "antenna was kind of up already" because "weird Asian fetishes" had made her accustomed to sexual attention before she began conducting research. Despite proceeding with caution, even Frances lost a gatekeeper when he suggested that she have sex with him in exchange for his help after she had informed him that she could not pay him.

Another reason participants reported pushing their instincts and safety to the side was their perception that dangerous ethnographies are the ones most glorified and rewarded in academia. Sociology, like anthropology, has historically idealized researchers who are courageous and "hardy."[16] And men ethnographers have described engaging in "one-upmanship on the horror index," attempting to show in conversations with other ethnographers that theirs was the most violent, most dangerous research site.[17] During our interview with Mary, a white woman who worked in the United States, she spoke about how ethnography "often deals with people going into these locations that involve the 'other,' and often the 'other' that's been sensationalized as dangerous." She mused about the implications of this for how we define good research as well as how women can do good research according to these standards.

Some participants were encouraged by committee members to stay at field sites where they felt uncomfortable or even in danger. Lena, an Asian American graduate student, reflected on this glorification of danger, observing that in her graduate program it was individuals who conducted ethnography on topics perceived as dangerous who received the most accolades and greatest financial reward.[18] She noted that these rewards are often overlaid with race as well as gender, with white sociologists who go into presumably dangerous settings in African American or Latino neighborhoods most often held up as the star ethnographers. According to Gina, there is continued exaltation of work that has a voyeuristic and exoticizing quality. In contrast, Lena felt black or Latino researchers who go into the same kinds of settings face suspicions about the legitimacy and objectivity of their research.[19] At the same time, she observed that in her program there was very little training on how *anyone* should respond to dangerous situations in the field. Furthermore, as Norman Denzin has noted, researchers may be discouraged from confiding in their advisers about danger in the field given that "victims" in popular culture are often considered "emotionally traumatized."[20] Concerned that their emotions will be either dramatized or belittled—concerns that are amplified by gender and race—researchers may decide that it is best to remain silent.

Not all women felt in danger during sexualized interactions with research participants. When Kista, a queer white woman, was interviewing lesbians, a few of her research participants engaged in sexual banter. But this did not make Kista feel threatened or unsafe. She explained, "I think that most of the sexual banter that took place was truly just a conversational lubricant. It was not sexual. . . . I believe that it surfaced because it was a safe environment, . . . and it was an easy, maybe nervous way to connect ourselves with regard to sexual orientation." However, even Kista edited out these interactions when discussing fieldwork with her committee members, worrying they would question her professionalism. And she added that these interactions would have made her feel unsafe had they involved men. Conducting research in queer spaces does not always diminish danger, however. Clark, a queer white trans man, eventually decided to quit working at a potential research site when a table of gay men and a bartender at the bar where he was working attempted to undress him to see if he had been "born a man." Although Clark's adviser was supportive of his choice, he told us, "I certainly never had, in any of my classes, a discussion about what it means to be queer and go into the field [in terms of] safety concerns."

Bob, a white environmental ethnographer working in the urban United States, observed that the glorification of "dangerous" ethnography is especially common in subfields that are numerically dominated by men: "There is this kind of, if not masculine, at least triumphant kind of narrative that you did things that were difficult, sometimes explicitly dangerous." Historically, these ethnographies have become the most celebrated and thus are more likely to be assigned, he said. In contrast, talking about vulnerabilities in the field is considered too feminine or even largely irrelevant to the craft. Bob drew attention to the ways that different types of fieldwork take on gendered meanings and are valued hierarchically: dangerous / masculine research is more valued and celebrated than safe / feminine research. Moreover, Bob's comment that the celebrated narrative is a triumphant one invokes an ethnographer who after significant risk has finally conquered his field site. Such a narrative conjures up images of battle, war, and domination, concepts associated with hegemonic masculinity.

While researchers have written about how to conduct research in dangerous settings,[21] scholars need to question the necessity and glorification of danger rather than accept risk as incontrovertibly valuable.[22] The glorification of dangerous ethnographies not only puts researchers at risk and valorizes androcentric approaches to research but also reproduces the exoticization of marginal lives, leading to knowledge that has more to do with the researcher than the lives of those they study.[23]

Intimacy

When explaining why she was initially reticent to tell others about the sexual advances made by her gatekeeper, Phoebe, a white graduate student working in Brazil, reflected that ethnographers are expected to develop "strong connections" with people in the field: "No one gets excited about an ethnographer who has awkward, strange relationships with the communities they are trying to work in."

Intimacy has long been a key benchmark of the quality of both ethnographic research and qualitative research more broadly.[24] More recently, the interest in embodiment as a methodological approach has placed heavy emphasis on the researcher's body as a tool to insert themselves into the worlds of others (e.g., Loïc Wacquant's "carnal ethnography" and Jeff Ferrell and Mark Hamm's experiential approach).[25] In order to get at the "pivotal practical and central existential problems" that actors face, Wacquant argues that we need to "foster long-term, *intensive, even initiatory, forms* of ethnographic involvement. . . . [W]e can and should work to become 'vulnerable observers' in our practice of fieldwork[,] . . . diving into the stream of action to the greatest possible depth."[26] Advocating for what he calls "carnal ethnography," he emphasizes the need for researchers to become as intimate with and integrated in the social worlds we are studying as possible, grasping the worlds of our participants by using our bodies in the ways they do. Feminist researchers, too, have called for closeness with research participants, expressing concern about the potentially exploitative character of research and advocating efforts that break down power hierarchies between the researcher and the researched.[27] As Brittany told us, the methods literature she read before going into the field gave the impression that she was "supposed to develop these really amazing, immense, intimate relationships with . . . informants." Worrying that she might not have achieved this while in the field, she struggled with concerns that the quality of her data was inferior.

Although our participants had varying opinions on the role of intimacy—or becoming extremely close with research participants by spending as much time as possible with them—many said it was a key evaluative benchmark in their minds as they entered the field. Many participants valued ethnographic intimacy, even though they recognized what seeking it might entail. While the intimacy of ethnography attracted Samantha, a white graduate student, "because you really get a picture of people's lives and experiences," she also acknowledged that establishing intimacy opens you up to a "continuum of sensuality," including desire as well as sexual harassment and violence. Indeed, Samantha chose to change her dissertation topic when she realized that the heightened context of unwanted sexual attention and potential risk in a fracking boomtown in the U.S. Midwest would make it impossible for her to carry out the kind of ethnography she valued.

For many, getting close to participants and spending time with them meant coping with assaults on their identification as researchers and independent women and even placing themselves in situations where they had to fight off attackers. For Phoebe, intimacy in the field was "very much a double-edged sword." She explained:

> Me doing a good job as an ethnographer means that I am intimate and having people share everything, but then it opens me up to, "Well, you should have

expected it, Phoebe. You are hanging out with this guy until 9 P.M." But it's like, I am taught that I should want him to want [me] to be around, right? [Laughing] What? . . . I am doing what I am supposed to be doing, which is having these strong connections with these people in the field, and that's what everyone wants, right? That's the goal, right?

In Phoebe's case, when she eventually told her adviser and graduate school colleagues that her gatekeeper had propositioned her, many responded, as she alludes to above, by questioning her behavior and suggesting she should have expected it. She reflected, "I wish we had more honest conversations about . . . the double-edged sword of intimacy and how I am expected to get it, but it can very easily be used against me in ways that aren't problematized or thought about at all."[28]

While intimacy is frequently held up as the approach that can create access to the best data, it also opens the researcher to unwanted attention or advances and blame and criticism when these occur.[29] For men, getting as close as possible to participants might mean reproducing hegemonic masculinity and masculine bravado and choosing to let homophobia, violence, and sexism "slide."[30] Of course, intimacy is also a contested notion, particularly within feminist methodological debates.[31] Nevertheless, as Katherine Irwin points out, researchers who become deeply immersed in their settings—the reigning definition of intimacy—continue to be "praised for having better data and much more complex and sophisticated renderings of their subjects."[32] Phoebe's reflection that the goal of ethnography is to establish strong connections and be intimate with participants demonstrates the degree to which these two ideas are conflated. It is as if intimacy were the only route to developing the connections with research participants that will lead to rich ethnographic data.

Some of our participants wholeheartedly agreed that achieving ethnographic intimacy was an essential part of good ethnographic craft. (Others disagreed, a point that is discussed further in chapter 3.) Gina emphasized that she expected ethnographers to develop close relationships with subjects: "I think I would judge a piece of work as lesser if I felt like the researcher didn't have strong relationships with respondents, familiarity with their lives." Still, she recognized the dilemma this could pose for women facing sexualized danger in the field: "I obviously don't think that women putting themselves in dicey situations [is a good thing], or that anyone of any gender needs to be in danger, but, yeah, it's really tough because I think I am totally subject to that norm as well." Gina stressed the systemic roots of the issue: "I am not sure that the academy can solve it by giving us a checklist of ways to be safe or . . . saying women can't do projects that are about violence, or about crime, or about sex—things that are going to expose them to dangerous situations. I think it's a broader problem; it's a systemic political issue." For Gina, the downsides of intimacy in the field for women would only be resolved when the broader problem of violence against women is resolved.

Maritza spoke about the contradiction between the standard of intimacy and being an objective instrument of research:

> It is impossible to be just an instrument. . . . On the one hand, we are saying, 'You have to establish close relationships.' But on the other hand, we as ethnographers are an instrument, and we are told to be careful not to contaminate [the data]. . . . This feels like opposing things, and there isn't a real discussion of how to be both an instrument of science and how intimacy works and how difficult it is for a person to be in the field. So I think, for me, we need more open discussions about what it means to be an ethnographer and a person as well, because we are not just machines. . . . It sounds very nice in theory and people can write all they want in their methodological appendixes and it sounds very nice, but it's more complicated.

Although intimacy can lead to nuanced and sophisticated understandings of our research subjects, a universal valorization of intimacy in the field can put both researchers and the researched in harm's way. In part, this is related to the breaking down of barriers between the researcher and the research participant.[33] Indeed, some participants reported that it was their closest research relationships that put them in the most uncomfortable situations. Moreover, the emphasis on the body as a tool with which ethnographers can achieve intimacy elides the different hardships researchers will encounter precisely due to what their particular bodies signify.[34] For example, all researchers will face certain dangers when they decide to sleep on the street or check in to a city shelter to study the homeless. However, not all must consider the risk of sexual assault that our participants Angie and Karen had to factor into their research plans when considering whether to sleep overnight in Occupy encampments or the sexual assaults faced by several of our participants.[35] And not all researchers have to acquiesce to flirtation to put participants at ease, as Bridgette, a black graduate student did. In her experience, in order to make men feel "comfortable" enough to be forthcoming in interviews, "you have to kind of be okay with them flirting with you" while at the same time not "encourage it." According to Bridgette, because of stereotypes about black women's sexuality, she has to navigate sexuality "in every aspect of my life."

Think about your favorite ethnographies or the first ethnographies to which you were exposed. What were these ethnographies about? Who wrote them? Do you think they valorized the fixations discussed in this chapter? How did those fixations affect how the work was conducted and presented?

Have you been exposed to the fixations we discuss here? In what context? Were they presented in a positive or a negative light?

The lack of discussion in ethnography about the diverse ways in which intimacy can be defined and interpreted (and the fact that it is perhaps not always necessary, as opposed to trust, for example) is a dangerous shortcoming given the messy and often perilous ways that sex and gender shape women ethnographers' efforts to establish intimate contacts in the field. Rarely do we ask students to consider what happens when research participants understand efforts to establish ethnographic intimacy as something more than that. Many of our participants noted that intimacy in the field can lead to problems because the meanings of intimacy and boundaries are not mutually understood or shared. Intimacy cannot be perceived only from the standpoint of the researcher but must also be understood according to the preexisting cultural categories and gender roles through which research participants filter and interpret the ethnographer's actions. Actively seeking time with participants, showing interest in their life histories and everyday activities, and breaking down formal barriers between the researcher and the researched can mean something very different to participants than it does to the scholar. How these actions are interpreted might mean there is a price to pay for intimacy and close access to their worlds.

CONTEXTUALIZING THE FIXATIONS

Here we propose two interrelated explanations for why these fixations might have stuck with the women we interviewed, becoming particularly salient when negotiating problems in the field. First, as with any other social institution, sexism and racism have structured relationships within academia and continue to wield systemic influence over academic fields and departmental relations. The ongoing dominance of the white androcentric perspective in academia has a silencing effect on women after they have experienced unwanted sexual contact in the field. Second, women ethnographers may interpret their own experiences as evidence of "polluted" research, worrying that the validity of their work will be called into question.

White Androcentrism and Positivism

Participants suggested that androcentrism and positivism, both of which deny the embodied nature of fieldwork, continue to influence qualitative methods. They felt that the positivist standard of objective research—in which the researcher does not contaminate the experiment or affect the findings—and the assumption that men's bodies are neutral research instruments meant they needed to direct attention away from their gender when discussing their research in order to approximate these ideals.

Although some view qualitative sociology as at least partially about challenging the notion of the transcendental, objective observer,[36] it is important to keep in mind that ethnography originated from the natural sciences in the nineteenth century.[37] According to Jo Reger, "The overwhelming tone in academia is one that privileges rationality, objectivity, and masculinity."[38] Of course, few qualitative researchers now espouse the view that ethnographers can be fully objective and detached observers. Instead, participants talked about gathering "valid" data. The dominant standard of validity that preoccupied our participants was one that has emerged from white men's experience of conducting research, which remains constitutive of hegemonic standards.[39] That is, even when it is recognized that gender shapes the data an ethnographer is able to gather, the implicit assumption is that data gathered by a man are more complete or more neutral, and thus more reliable, than data gathered by a woman, which are skewed by gender bias. According to Kari Lerum, researchers use "academic armor"—for example, changing one's way of dressing or other aspects of self-presentation—to strive for objectivity and meet the standards set by the default body.[40] Indeed, the manner in which many ethnographies are presented perpetuates the notion that good data are gathered only once a researcher has become fully integrated into their research site, shedding those characteristics that differentiate the researcher from their participants. The iconic field researcher heeds Goffman's call to become a "full member of a scene[,] . . . [to] settle down and forget about being a sociologist."[41] This focus on full immersion and integration as *the* means by which we evidence ethnographic validity and neutrality often obscures the embodied nature of ethnographic data by defining what differentiates the researcher from research participants as barriers to be overcome. In other words, it directs attention away from the ways in which the practice of ethnography as a "practice of intimacy" is differentiated by gender, class, race, and other embodied factors.[42] While researchers may no longer strive to access a reality independent of their own perceptions, in writing about race, class, and gender in the field as obstacles over which we must prevail or which we must set aside,[43] we miss "the opportunity to reflect on how being a gender [or race, class, etc.] outsider impacts the actual process of field research."[44]

Yvonna Lincoln, Susan Lynham, and Egon Guba explain that because most constructivists (or interpretivists) do not believe in "objective" reality, validity is derived by means of community consensus.[45] That is, how a community of scholars assesses the validity of one's work is the key to its reception. Similarly, Bourdieu declares objectivity desirable and possible by redefining it as achieved through individual and collective reflexivity, as critically analyzing the researcher and the tools, assessment procedures, and so on, of the field as a whole.[46] However, assessment requires agreed upon standards. The evaluation of validity, regardless of how it is defined, is only possible because of ideological forms, of which the standards (or fixations) we are discussing are examples. Thus even when objectivity itself is set aside as a central concern, qualitative scholars remain answerable to a broader community—including constructivists and critical scholars as well as postpositivists—that will evaluate the validity of their work. Our findings indicate that the certification of research decisions, processes, and outcomes—the process Sandra Harding has termed the "context of justification"—continues to be dominated by androcentric norms.[47] It is when interviewees anticipated the "rigorous justification procedures" their peers would apply to their methods and data that they were silent about certain gendered and sexualized experiences.

Positivist origins, too, have left an indelible mark on ethnography, producing contradictory expectations for researchers seeking to collect "valid" data through full integration. Mary saw these contradictions embodied by her mentors. She described this situation as follows:

I have two competing theoretical perspectives at once, or three, I'd say. There are three people who have been really influential in my training. And none of the three agree on anything methodologically. And so I carry all of that baggage with me when I go into the field and when I come out of the field. . . . One of those people said getting too close to people was a bad thing and that makes it too messy and complex and you lose your theoretical angle. . . . One of those is all about being fully embedded in the field but paying more attention to behavior than talk. And one of those is more full embodied ethnography, being one of the people, sharing yourself, having them share with you, come to this full loving communal understanding of the research. I think that made doing research really hard because I was always competing with these different perspectives on what was best.

As Mary pointed out, on the one hand, we are to be rational, objective, and aloof, but on the other, we are to develop intimate, warm relationships with participants to solicit the "truest" data possible, seeking out our participants' "essence or inner core."[48] This presents a quandary for researchers, who understand the need to demonstrate vulnerability and intimacy but must also sanitize their research narratives to appear objective and neutral. Women in particular must be careful to erase their bodies from the process of gaining intimacy. This is because women's bodies have long been considered the opposing complement to men's rational minds and because the meanings associated with our bodies—passive, helpless, in need of protection—stand in contrast to the ideal ethnographer.

It is essential to note, however, that even when in contradiction the fixations affirm one another. While intimacy and objectivity seem to be opposed, Markowitz and Ashkenazi have noted, participant observation is paradoxically "based on the epistemology of positivist empiricism and assumes that (a) culture can be known by sensual experience."[49] In order to "meet the natives on their turf" we are trained to embrace and become engulfed in their experiences but also to negate our bodies in the process.[50] By displacing our own bodies in the research process, we can both achieve a deep understanding of those we study and remain sufficiently objective to step back into our analyst suits—or so we are told.

Some felt the lack of discussion about unwanted sexual attention in the field in methods classes and with peers, mentors, and committees evinces the hegemony of the white androcentric narrative in academia. Karina, a white graduate student in sociology, explained, "I think the reason why it doesn't happen is because the discipline is historically dominated by men, just like others. So the stuff that's been written about this has been written from a male perspective just like it's historically been written from a white perspective." Bob likewise associated the lack of reflexivity among sociological ethnographers with the homogeneity of those who historically were able to achieve access to their ranks, a homogeneity that often extended to the populations they studied: "If you think of Chicago school and then even sort of second wave stuff[,] . . . it was men often studying, and encouraged to study, people like them." Bob also linked the lack of reflexivity about gendered components of fieldwork to a continued adherence to positivism, a theory of knowledge that feminist scholars have long critiqued as prioritizing masculine experiences and ways of being in the world.[51] This commonsense understanding of what is of interest, of what is relevant, silences those experiences that do not "make sense" from the dominant perspective.

As Eva Moreno writes, "A central aspect of academic life is the denial of gender at work," such that "if we bring up issues that are specific to us as women in the academic context, we run the risk of doing damage to our identities as [scholars]."[52] Indeed, graduate school teaches silence on these issues. Bridgette observed that she learned to "be polite and laugh off" harassment by men professors, an approach she later applied in the field. Jenna, a white anthropology graduate student working in South Asia, was reluctant to tell her adviser about the harassment she was experiencing in the field because she feared that the adviser, a woman, would think she was an incompetent ethnographer. She added that to the extent that being harassed in the field made her feel physically unsafe, it *did* affect her ability to perform competently. She may have been less reluctant to seek help from her adviser, however, if it was not assumed that everyone has "equal access to field material" and is equally able to participate in the ethnographic "community." Knowledge production is not only gendered but also racialized. Cristina, a Latina who conducted fieldwork in the U.S. Southwest, argued that white men in sociology are not forced to justify their positionality in the field in the same way women and people of color are. She saw this as related to historical processes of distinction in the discipline, recalling as well that subtle and overt forms of racism in graduate school made her feel like she didn't have a community from which she could seek reassurance in the face of the racism and sexual advances she experienced in her field site.

Harriet noted that "women get a lot of flack for writing about women's issues," suggesting that even writing about gender (much less sexualization in the field) can result in women being taken less seriously as scholars. She also observed that even for women ethnographers who do not enter the field intending to study gender, it frequently becomes relevant: "You're in this environment where those power dynamics are so clearly being played out over your own body as well as others. And how can you not write about that? And it would be exactly the sort of thing that would not be made perspicuous to [a young man in the field] at all." As Harriet said, many women cannot avoid noting the ways in which their bodies have an impact on their research and relationships. Maritza confirmed Harriet's observations:

> When I started off I didn't have gender in my mind, but it's being brought up in these interactions [in my fieldwork with community organizations] and in the streets, I get cat-called very often. And so it's not the same for me to be a woman in the streets as it has been for [the] men who have written most of urban ethnography. And the women who have done urban ethnography, they are pushed to study women, interview women, all of this because these other places are not very friendly to us.

In Maritza's opinion, this problem is compounded by the fact that as a discipline sociology has not given it importance.[53] In her own experience, men are often oblivious to issues of gender and sexuality and women are reluctant to speak openly about them (for reasons we continue to explore below). She also spoke of a disciplinary norm of concealing vulnerability: "There is a culture that you have to be very put together and perfect and [not] show vulnerable spots, and this is something very vulnerable that people don't want to talk about."

That many women have to consider issues of gender and sexuality in their field sites even if they did not set out to study these topics stands in contrast to men colleagues who stated they had never thought about the gendered nature of their research. For example, Lena described a conversation with a graduate school colleague who conducted ethnography in an urban area in the early hours of the morning. During one conversation she asked him if he thought he would be doing the same kind of work if he were female-bodied. His response indicated a lack of reflexivity about the ways his embodiment facilitated his research. Lena reported, "He said, 'You know, I hadn't thought of that, but I guess I would just try to wear big clothes and a hood and look threatening.'" The response by Lena's colleague elides the fact that his embodiment shaped the fieldwork he felt comfortable doing and the data he ultimately collects.

The fact that most women *have* to think about gender and sex (and their intersections with race and other factors) while in the field and men *may or may not* is largely a product of whose behaviors and interactions are at the center of the social world—and our disciplines—and considered the norm by which all others are compared. Of course, academia is no longer completely dominated by white men. Nevertheless, the othering produced by this historical norm made many of our participants feel alone in navigating sexual politics in the field. It convinced them that this was a topic their men colleagues and mentors would not understand.

Concern over whether or not one is considered competent (much less professional and authoritative) can be exacerbated by experiences beyond fieldwork. For example, some participants talked about being hit on at conferences by senior colleagues. Some also experienced sexual harassment and threats of sexual violence at professional meetings, confirming for them the pervasiveness of patriarchy within academia. For Sofía, experiencing sexual harassment at the hands of colleagues was particularly troubling: "Patriarchy. See, the thing is, . . . it's everywhere. And the problem is that I think in our case when you see it at the more horizontal [level, . . .] these men [who subscribe to the patriarchy] have intellectual skills [and] can actually become more sophisticated. More sophisticated. And that's very dangerous, you know?"

Participants reported mixed reactions when they spoke to men who were their colleagues and mentors about their experiences. While some expressed concern, others laughed or told women to "suck it up," framing harassment as just one more difficulty researchers had to cope with in the field. Cathy noted that this (white) men's privilege of ignoring the role of embodiment in the field is compounded by the discomfort of some men professors when it comes to talking about sex and gender politics in the field; both factors contribute to institutional silence surrounding these issues. Because the oft-idealized intrepid ethnographer is implicitly scripted as a white man, failing to grapple with sex and gender in the field works against ethnographers' safety and also against thinking about how our ethnographic fixations cloud our vision about what makes work "good."

Perhaps just as important as asking whether men would understand these experiences or how they would react to women speaking about them is asking why many women silenced themselves before talking to colleagues and mentors. The fixations of danger and solitude keep researchers from talking openly about the multiple types of vulnerabilities they experience. Despite the training of some of our participants in feminist methods, when faced with harassment in the field, many participants reverted to epistemological assumptions rooted in the experiences and worldviews of elite, white, cis men about how the construction of knowledge is supposed to proceed. Mary, whose field site in the U.S. Midwest was dominated by men, reflected on the continued dominance of these fixations despite the existence of "many great feminist texts." She felt the sociological ethnographic model still seems to privilege a notion of objectivity: "Even as I read all this feminist research and know better on one level, that . . . notion of the removed person sticks in your head and kind of affects you." The assumption that neutral observation is both possible and desirable contributes to the silencing effect the three fixations have on women ethnographers.

Polluted Research

As mentioned above, ethnography originated from the natural sciences, and understandings of validity and objectivity from a positivist past continue to undergird ethnographic standards. As Bob observed, "I think . . . while people would contest this if you said it explicitly, . . . there still is kind of this fly-on-the-wall idea, far more in sociology than anthropology." "Fly-on-the-wall" ethnography refers to the kind of research where the ethnographer is noticed as little as possible and has minimal impact on the scenes they observe. However, it is hard to conduct fly-on-the-wall ethnography when one's body draws attention or becomes a target in the field. This is not to say that only women's bodies affect the scenes they study but that even when cis white men ethnographers are studying people very different from them, they generally are not called on to account for these differences in academic circles. In other words, cis white men are more capable of selling fly-on-the-wall ethnography because their bodies draw less attention in academia, even if they draw attention in field sites. As a result they are not asked to consider how their gender and bodies shape fieldwork. Even when a man's body becomes salient in research, it is more likely to give credibility to knowledge production as long as it adheres to other expectations of neutrality (white, cis, heterosexual), whereas the body scripted feminine delegitimizes these claims.

Concerns that their academic community might consider their research polluted or invalid led some participants to avoid talking openly about their experiences with sexual harassment in the field.[54] For example, Karina was conducting research in Rwanda when a government official grabbed and tried to kiss her in his office. Based on this experience and other sexualized interactions, as well as the general lack of security in the country, she eventually decided to change her dissertation topic. However, when people ask her about the decision, she sticks to the political context. She reflects, "Particularly as women there's a lot of fear of being accused of overreacting or being too sensitive. Or, you know, the backlash." She added, "There's this idea that if I talk about things that are quote-unquote emotional or sexual in nature I'm not being professional."

To present themselves as professional, our participants felt they could not risk sharing experiences that might evoke these traits in the minds of others. Acutely aware of these stereotypes, Karina, Kista, and others adapted and redacted their field experiences in order to present themselves as professionals, not feminine caricatures driven by emotion. This self-imposed silence demonstrates the degree to which women ethnographers can—sometimes consciously—become carriers of a discourse that marginalizes their own experiences. It was evident in our interviews that few participants worried about adhering to positivist notions of objectivity (even as they may have worried that they were being held to the standard of the neutral observer); however, concerns that peers and mentors would deem them incompetent or their research less valid because of the gendered nature of fieldwork were a principal source of anxiety for them. Our interviews suggest that internalization of the commitment to validity and accessing "genuine" data, combined with their experiences in academia, has led women to perceive talking about sexual harassment and other sexualized experiences during fieldwork as potentially damaging to their data as well as their careers.[55]

Some participants even voiced reservations about participating in our study; they worried that it could reinforce the inaccurate notion that women do "worse" research than men. As Mary put it, "As a woman who's going into the field, on one level you don't want to admit that there is fear and vulnerability because you don't want to be seen as doing less than [a man.]" When the ideal field worker is a man, any admission of how feminine embodiment (and the social relations this entails) shapes the fieldwork experience puts you at risk of being judged as inferior or not being taken seriously. Kista embedded her concerns about discussing sexualized interactions in the broader sociological community, which she believes devalues qualitative work: "I think that should be a concern for women, particularly because [many] are doing qualitative research. . . . So that alone is grounds for them to mess with us. I'd say let's not give them [men critical of qualitative research] any more ammo." For Kista, discussing sexualized interactions could provide other reasons to discredit qualitative work, particularly qualitative work conducted by women. From her perspective, discussing the vulnerable experiences one has in the field can make one more vulnerable in academia.

Because these kinds of interactions are rarely discussed before students enter the field, students have, as Michelle put it, "a limited basis for knowing at all how anyone would react." For example, when Michelle was conducting preliminary research in another country she met a friendly expatriate who offered to help her acquire contacts in the town where she was hoping to launch her project. Though she felt uneasy about his overtures, she accepted his offer and met with him to discuss how to proceed. Over the course of their interaction, this man was sexually aggressive, both verbally and physically. When Michelle asked him to stop, he ignored her. When she then attempted to take leave of him, he assaulted her. Michelle was able to fight him off and escape. Afterwards, she hid in her room for two days, worried that he would find her if she went out. Michelle spent these days agonizing over whether to call her adviser but finally did, reasoning that if she disappeared, "no one would ever know." Her adviser responded with great concern for her safety and emphatically told her to leave the town immediately. Yet in the days she spent locked in her hotel room she had worried that he would respond by telling her, "Suck it up," or "You're being a wuss. Just go out there and do it."

During her interview, Michelle observed that women often keep the things that happen to them in the field a secret because of "fear of not being taken seriously in academia." Or they worry about being challenged about their decisions. "Why did you cut off contact? You shouldn't, they didn't actually attack you, why didn't you continue, you know?" These are the kinds of questions Michelle reported that she and others anticipated being asked if they spoke up about their experiences. Indeed, when she tried to organize an event in her department addressing issues faced by women in the field, many women declined to participate. Michelle told us, "I was surprised a little bit when the female researchers told me that they didn't even want to be in a discussion in the department because of fear of not the professors but the males who were ultimately their colleagues. I mean, when we graduate these are the people we're gonna see at conferences, you know, these are the people we're gonna have reviewing our work." The fear of judgment based on the privileged position of men in the academy places important limits, then, on actually addressing the safety of women in the field or the implications of these experiences on the construction of knowledge.

The judgment Michelle feared was reflected in the mansplaining or criticisms leveled against participants when they did discuss their experiences with harassment with men colleagues and advisers. Such comments suggest that women are in fact seen as polluting their field sites when sexualized interactions occur. Again, these experiences are often shaped by intersections of sex and gender with race and other factors. Monira was a Muslim who wore a hijab when she participated in a master's-level class for which she interviewed a young man about educational outcomes for people in the foster system. He became "creepy," asking to see her hair and then saying, "Is that like asking to see your boobs?," and later touched her when she drove him home. Earlier in the evening, she had realized that the interview had not been recorded, and they made plans to redo it the following day, but after the disturbing interaction, she decided not to go back. She told her professor about it, and she was supportive of her decision, but not all of her classmates were.

> I remember my professor asking me to share this experience in class to speak about methodological, unplanned incidents that happened, and how to work around them and how to react to them and how to handle them. And I had shared this experience in class, and one of my classmates, who was in the Marines and so he was very built, he was tall, he was intimidating to look at, he told me that that was bad research. And I was taken aback, and I said, "Excuse me. What do you mean?" And he said, "If I was in that situation I would have gone to his house the next day." And I said, "Well, you're also like a hundred pounds heavier than me. And you can lift your own weight and then some. I'm—these are two different situations."

The professor backed Monira up, explaining to the man how women may experience things differently than men. Monira recalls, "And I just thought to myself like, 'How did this become a class on, on empathy?' [Laughs]" Her fellow student judged her on the basis of the (cis white man) neutral sociologist, failing to take into account how race, religion, and gender all combined to structure this interaction in the field, leading Monira to feel endangered. Experiences like this drive home why women ethnographers might be resistant to being open about sexualization and gender-related safety issues in the field. They also suggest that women's suspicions that their fortitude as ethnographers and the validity of their research will be called into question are well founded.

At the same time, a rejection of paternalism shaped Gina's feelings about talking about these issues. Just as there was a fear among some participants that our study could lead people to think that women were doing less good research, Gina feared that it could lead people to say that women should not do certain types of research: "It cuts both ways. I don't want my committee to say to me, 'No, you can't study sexuality because you are going to find yourself in these dangerous situations,' whereas men would be fine with it." Phoebe likewise spoke of the fine line between talking about the relevance of sex and gender as a way to be patronizing or denigrating women's abilities as opposed to a way to support them and recognize the validity of their experiences in the field. But the point, of course, is not that women should not do certain types of research or that women's work is less valid as a result of these issues. It is that embodiment and the accompanying social meanings shape *everyone's* research: what data are available to them, how people will receive them, what settings might present danger and therefore warrant different safeguards, and so on. This interpretation was outweighed for many participants by fears that they would be seen as bad ethnographers if they fully acknowledged how sex and gender shaped their fieldwork experiences.

Some participants worried that their projects would be viewed as contaminated or less valid because their gender kept them from being able to gain access to certain sites and populations.[56] Brittany recalled being invited into the van of some men performers during a hailstorm, on the promise that it would be a chance to talk about her research. She declined. Later, rather than empower her to propose an alternative meeting space should a similar opportunity present itself in the future, some of Brittany's mentors, who were men, told her that she "probably should have gotten in the van. Maybe that was a great opportunity."

Others were concerned about the quality of their data when their gender and attractiveness to men *created* access and opportunities. According to Joan, who conducted fieldwork with Central American elites in the early 2000s:

> I felt like it was like cheating. You know, every female in any position, you wonder how much of your position is how attractive you are or aren't.... I felt like it skewed the data that they were flirting with me. I mean if you are trying to get genuine interview data you don't want someone who is trying to push themselves as a potential sex partner. [Laughs] Like that's not very valid data.

In sum, concerns that their peers would interpret their gendered and sexualized interactions in the field as polluting their work, thereby rendering it invalid, shaped participants' willingness to share these experiences openly.

Do you agree that positivism and androcentrism still influence academia and the production of knowledge? Why or why not? To the extent that it does exist, is this influence largely positive or negative in your estimation?

What epistemological traditions are most influential in your own research? How do these traditions evaluate knowledge production? To what extent do they account for researchers' embodiment?

If validity is defined by community consensus, how might scholars go about redefining validity in ways that do not privilege research conducted by particular bodies? How do you think validity should be defined? How can we evaluate validity without ignoring or reinscribing inequalities among researchers?

CONCLUSION

Our interviews indicate that the standards to which many ethnographers hold their work discourage open dialogue on sexualized interactions in the field. Participants in our study (and here we include ourselves) frequently turned to particular narratives and fixations that narrowly define what counts as valid data to measure and evaluate experiences, even though these leave little room to understand and articulate the embodied paths by which data are gathered. As others have noted, ethnographic training still tends to overlook the ways in which gender and sexuality not only shape our work but also constitute it *throughout* our time in the field.[57] Indeed, for much of their history, ethnography and sociology more generally have not recognized or provided a vocabulary with which to discuss gender, sexuality, and embodiment as issues centrally important to the production of ethnographic knowledge for all researchers. Our data suggest that this remains true, at least to some degree. Aside from some who had feminist mentors, participants reported little to no discussion of gender and sexuality as they prepared to enter the field.

The lack of discussion in sociology and other disciplines on the sexual harassment, advances, and violence that may be faced in the field operates as "vocal silence" that communicates and reproduces values, standards, and norms by circumventing discussions of them.[58] Perhaps it is unsurprising, then, that when participants dealt with fieldwork challenges, they turned to ethnographic fixations predicated on the "default" body: that of a cis white man. In other words, the vocal silence surrounding bodies and fieldwork led the women we interviewed to turn to fixations that most delegitimized their own experiences. These fixations sustain a false division between scholar and woman, a division requiring that to be a scholar one must "deny gender" at work; however, this division collapses in the field.[59] There is no neutral body, a fact that can become especially clear in the context of fieldwork. By fetishizing the ethnographic journey that adheres to these fixations, we reproduce this false division and limit the ways in which students and scholars design and evaluate projects. This is a problem, then, of the logic of evaluation as well as an epistemic issue of what counts as valid ethnographic knowledge, an issue that is discussed further in chapter 5.

The delegitimation of sexualized and gendered interactions as constitutive of our fieldwork and data has promoted a "fiction of a genderless self," contributing to a disembodied presentation of research and further obscuring the fact that the cis man's body remains the default in research.[60] It encouraged our participants, concerned with meeting a standard of validity based on an experience that is not their own, to relegate these interactions to "awkward surplus,"[61] perpetuating the notion that the identities that set the researcher apart from those they study must be shed at the beginning of any worthwhile project.

There is good reason to believe our participants' adherence to these standards is not idiosyncratic. These fixations have a long history and continue to be taught in courses on ethnographic methods. Ethnographers, like other academics, make choices as members of broader communities.[62] As in other communities, disciplinary norms shape individuals' behavior and understandings of their experiences. Our data show that women's experiences of harassment and sexualization in the field are shoved aside, marked as unimportant and irrelevant to the construction of knowledge. In contrast, we need to recognize that *all* ethnographic data are shaped by gendered and sexualized experiences that create particular opportunities and constraints for differently embodied individuals. Work produced via a different path is not necessarily better or worse but simply different. Having demonstrated the need to move beyond these underpinnings, the following chapters draw from our interviews to discuss gendered embodiment, harassment in the field, and the costs of harassment while also providing researchers with guidance for thinking about traditional concepts like access, power, and documentation from an embodied perspective.

Gendered Bodies and Field Research

THIS CHAPTER DISCUSSES THE METHODOLOGICAL ISSUES of access, trust, and building relationships in the field from an embodied perspective. A recent interest in embodiment as a methodological approach has placed heavy emphasis on the researcher's body as a tool to insert themselves into the worlds of others. However, this perspective, concerned primarily with researchers' bodies as instruments of discovery, does not differentiate between the hardships researchers will encounter precisely because of these bodies. Indeed, these approaches take embodiment into account only to the degree that "the body" allows the researcher to turn themselves into the phenomenon;[1] they do not consider the ways in which different bodies are vulnerable to different sensations, suffering, and violence in the field. These considerations of embodiment are constrained by enduring standards of long-term and intensive presence and participation in the field that ignore the different positions of power from which men and women approach fieldwork.

The goal of this chapter is to consider three issues. First, we look at how expectations (gendered, raced, etc.) in the academic field encourage researchers to adhere to "neutral," disembodied narratives of fieldwork. Second, we analyze how stereotypes of different bodies result in distinct opportunities and drawbacks over the course of fieldwork for all researchers. And third, we engage with issues of flirtation and sex in the field, topics that tend to be overlooked in methods books and courses. We use vignettes from our interviews to explore these issues and encourage readers to think through their implications. Thus we echo Maree Burns's call for "interrogating the impact of the body on the knowledge and meanings produced" through research.[2] At the end of the chapter, we discuss ways to present embodied ethnographic and interview data.

The term "embodiment" has multiple lineages, some of which essentialize bodies and experiences. Throughout this chapter, we attempt to analyze women's experiences while avoiding this essentialism. We do so by taking into account the ways in which bodies and experiences are differentially structured by power relations. Women's bodies do not produce universal experiences, nor does experience arise for all women "by virtue of their womanhood alone."[3] Following Barbara Sutton, we consider "women's bodies as sites through which women experience both differences and similarities, as dynamic entities that contain, express, and resist social relations."[4] To adequately examine embodiment in both the field site and the academic field, we must take into account how intersecting forms of domination produce different and similar experiences and strategies.

THE ACADEMIC FIELD

Gender and race structure academic fields, which influenced participants' experiences in and narratives of their field sites. Similar to the ways in which ethnographers and social scientists have othered the people they study—on the basis of race, culture, ethnicity, geographic location, and so on—researchers from groups that have historically been marginalized are also othered within the academic setting, where straight, white, (often elite) cis men's experiences stand at the center of the social world.[5] This is not to say that power is static and universally "held" by straight white cis men across all contexts. Power is dynamic and, like a researcher's social location, varies depending on the context and the field.

Nevertheless, the university is a hierarchically organized institution in which researchers must seek academic capital and prestige from established scholars, which creates an unequal relationship of dependency.[6] Scholars must gain academic recognition for their work and contributions to be legitimized, and the ability to provide this recognition is not evenly distributed throughout the academic community. Because of these unequal relationships, women, people of color, and other subordinated groups may feel that it is necessary to reflect the perspectives and ideas of colleagues in dominant positions if they are to advance in their careers (or simply secure their current positions). Academic socialization and the distribution of power within the university pressures scholars to accept "race-neutral" and "gender-neutral" methodological and epistemological orientations.[7] Tukufu Zuberi and

Eduardo Bonilla-Silva have discussed race-neutral orientations as the silencing of nonwhite perspectives by "white logic." White supremacy has "defined the techniques and processes of reasoning about social facts," and this historical posture "grants eternal objectivity to the views of elite Whites and condemns the views of non-Whites to perpetual subjectivity."[8] Academics who are not white may develop a "scholarly" double consciousness, looking at themselves and their work through the eyes of white researchers.[9] Gender neutrality, we would argue, is part of this white logic, also relegating women's experiences to the subjective and projecting suspicion on research by women of color on the basis of their race and gender and the intersection of both. As Jo Reger has written, "To experience emotion is to be seen as experiencing 'irrationality' in the research process. In sum, it is to experience femininity and marginality."[10] Accusations of irrationality, bias, and subjectivity from those adhering to the dominant paradigm keep many researchers at the margins, despite the fact that some ethnographic work by women and people of color has garnered attention and acclaim. By and large, members of subordinated groups must continue to act, talk, and write with the "eternal objectivity" crafted from the experiences of cisgender white men in mind.[11]

Just as Dorothy Smith wrote of how "women's means to reflect upon themselves is a reflection from outside themselves, the structuring of themselves not as subjects, but as other,"[12] the women we interviewed talked about considering the perspective of men colleagues before sharing their tales of the field.[13] This was true of Karina, whose story is told in chapter 1; she did not tell others about the assault she experienced in the field for fear that she, and her work, would be deemed emotional or illegitimate. Maritza, a Latina doctoral student also talked about fears of being delegitimized and silenced within academia if she talked about being hit on by a professor at a national conference. While the settings are different, the responses that Maritza and Karina felt they would receive if they spoke openly about these men's actions are quite similar.

This is not to say that all women ethnographers (or even all women we interviewed) face the same expectations or have the same experiences. Gender is fluid and diverse, and experiences structured by it are neither uniform nor homogeneous. For example, not all of our participants interpreted sexualized interactions as disconcerting. However, if expectations are diverse within the field, the women we interviewed seemed to anticipate similar reactions from mentors and advisers. This is because although gendered experiences and practices are diverse, they are ordered by hegemonic scripts not written by the social actors who perform them. Aware of these scripts, others echoed Karina's concern that "as women" they risked appearing overly emotional or hysterical when discussing the issues they confronted during fieldwork.[14]

Maritza, who conducted fieldwork in a major U.S. city, worried about another stereotype that might bring her academic rigor into question: women use their bodies in exchange for something else (in this case, data). She explained, "I know it's not my fault, because I didn't do anything. But you never know that some people might think, 'Oh she's a flirt. Maybe she was using her gender to get interviews.' You just never know what will cross people's minds, and it means giving explanations about something that happened." She worried especially about being vulnerable about this with her professors, who were men, because of the power they had over her. Gendered expectations, both in the field and in academia, shaped Maritza's trust in her professors and her sense of how they perceived her.

Joan, a white sociologist, explicitly linked doubts she had about her academic career to doubts she felt in the field, explaining, "At that age I had been worried for years that part of my academic success was due to appearance." These worries came with her to the field: "I mean, [like] most women, I just worried about my capability as a researcher, . . . and the fact that [the men I interviewed] patronized me incessantly did not help anything." When asked how she feels about this now, she replied, "Partly annoyed at myself in the lack of faith in my own abilities and also I think that I completely overestimated the amount of power being an attractive female gives you." Here Joan connects her confidence in the field to her embodied experiences in academia. Because she felt her appearance helped her succeed in academia and in the field, she questioned her capability in both areas. She also noted that she has come to believe that attractiveness is a less powerful resource than she thought when she was younger, linking her feelings about her capabilities to a broader societal norm, that a woman's most important resource is her looks. Gender, however, does not operate in isolation, as we discuss throughout this chapter.[15] Instead, it intersects with other facets of identification and systemic inequalities to structure opportunities and constraints within academia. For example, race also entered into some women's considerations of validity. Lena, an Asian American student, talked about how sociologists are often critical of people of color for "studying their own." Cristina, a Latina participant, also felt that she would be less likely to have her neutrality questioned if she were a white middle-class man rather than "similar-looking" and with "a similar background" of the people in her field site.

The repetition of these themes in our interviews suggests that gendered and racialized scripts in academia (also informed by sexuality, able-bodiedness, and other factors) continue to reproduce standards based on (white cis men's) neutral bodies and disparaging stereotypes of women. Even before entering the field, women learn through their academic socialization that performing different gender scripts (whether that be by "playing up" femininity or neutralizing their bodies) is in their (career's) best interest. These scripts, as Smith wrote, create a cyclical effect that keeps women from producing authoritative forms of thought—in this case, field narratives—that depart from the themes, problematics, and assumptions that keep in place hegemonic structures.[16] In her words, women in the social sciences "have learned to live inside a discourse which is not ours and which expresses and describes a landscape in which we are alienated."[17] The power dynamics within field sites, discussed below, are exacerbated by those in academia, where researchers must convince peers and mentors that things like their race and gender do not invalidate their work.

PRETTY GIRLS, DUMB GIRLS, FRIENDLY GIRLS

Performing, or "doing," gender in expected ways can legitimize social actors, while performing gender in nonhegemonic ways can discredit them. In other words, our self-presentation and performance have consequences for us as social beings and, thus, as researchers. The women we interviewed were acutely aware of gender as performance and how their performances—regulated by local context and actors—could facilitate their research. In this section, we look at three intersecting "types" that women described being cast as while conducting research, which we refer to as the dumb girl, the pretty girl, and the friendly girl.[18] Each of the types intersects with expectations and stereotypes related to race, sexuality, nationality, and so on, and each resulted in distinct opportunities and drawbacks over the course of fieldwork. These opportunities and constraints demonstrate how social meanings attached to bodies transform those bodies into tools or targets, depending on the particular context in which an ethnographer is working.

Niceness, whiteness, and thinness can all mark the researcher as "pretty" in certain contexts. Mary, whose body conforms to these markers, worked in a men-dominated field site in the U.S. Midwest. She explained, "I think that there were benefits to being a woman in, I guess, ... the packaging that I come in." For some participants, then, meeting hegemonic standards of beauty and femininity was inadvertent. Others very consciously played up their appearance in order to facilitate access. Some participants chose to dress professionally; others emphasized certain aspects of their femininity. Harriet, a white organizational ethnographer, explained, "I know to my field site people, I look kind of cute and innocuous. And I don't look like I have any power. And that's . . . a line that I often play with. Because it allows me to get the access to the moments that I need. Because I can fade into the background."[19] Regional characteristics were also played up. Amy, a white woman whose work focused on families in the United States, described enacting proper and conservative femininity: "I think my presentation of self was very sweet, very nice. I would pull out the southern thing sometimes."

Young women are often interpreted as dumb, innocent, or naive—and thus inferior—in the field, even while doing a job that places them in a position structurally superior to that of their male informants.[20] These perceptions can work in the researchers' favor, even though it requires playing into disempowering stereotypes. Phoebe, a white woman working in South America, reported that she got great data from playing up both stereotypes, as others perceived her as cute and dumb. She went so far as to observe that if her gatekeeper had not eventually propositioned her (at which point she called him out) she would have continued doing so for fear of "squashing his desire or fantasies" and thereby losing access. She explained, "I know that stuff is so intertwined with my ability to make contacts in the field. And I am not naive about that. In the same way, it's part of my tool kit to get through the day-to-day, you know? And I am not going to pretend that who I am or what I look like doesn't affect the research that I get." Although being cute and dumb did not fit the way she understood herself, Phoebe recognized that assumptions about intelligence, gender, race, and nationality all intersected to influence her ability to get data.

Like Ruth Milkman, who noted that her access was facilitated by men who found her inquiries those of a harmless girl, Joan admitted to playing into the unthreatening girl role in order to gain access.[21] She noted that the relative lack of women in professional roles in the Central American countries where she worked meant "there is very little expectation among the men there that a woman is someone you should take seriously." As a white woman from a prestigious U.S. university, she did not anticipate that this would affect her own fieldwork, but it soon became clear that she was mistaken. She remarked, "It was pretty immediately obvious to me that being female and young . . . and not being taken seriously could actually help with access." She described going to an open meeting of an important business association early on in her fieldwork in El Salvador: "I had so much attention, you know, just for being a young gringa there, I was like, 'This is great!' [Laughing] This is how I get access, you know, because everyone was super flirtatious and willing to talk to me." Joan always dressed conservatively, but after realizing that her appearance was useful for gaining access she altered her strategy: "I femmed up more and more with perfume and shit that I would never do in the United States. But when in Rome, right?" Joan also explained, "It got very tiresome after a while. . . . I spent more time on beauty there than I did any other place in my life or any other time."[22]

Joan contrasted her experience to that of a colleague: "I had a male friend who had done some similar interviews and had been threatened at one point. He had been jumped and had his fieldnotes stolen after a scary interview. Nothing like that ever happened to me, partly because I was so nonthreatening to them." Joan was uncomfortable playing up the feminine aspect, and ultimately it had costs, but she was frank in her acknowledgment of how gender, race, and nationality combined to facilitate her access to Central American elites. Joan now believes appearance was a less important resource than she had assumed, but it was nevertheless one of the tools she used to gain access at the time.

A Latina student, Jackie, conducted interviews for a professor's project on Latino construction workers in a context where she felt that coming across as friendly was an asset for gaining access because it put the men at ease.[23] However, cultural norms related to the separation of spheres can shape how women's friendliness—and even their mere presence—is interpreted in the field. Michelle described anticipating that she would have some difficulties in the field because her research focused on the public sphere, which was dominated by men.[24] As a result, she knew she would not be abiding by the normal gender expectations for women. She described what this meant for conducting research and the measures she took to cope.

> I knew from pre-dissertation research that their initial reaction to me was going to be to hit on me. [Laughs]. . . . I had spent quite a bit of time there in multiple visits before doing my dissertation research, and so by this point I had already learned that it was important to really draw the line. . . . When I first did my pre-dissertation research I thought, "I'm a qualitative researcher. I need to meet as many people as possible and be open to everyone." So I was friendly to everyone and after doing that for a couple months realized that

I was not getting the response [laughs] that I wanted from men, who really misunderstood all of what I was trying to communicate and thought that that just meant I was seeking lovers or something. So by the time I did my dissertation research I had already developed this different attitude, which was kind of coldness and aloofness to men in general, unless [I was] personally introduced to them.

In the context where Michelle conducted research, men understood her friendliness as something very different from what she intended. She had to alter her performance of femininity to adhere to local expectations and understandings of appropriate behavior. She also learned that she would not be able to do "full-on field participant observation" because both men and women misinterpreted her desire to spend time with men. In other words, her gender kept her from hanging out with certain groups of participants and becoming a part of their daily lives, resulting in a departure from ethnographic expectations grounded in the search for intimacy and closeness. In addition to scaling back the scope of her participant observation, Michelle said, "I made sure I knew their wives very, very well if I was going to spend any amount of time with them [men], that I was clear that I was more friendly with their wives than them, things like that." While some might view Michelle's calculated moves as failing short of ethnographic standards, they were key to building and maintaining the relationships that she needed in the field.

As Michelle's case indicates, building barriers and drawing lines in the field are important for data collection as well as physical, psychological, and emotional safety. Sometimes becoming "cold," "aloof," and less friendly with men is important to make the researcher feel safer or less uncomfortable. In Michelle's case, she most likely would not have been able to collect her data if she had not adopted an aloof stance with her research participants, who were men. However, being cold and drawing boundaries collide with the expectation that ethnographers should develop close and intimate relationships and willingly face danger in the field. In other words, women can draw on certain forms of self-presentation in the field to stay safe (and sane), but these are choices for which they may later be criticized.

Age is another factor that affects participants' interactions with women. Virginia's experience as a white researcher in Asia made her feel that age was an important factor in accounting for how people interpreted her body: "There, there's sort of a role for academics [where I work] because I'm this unmarried, nerdy, working woman. There's sort of like a movie stereotype for that. So as I've gotten older I feel like people kind of have more of a niche for me. . . . They're less confused by the fact that I'm not married." Virginia shared the advice given to her by another woman who worked in the same region: "She said once that as you get older people start to see you more as more asexual than anything else. . . . I think it's just a combination of the way you dress and the way you present yourself and this really twisted idea that women with power are not real women." While age might change how women are understood and treated in the field, this varies by cultural context. And it also does not mean that harassment becomes a nonissue. Indeed, coauthor Patricia reports that in her experience harassment has not disappeared from the field, but its instigators have grown older as she has. Still, with age comes experience, such that women researchers may become more adept at preventing, staving off, or handling harassment when it does occur.

Often when a woman's appearance created access, it came with a cost. For example, coauthor Rebecca conducted her fieldwork in Venezuela when she was in her late twenties but was consistently taken for twenty-one or twenty-two, an age when people (especially women) are often considered naive. These perceptions—that she was young and innocent—facilitated her access to men police officers. However, she was often made to feel dumb and inexperienced by these same research contacts. For example, her research decisions, such as living in lower-class sectors of town, were chalked up to naïveté by police officers, despite the fact that she explained to them that she had spent years working in these areas. For Ronette, a white PhD student, being viewed as an incompetent woman made her feel like a target at the beginning of her research. She drove a truck for a tour associated with the organization she was studying. She told us, "On the first tour, I had no idea what to expect. I had no idea I would be in this space with all trucker men who would target me in a lot of ways, for their own little camaraderie kind of thing." For example, after her first day on the road she was waiting for a shuttle to a local hotel with the other drivers, all of whom were men. She recounted:

> One of the drivers . . . started talking about, "Oh yeah, remember that last woman driver we had before?" . . . They told the story about how she had no idea what she was doing and she was not a good driver, and they were all laughing about it and stuff, and it was very obvious that it was targeted at me. And so I just kind of sat there and listened for a while. That was the first day, and it was really isolating. . . . I felt like I was in the spotlight, but there was nothing I could do to respond or interact.

Friendliness was not a universal benefit in the field either. Jackie, whose friendliness facilitated access to Latino construction workers, said many of the men asked her and her co-interviewer, also a young Latina student, out after the interviews. She wondered if this meant that the men were not simply put at ease but had ulterior motives in consenting to be interviewed. Several participants observed that women's friendliness can be misread as flirtation. This is true whether the researcher is an "insider" in the cultural context in which she is working or an "outsider."[25] As Jackie noted, this sort of misinterpretation is common outside of fieldwork, too. She joked, "Guys—just because you smile at them, they think you want to sleep with them!" Brittany, a white woman, described how friendliness in the interest of access creates a dilemma in a heteronormative fieldwork context.

> In talking to women, they don't necessarily assume that the reason that I'm talking to them is because I'm interested in them. Right? I mean, interested in them in a sexual way or, you know, any kind of attraction that way. Whereas for a lot of the men I was working with, just the very idea of me wanting to talk to them gave them the impression that . . . underneath all my research questions was some sort of emotional, physical attraction to them that really wasn't there. And it doesn't matter how much you try to show them or tell them that you're not interested in that way. That assumption is always there.

She talked about the difficulties that combating this entailed.

> You want to be friendly to your research [participants]. You wanna smile. You wanna make them comfortable. But there's certain individuals where any form of comfort to them will be interpreted as a come-on. And then if you take that away all of a sudden you're left with something that they're interpreting as being really threatening. So I'm either being interpreted by my [participants] as overly interested in them, sexually interested in them, some sort of attraction, . . . or I'm completely threatening and I'm trying to emasculate them and I'm trying to attack them for their views. There wasn't always a lot of middle ground.

As Brittany's experience demonstrates, gendered social interactions in the field are constituted by multiple meanings that often do not allow for shared interpretations.

Choosing to alter one's self-presentation in the field can have other emotional costs. Playing into gender expectations results in ethical questions for the researcher. Presenting a "false" version of themselves to participants seemed unfair to some of the women we interviewed given that they were

Think about your own research context or one of the contexts in which the researchers in this chapter worked. What kinds of embodied performances (including identifications like race, class, gender, nationality, etc.) and expectations might you be held accountable for? How do you think this would affect your research? How do you think this would affect your sense of self?

Would you play up (gender, race, class, etc.) expectations to facilitate your research? Why or why not?

asking participants to open up and be honest about themselves and their lives. They felt this was an ethical issue but also one of building trust and rapport through honesty and openness.

Our women participants generally felt that if they were men, they would not have confronted these particular stereotypes; nor would they have spent as much time negotiating being infantilized or sexualized in the field, either by resisting it or allowing it to happen. This is not to say that men do not navigate bodily expectations that place them at a disadvantage, however. Indeed, to prepare all researchers for fieldwork, researchers and educators must also recognize and discuss the disadvantages and risks men face in the field. Men researchers may be placed in competition with their participants.[26] Men, too, can be sexualized (e.g., assumed to be hypersexual and sexually aggressive); they face different risks associated with expectations of hegemonic masculinity depending on the context in which they are working. As for women, there are divergent stereotypes of men associated with their race, class, gender expression, and so on, that can put them at risk of various types of violence.

EMBODIMENT AND ACCESS

Our participants described numerous ways in which their bodies—or perhaps better, the social meanings associated with their bodies—created advantages and disadvantages in the field. In this section, we discuss some of the ways researchers' bodies can facilitate and constrain access, beyond the stereotypes discussed above.

Access

In certain contexts, feminine embodiment can facilitate trust and access, particularly with other women and children. As discussed above, many of our participants felt men and women alike were more likely to trust and open up to women ethnographers, giving them access to thoughts and experiences they may not have shared with men. Sabine Grenz found this as well while conducting interviews with men and women about sexuality. When asked, all of her participants stated they would rather be interviewed by a woman than by a man when discussing this topic.[27] Similarly, Sofía, a Latina associate professor, observed that participants in her research treated her as a person they could safely tell about their experiences of family or sexual violence.

For some women, when interviewing men access and trust were facilitated because they were not perceived as a threat to their participants' masculinity. As Nancy, a white researcher, explained regarding her work in men's prisons: "They just told me stuff that I don't think they would have told a man. I think I felt safe to them because I was not a threat to their masculinity." In a sense, she said, her interviews with the prisoners were an opportunity for them to display their sensitive sides: "I think they were able to be vulnerable with me in ways they wouldn't have been with a male researcher." Will, a white man, concurred, noting that women who did some interviewing for him managed to elicit more emotional vulnerability from gang members than he did. Annie, an Asian American woman, found that being perceived as unthreatening facilitated people's trust in the rural Latin American communities where she did her work. She added that although participants' perceptions of her as passive ran counter to her temperament, it was essential for maintaining access as well as physical security in her field sites. Nevertheless, these two goals sometimes ran counter to one another. She explained:

> I will lose my field site if I appear to be a threat to the gangs, or to the narco traffickers in the barrios. I will lose my site at best, and I will have to [leave the country] at worst. . . . So while I am loath not to be my ideally projected strong independent self, I also feel like I do need to convey a particular weakness and nonthreateningness that is completely counter to my nature. The

work that I am doing is not threatening to them, but I am a woman alone from the United States, and that is so often associated with being a spy in these parts.

While being a woman made her seem unthreatening, the fact that Annie was from the United States mitigated this benefit to some extent and required that she act very different from her "self" as she understood it.

Many participants spoke specifically about how their gendered embodiment gave them easier access to women and children. Some contrasted their experiences with women directly to the difficulties they had with men. Joan, for instance, reported that women seemed to take her more seriously.

> I remember noticing afterwards going through the transcripts and stuff that the women told me a lot more than the men did. They were some of the best interview subjects, the handful of them that I had. And actually they were great. And these are right-wing women. There was no meeting of the minds, but they were straightforward, they took me seriously, they answered my questions. Which the guys didn't do.

Likewise, Angie, a white researcher who worked on the Occupy movement in the United States, said that women "really saw me as another activist," while men tended to sexualize her.

In some cases, the cultural context in which researchers were working meant that only women could gain access to women and children. Susie, a white woman who did her research in Madagascar, explained how this played out for her.

> Men and women in Madagascar have sort of separate social lives, even if they're married. I felt like being a woman allowed me to be more friendly with other women who I was doing research with. I don't know that a man would have not been able to do the same type of research that I did with the women, maybe he would have, but women are very deferential to men. So the fact that I was a woman, I think they were more comfortable talking to me without their spouse present. Like if [I] had been a man maybe they would've wanted their spouse to answer for them[,] ... which happened at the beginning of my research.... Some women, not all women, some women would just sort of bow their heads and let their husbands respond for them. So I think the fact that I was a woman, their husbands were okay with me coming by the house [laughs], which would not have been okay for some men.

Thus patriarchal gender norms can facilitate access for women researchers in some cases.

Interviewing women also gave some participants access to spheres of life rather than shutting them off, as sometimes happened in spaces dominated by men. A Latina participant, Marina, explained that while she could not go to the cantina with men day laborers without being thought of as a prostitute, when she was working on a different project with women, who were also day laborers, she was able to gain access to more parts of their lives. They invited her to go to Mass with them on Sundays or to go shopping with them. This was particularly important to her research because she was interested not only in their lives on the corner, but in their commutes and household and neighborhood dynamics. Her research with men was for an interview-based project for another professor, which did not require that she accompany them in this way. But she felt that even if she had wanted to, it would have been too difficult to navigate access to other parts of their lives.

For some participants, similarities between themselves and their participants—related to gender presentation and performance as well as other factors—facilitated trust and access. When studying the experiences of women in the Occupy movement, for example, Angie found that her own prior experiences with street harassment, sexual harassment, and stalking meant she "could relate and sympathize and know what kinds of questions to ask" when her participants mentioned their experiences with these issues. Men, she observed, might not find these experiences important enough to pay attention to them in their research. Though she did not doubt that men could get access to the same data that she did, the larger obstacle was that they would first have to view gender inequalities in movements as an important issue. Her observations highlight that what we as scholars perceive as important enough to study can perpetuate power inequalities, thus shaping the overall body of what counts as valid or important ethnographic knowledge. For Brittany, it was much easier to build long-term relationships with women who had been ignored by others. She reflected:

> A lot of the women ... were supportive of me, just being a woman doing research or taking an interest in them. . . . Or they were excluded or kind of ignored by other high-power people. So I think they saw me as an outlet, in the way that the men didn't really need me. They didn't need me to get their story across. They already had a lot of networks and contacts and power that my female informants didn't have.

In contrast, when she was studying historical reenactments, the men Brittany talked to would sometimes refuse to drop their eighteenth- or nineteenth-century character roles in order to avoid answering her questions about the race, class, and gender politics of the scene.

Older men, however, were more likely to take Brittany under their wing, treating her as a granddaughter. This was also true for Janet, a black sociologist studying social class. She described this tendency as a "very paternal thing that allowed me to be able to get more information. And you know, I am not saying that I acted like I was younger than I was, but I definitely allowed them to treat me like I could be their granddaughter." This role sometimes came with unsolicited advice (e.g., about her dreadlocks), but it did facilitate access. In these situations, women's bodies can allow for the development of intimacy in ways that do not put the researcher at risk of sexualization or sexual harassment. Intimacy between older men and women like Janet and Brittany was not a sexualized intimacy but rather a familial one.

Gender facilitated access for men in certain contexts, too. Especially when it came to accessing spaces of power, being a man (particularly a white man), and thus being considered a legitimate holder of power, can be a key embodied asset. Men are able to participate in particular activities or draw on hegemonic masculine scripts that help build trust and intimacy with other men. Sergio, a Latin American mestizo who works on crime and violence in the Global South, explained that among the many strategies he used to build rapport, some were facilitated by his gendered access to men's spaces and activities.

> I have established good bonds or good trust relationships mostly with men. . . . I think it has to do with the type of things we have in common. Like the spaces where I can hang out with them. I think one of them is just being able to drink with them, right? To share beers, spend time with them just drinking. That says a lot about your capacity to create bonds with them but also that you are capable of doing it as a man, right? And then soccer games. Soccer games were key also in developing a trust relationship with them.

Because most of the community leaders in his field site were men, being able to participate in these activities was a key strategy for gaining access. Will engaged in similar activities, and although he was reluctant to flirt with women in the field, he considered his approach to interacting with men a form of flirtation, a strategy to interest men in a friendship with him and keep their attention. Albert, a white-multiracial ethnographer working in a school setting, noted that drinking was a key activity that allowed him to gain access, too. Although he recalled drinking with other men teachers in "shady" bars, their young women colleagues would usually not stick around in those situations, suggesting the gendered character of this access. As Albert observed, in general, men ethnographers have more access to certain spaces of power simply because there are more men in those spaces. Women might gain access to such spaces, but the politics of decency that regulate public space may lead participants to misinterpret women's motives when they do, potentially shutting down other avenues of access. Daisy, an Asian American researcher who studied entrepreneurship in China, explained that there were places and times of day that she did not have access to her men participants. She spoke of a man she knew who was studying similar issues and would accompany men to hostess bars. Daisy reflected that, as a woman, it would be difficult to maintain her impression management if she entered those spaces, because she would be perceived differently as a result.

The men we interviewed recognized that women ethnographers were more likely to face sexualization in the field as well as distinct safety concerns. Bob, a white environmental ethnographer working in the urban United States, described one experience that confirmed this for him: "I remember when a woman came around, a young woman who wanted to make a documentary. And in the end she did make her documentary, so it's not that she couldn't do the work, but . . . as soon as she left the guys were talking about how big her 'tits' were and all this other stuff. And I felt like, 'Oh my God, like, does she know what she's getting into?'"

According to Bob, this woman actually got access to a couple of men he never did, and he surmises that it may have been because she was working on a documentary rather than an academic book, which meant more exposure for the participants. He has reason to believe, though, that it also had something to do with gender: "They were the [same] guys who made tons of sexual innuendos about her when she wasn't there." So in this case (and as confirmed by the experiences of many of our women participants) gender did not prevent this woman from getting access, but, as Bob observed, it was intertwined with sexual objectification. In contrast, he reflected, "I cannot recall a single field encounter where I felt that there was a sexual connotation—with men or women." It may be the case that Bob has experienced sexualized interactions without recognizing them as such. However, Bob's understanding that all of his field encounters were nonsexual speaks to his ability to successfully navigate social spaces without being affected by sexual connotations, suggestions, and insinuations—a privilege that not all researchers enjoy. Moreover, the access facilitated by masculinity is usually not dependent on denigrating self-presentations by men or men's complicity in their own disempowerment (though it can imply complicity in the denigration and disempowerment of women). For example, David, a Latin American researcher of social movements, felt his youthful good looks helped him but not because he was sexualized by participants. Instead, it led older women to help him with his work.

Several white participants noted that their race facilitated their access in the field. Mary, who discussed numerous disadvantages related to gender, pointed out that her race was a significant advantage to her work. According to her, the research she conducted in the rural United States may have been next to impossible to do as a person of color. And Susie reflected on the relationship of whiteness (and being from the Global North) to certain freedoms.

> The fact that I was a white woman, as opposed to a Malagasy woman, did give me a lot more freedoms. So being white made my gender less of an issue, if that makes sense. . . . I mean, it was sort of suspect if I was spending time alone with a man, but [I was] definitely not [held to] the same standards that a Malagasy would be held to. Or the fact that I was able to continue my education to a PhD level and not have children at my age and not [be seen] like my life is over.

Susie admits she did not reflect on this while in the field, but in retrospect, it was clear that, despite the issues she did face, a lot of restrictive gender roles did not apply to her.

Some women of color also felt that the intersections of gender and race protected them in some respects. Annie felt she benefited from her racial ambiguity in her fieldwork as men did not quite know what to make of her. Frances, who is also Asian American, described how intersecting assumptions regarding race and nation entered into her fieldwork on immigration in Europe. As an example, she described making initial contact with participants.

> Because I have a fully American accent, [if] they didn't meet me initially face-to-face and a contact was made through phone or through snowball [sampling] or something like that, . . . then they expected me to be this white American woman. And so [laughs] when I showed up, and then I'm this small Asian woman, they're surprised. I had this one guy who was waiting for me at a café. And we were right next to each other and texting, "Where are you? Where are you?" And I'm like, "I'm over here." Suddenly he turns

around and I'm waving to him, and he's like, "Oh, I thought, I was expecting an American." And he meant white American, of course.

While exchanges like this reinforced her outsider status, Frances felt being an outsider in the communities she researched helped her generate trust in the long run. Maritza, despite her many negative experiences with harassment in the field, felt that her gender protected her in some ways.

> If I were walking down the street as a brown or a black man, I could be subject to violence. That's not going to happen to me. I would rather get cat-called than suffer physical violence.... I mean, I have never feared that anyone would rape me or anything, but I know that if I were a black male or a Latino male or whatever, ... I might fear for my safety or be subject to police surveillance or something.

Even though Maritza faced racialized sexual harassment in the field and in academia, she felt she was safer in certain ways than black and Latino men would be if they were working in the same neighborhoods. Her reflection speaks to the different types of violence and vulnerability that men—particularly men of color—face in the field, vulnerabilities that require further exploration in men's ethnographies. In Brittany's case, the mostly white men she worked with in the U.S. South were often suspicious of her agenda. Still, it was there that "being a white woman from a southern institution" brought its greatest advantage. "I can blend into southern and do the southernisms. . . . And I would wear the [Southern University] T-shirt every once in a while to let people know that's where I'm from." In many cases, she felt that researchers from other regional, racial, and ethnic backgrounds would be able to get "equally fascinating," if different, data. But in certain social environments, they would also be at "a distinctly different disadvantage," as Brittany put it. That is, Brittany's whiteness gave her access—and protected her—in white supremacist settings. Conversely, as a queer white woman studying queer populations, Kista described being checked for exercising her racial privilege, like when a participant asked, "Why should I let you interview me? Why should I help some white chick get her dissertation?" She explains, "I was directly held accountable for how my white privilege is being used in the interview process to access information from oppressed black women." According to Kista, this interaction "was a consciousness-raising moment." She explained, "I wasn't conscious about how my own political position was being played out in my research until that conversation."

For some participants, even as gender and race facilitated access, they also turned their bodies into a target in the field. Karina explained, "Well, I think here is where race really comes into play. Because, you know, when I'm walking around Rwanda there's the sexualization of everyday life, but there's also, I'm a white woman and that's really rare. I felt like I was just standing out [laughs], you know? I felt basically like neon. So not only like a target but a very visible one. . . . It didn't matter how fast I moved or how many other people were around, I was still very obvious." Whereas in the United States she is sometimes able to avoid harassment by blending in, she was not able to do that in Rwanda. Though her whiteness facilitated her access to government representatives, it made her a visible target in the field, which resulted in costs that Karina had to navigate. Lori also stood out as a "tallish, blondish woman" in South America. For her, too, this could be uncomfortable and made her vulnerable to street harassment, but it also created access: the men athletes she worked with liked having her around because of her appearance.

Some participants talked about navigating ethnicity and skin tone as well. Linda, a Latina participant who described herself as a coethnic vis-à-vis her participants, observed that in her work on a multisited project about immigrant organizations ethnicity, more than gender, defined her research relationships. Among other things, she tried not to appear too authoritative with participants, lest they think she was too assimilated and thus untrustworthy. Moreover, because her accent is difficult to place, it was easier for her to work in contexts where there were tensions among Latino groups than it might have been for someone more clearly identifiable as from a particular country. Being Latina also facilitated her access compared to white researchers who worked on the same project. Similar to Mary's and Brittany's observations about working in field sites dominated by white people, conducting research with communities of color was facilitated by race and ethnicity for some of our participants.

This does not mean that researchers of color automatically gain access because of their skin color and/or identification, however. Bridgette described negotiating differences related to class and skin color with her participants, who were also black.

There's some interesting dynamics within the black community around class and gender. As a researcher, I have to further legitimize myself because a lot of African Americans kind of distrust science and research and government and that kind of thing. So as a person who is affiliated with a university and science, I have to further legitimize myself. Also, the fact that I am highly educated, and even my skin color—I am lighter-skinned—and so those dynamics kind of play into [it] because people may think that I am not trustworthy or I am on the side of the universities or I don't understand what it's like to live in a poor neighborhood.

Bridgette worked to gain trust by being visible in the community where she was working. She is bisexual, and she faced questions in the black gay community about her sexual identity: "They'll ask me, 'So are you gay?' Like if that's a legitimacy to why I am doing this research. So you know, 'Are you family?' They will ask it that way." Thus Bridgette's race and sexual identity undoubtedly created access for her, but access was not unfettered. Like other women of color we interviewed, Bridgette's experiences illustrated how multiple identifications—including gender, race, and sexual identity as well as education, occupation, and religion—intersect to create different opportunities and constraints in different contexts.

Men also noted the ways that different aspects of their identifications became particularly salient in the field. For Sergio, a mestizo Latin American working in his country of origin, race and gender were both salient in his interactions in the field. Indigenous men who lived in the city where he did his fieldwork often joked with him that he should hook up with indigenous women. On one occasion a man tried to pick a fight with him by accusing Sergio of calling him an "Indian." Sergio saw both of these as attempts on the part of the men to assert their masculinity. Despite these tensions, he noted that his race and gender helped with access, as being perceived as a white man in his country (as he was) connotes prestige and access to resources, as it does in many other parts of the world. He was also perceived as a foreigner (he studied abroad and introduced himself as someone who lived in the United States). This granted Sergio access that he might not have had if he had been perceived as a local.

Lack of Access

Participants talked extensively about how gender negatively affected their access in the field. A Latina associate professor, Elena, talked about one of the first research projects she was involved with, which focused on fishing communities in the northeastern United States: "I was very young at that time, and they perceived me as someone, that I was not going to do any harm to them and that I was innocent in some ways." Later she began research in Mexico, where she did not experience the same advantages. She explained, "Because I have been working in a part of Mexico with very traditional gender roles, women are not allowed to interact with men, so that really was a constraint to me, for my research." Ethnographers, as Elena points out, cannot expect to operate outside the social norms and expectations that govern their field sites (even as being an outsider sometimes confers certain freedoms).

In some cultural contexts women's access may be restricted, or they may be banned from certain spaces altogether. Researchers who study religion or work in fundamentalist contexts are likely to confront this issue. For example, Mercedes, a Latina researcher, described how at one Evangelical church where she collected interviews, the young men refused to meet with her one-on-one. She was able to interview them but only when others were around. And while Bridgette generally felt her gender was an advantage in her work on sexuality and religion, she described sometimes feeling like she "wasn't treated as an authority." She recalled an instance in which her access was curtailed while recruiting participants at a mosque with a group of two other women and one man. A leader there agreed to talk to the group, but as they entered, he stopped the women, telling them they had to enter via the women's entrance. "In shock," as Bridgette described it, they paused to regroup and think about how to proceed. They ended up sending their man colleague to talk to him, and the women went through the women's entrance as instructed, where they found "a lot of toys and kids." She reflected, "Normally I experience racial discrimination, and I've experienced harassment too, but that was the first time it was just like specifically because I am a woman I cannot come in." Although a researcher might prepare for fieldwork by reading about participants' beliefs and practices, experiencing inequality firsthand in the field can still have an unsettling effect.

Cross-gender access in seemingly more egalitarian spaces can also be challenging. Lisa, a white associate professor, for example, was interested in studying the men's cycling scene in a midwestern community. Although she had a willing gatekeeper, other men would engage in creepy innuendo when she was doing observations or trying to set up interviews. Very few agreed to formal interviews, or they sabotaged the interview by turning it into a sexualized encounter. After many months, she decided to abandon the project. She explained, "I came to the conclusion that I'm not the person to do that research. And I knew that right after because I had a graduate student who actually was a cyclist. He was male. And for a class project he went in to interview cyclists. He came back with, like, twenty-five interviews, no problem at all." From Lisa's perspective, her identification and self-presentation as a woman prohibited her from being able to complete this project. In contrast, in the case of her student, the men were just "helping out another guy." Of course, it might have been the case that if Lisa had "persisted," if she hadn't "back[ed] off instead of pushing forward," she might have eventually made contacts, pushed through barriers, and been able to gather the data she sought.[28] Nevertheless, while some researchers might chastise her for lacking stamina or endurance, we would suggest that Lisa made the healthy decision to remove herself from a toxic research environment.

Like the women in our sample, several men said there were spaces they could not enter when interviewing across gender. Indeed, it is important to consider the ways in which men's bodies also shape access, especially given that cis white men's bodies have historically been treated as neutral. As Adam Baird writes about conducting research with gangs, although his "male patter" opened up certain avenues to gang members, it "set a particular tone, meaning that gang members were less likely to discuss the emotional burden of quotidian violence, fear or loss."[29] In some cases lack of access was interpersonal, as in the case of Sergio, who noted that it seemed harder to build trust with women. In others, it was institutional. For example, Claude, a white researcher, recalled that his access to women in a drug treatment program he was studying was restricted because women residents were not allowed to speak to men there. Albert also worked in a gender-segregated field site and had to figure out ways to enter young women's spaces and develop relationships with them.

Concerns for one's safety can also restrict access for women in some circumstances. Annie described a monsignor in the Latin American country where she worked who told her that because she was a woman she could not move to a particular neighborhood (she had been living in the seminary before that). While Annie knew he was likely concerned for her, it enraged her to be told that she was unable to do something just because she was a woman. This constraint upset her even though she described her field site as "lawless" and acknowledged that it was a context in which she felt vulnerable in some respects. Mary described not going to bars and strip clubs in the midwestern fracking community where she did her research. In her case, safety and the politics of respectability were both at play: not only was she concerned for her safety, as men vastly outnumbered women in the community, but she also worried about what people would think of her in that conservative small town if she spent time in those spaces. Samantha, who also worked in fracking country before changing her dissertation topic, noted that access was gendered in the sense that the "man camps" were not safe for women. She noted that ethnographers who were men could live in the camps and work alongside the other men, creating possibilities for ethnographic intimacy that were not available to her. In fact, Mary recalled that just as she was leaving the field, an ethnographer who was a man arrived at the same field site and easily entered spaces in which she may have been in danger.

Although women participants often felt more comfortable and safer when working with women (even when those women were hitting on them, as was the case for Kista and Louise), this did not mean they always had unfettered access to other women either.[30] For example, in coauthor Rebecca's experience, unlike the men, the few women police officers she got to know "had no motivation to hang out with me." She explained, "They were women and they have families and lives outside of their work, so when they weren't working, most of them had small children and things like that. So it was much more difficult to motivate interest in them to be around me." In contrast, men's interest in her, as debilitating as it was, did help create access. For Elena, getting the women in the Mexican rural community where she worked to trust her enough "to invite me to their houses and feel comfortable around me" took almost a year. She perceived that they felt threatened by her and suggested this was more likely to be the case in contexts with rigid gender norms that associate men and women with separate spheres. The women had a lot of questions for her before agreeing to participate: they wanted to know about her intentions, as well as personal matters such as her background, clothes, and lack of makeup. She had imagined it would be easier to work with women than with men, but for her the opposite was true: in her field site men actually got upset that she was not asking them more questions because they wanted to show off their knowledge. Likewise, for Linda, a Latina student who worked on immigration in the United States, women were more guarded than men. Some women said they had to check with their husbands before agreeing to participate but then did not get back to her. Jenna, a white graduate student, noted that even though being a woman was essential to getting access to women in her South Asian field sites, it was men who were more willing to talk to her at first (to the point that she faced harassment, as discussed in chapter 3).

Depending on how a researcher's actions are (mis)interpreted, women may be wary to participate. When Cathy, a white researcher, was working in Mexico she perceived "aggression from a lot of women," particularly from women around her age, in their twenties and thirties. She believed jealousy among women, as well as their prior interactions with and stereotypes of U.S. American whites, contributed to their hostility. June, a white woman from the United States who was studying the health and well-being of Mexican women whose husbands were transnational migrants, faced similar issues at the beginning of her fieldwork, connected to her gender, race, and nationality. She explained: "Because I was working with women who had migrant husbands, a lot of them had had experiences of their husbands having other relationships with women in the United States and not sending money back to them, and so I think a lot of the women had a particular image also of American women as kind of stealing their husbands." Phoebe, too, described her relationship with the women at her field site as pleasant but cold, noting that they viewed her as just another one of her gatekeeper's "girls." Thus racial and national politics intersect with gender to influence access. Educational and class differences also created some uneasiness among participants. None of our participants were particularly surprised by the difficulties of approaching women in the field. As a whole, they were reflexive about the ways their race, nationality, education, and class afforded them power in the field and viewed the pushback they received in such instances as understandable.

FLIRTATION

The topic of flirtation, touched on above, merits further attention. Flirtation is an important way in which gendered embodiment, and the sexualized meanings attached to interactions during fieldwork, enters into the ethnographic field, reflecting and reproducing broader power relations. As Shamus Khan, influenced by Foucault, writes, "Our bodies are expressions of the larger power relations of society, and each act of the body works to express itself relative to its own position within these power relations."[31] Several women felt men participated in their projects only because of their desire to flirt or their expectation or hope that doing so could lead to something more. While men might have participated because they felt safe with women, as discussed above, it must be noted that flirtation and feelings of comfort and being at ease can overlap, with the latter often facilitating the former.

The issue of access is central to understanding the role flirtation can play in women's fieldwork, especially when their participants are men. Annie explained that she let men flirt with her to keep from shutting down access, but tried not to reciprocate. In one extreme situation, the sixty-five-year-old owner of the stable where Annie took riding lessons, who had become her gatekeeper and source of local cultural knowledge, proposed to her. She explained:

> By the end of the summer, he wanted me to marry him. So now I am in this situation where [there's] this really, really rich source of cultural contact [who] validates me to the people in the rural area, but at the same time, every interaction with him is annoying because I have to deal with advances from a sixty-five-year-old man. It's really frustrating.

Annie clarified that she found the situation annoying rather than threatening, but working out "how to preserve his ego while making my boundaries clear" proved to be a daunting task.

Daisy spoke of the difficulty of dealing with suggestive texts from her participants in China, where she studied entrepreneurs: "A lot of times I'm getting these texts from these male contacts, and it's not like I could just ignore them. Because my ulterior motive is . . . to pick their brains for the things that I want to know about. And so I need to maintain that relationship." Nevertheless, she described the burden this entailed: "I don't want to mislead them or give them mixed signals. It's a really tough line to balance."

Like several others, Marina observed that it was easier to get interviews with men than with women, and she, too, surmised that this was because of the sexual possibility. Kista argued that if she had shut down sexual banter with women, it would have restricted her access: "I think that the normalization of sexual banter among some queer populations makes it not a threatening thing, makes it not a sexual thing, frankly, [but] makes it a rapport thing instead." She explained further:

> It would have shown me to be an outsider, right? If I can't engage in the same banter that they can engage in, then I must not be like them. And if I'm not like them, then I'm not who they thought I was. And if I'm not who they thought I was, then we're not having the conversation they thought they were gonna have. And it's all tanked at that point.

Again, though, she confessed that she would not feel the same if she were interviewing straight men.

Some of our participants completely shut down flirtation in the field. This was true of Angie, who would cut off conversations with men in the Occupy movement if they began flirting with her (although it is important to note that men were peripheral to her project, which was on women in the movement). But most tried to either manage or use flirtation to their advantage. This was certainly true for Joan, who, as noted above, was initially surprised when Salvadoran elites flirted with her in the field but used their interest to get them to agree to be interviewed. Some expressed the belief that flirtation is just a part of life, and it makes sense that it would enter into fieldwork. Reflecting on her work in the prison system, Nancy said:

> Flirting is part of our sociality. I guess for some people they don't like when we acknowledge that, but I flirt with everyone, right? I flirt with men, I flirt with women, and it's fun, right? I mean flirtation makes it sound like you are trying to get in someone's pants, but to be human is to be flirtatious. You show interest, you make eye contact, you ask people questions, you sort of indicate a level of interest [in] them.

She noted, however, that the prison officers did not like to see her flirting with inmates.

Indeed, flirtation was not always a concern or a problem for researchers. Some enjoyed engaging in flirtation and found these experiences pleasurable, so that pleasure and possibility combine to facilitate access. Reflecting on her work in rural Latin America, Tammy, a white researcher, revealed that she enjoyed flirtation: "I have to admit ... sometimes that kind of attention is kind of fun. Have a good time and flirt back a little bit. It seems sort of harmless, at least when you are well known in the community and you know that, well, there's a dozen people here that will watch out for me if anything happens, you know, or if anyone tries anything." Tammy's ability to find pleasure in these kinds of interactions was context dependent; she remarked that she would not engage in flirtation in a place where her social networks were thin.

A few participants talked about the crushes they developed in the field, which similarly led to difficult balancing acts.[32] Rosie, a white graduate student, studied music festivals for her dissertation. While interviewing "an incredibly articulate young man, probably just within a couple of years of my own age, ... I was cultivating a little bit of interviewer-participant crush." When she had a hard time hearing him at the campsite because of the music and crowd noise in the background they went to her car to finish the interview. During the interview Rosie described the interaction as "very comfortable," similar to a conversation between friends. When her participant started asking personal questions, however, the situation changed.

> I had the sudden realization [that] there is a strange man in my car, asking me intimate questions. . . . I felt as if my own sort of individual ambitions [were] conflicting with some of my research intentions. . . . So I had to ask him to leave, and he's like, "Well, what's wrong?" And I am like, "I invited you into my car, and the interview is now done. You need to leave." And he's like, "Oh, okay. Well, then."

Even though she cut things off, the crush ultimately created tension for her in the field. After the interview her participant continued to come to her campsite during the festival to hang out, and for her "there would always be this overtone of, like, 'We could make this work. I know you are attracted to me. I am attracted to you.'"

Confronting and managing flirtation was complicated and riddled with tension and contradictory desires as well. Harriet told a story that encapsulates how attempts at ethnographic intimacy can go awry in the field. First, she reflected on how this can happen.

> I mean it is flattering, you know? Some young, pretty girl comes in and starts asking you all these questions about your work that your wife doesn't even care about anymore, and seems super interested in your life. And there is a way in which the more they tell you builds a kind of intimacy or an intimacy assumption for them, even though for you, you're gathering data.

She went on to talk about a young man in her field site who was very flirtatious with her.

> I kind of returned some of the flirting because, you know, . . . he's cute, he's my age, [and] friendships in the field are super important. He asked if he could come over, we could go out and get a cup of coffee or something. And I was like, "Sure that'd be fine." I had seen him a lot on his turf, so why not?

Harriet interpreted this as a research opportunity, albeit a pleasant one. But when the man arrived for coffee, he was carrying flowers. When he suggested they take a walk on the beach instead of getting coffee, Harriet agreed. As they talked on the beach, he suddenly began kissing her. Harriet spoke openly about how difficult it was to categorize this interaction and how conflicted she felt about how to manage it. In one moment, they were "talking a little bit about, you know, where I come from and so on. And then the next thing I know he's kissing me." Harriet described her thinking at the time.

> And that is when I hear in my head, I hear that, like, "Sleep with a native, it's the only way to know what's going on." And the other side of my head is like, "No, this is, this is so, you need to get out of here [laughs]. You need to get out of here." . . . You don't really know how you feel in those moments. Because you're totally conflicted. Because you're in the field, but you're also, you're also being sexually, I don't know. Most women don't say sexually assaulted in those [situations], most, because, you know, I knew him, he knew me, but there's a moment where, you know, he's sticking his tongue down my throat and I'm like, well . . . [laughs].

She managed the situation by telling him her professional ethics did not allow her to have this type of relationship with a participant, but it was a surprising and confusing moment from which it was hard to extricate herself.

For some, "fieldwork crushes," along with flirtation, were viewed as valuable for data collection. But others wondered if flirtation actually *was* helpful in the data gathering process. While it helped with access, Marina said, it sometimes seemed like men just gave the answers they thought she wanted to hear, which made her question the validity of her data. Nancy likewise wondered, "Is it real data because they are flirting with me?" This made her reluctant to talk with her committee and others about the role flirtation had played in her data gathering.

> No one talks about that. What does it mean to establish rapport? The idea that there might be a charm aspect to that that might be gendered or classed or raced, or gendered primarily, but I can't do my gender without also doing my race and class. And, like, what does it mean that I play the dumb white girl sometimes, like, "No, I don't understand, can you explain that to me?" That is a tool that I used in these interviews. Is that professional? Can I call it data?

Nancy recognized that acknowledging using her embodiment as a tool in these particular ways could open her up to critique, even though, as she noted, all qualitative scholars use tools that are specific to their particular embodiments and positionalities. Still, she reflected, "I can't say that to my committee! . . . They are going to tell me not to do this, that I am wrecking my data."

Indeed, women may face the judgment of their peers if they deliberately engage in flirtation in the field. Will, who worked on gangs in South America, observed, "I think women using sexuality really, really raises the hackles of the misogynists. They'd be like, 'How dare women use their competitive advantage in sexuality to get better data than men. The bitches.'" At the same time, he added, men take advantage of being the "exotic, wealthy man" to get data (and attract women), too.

Of course, sexualization affects men's research as well, and they also may face negative implications when sexualized. But how sexualization shapes research varies according to gender and other aspects of embodiment. For example, at social gatherings women sought Will out to dance and suggestively pointed out that his girlfriend was in another country; a few women propositioned him. However, he noted that these advances were always contextualized by his Western white man's privilege, such that his social location provided him with resources he could use to navigate the situation in ways that did not put him at a disadvantage. Rather than negotiate a lack of power, Will found that as an exotic, alluring, and powerful foreigner in the field he had to maneuver interviews and fieldwork with women carefully. He avoided personal relationships with his participants, considering the possibility that these might lead him to exploit his privileged position and generate sexual rumors about him.

Brian, a white graduate student, felt the same way. In Central America, people often teased him about dating someone, making sexual jokes and encouraging him to have a "girl on the side." This teasing did not threaten his research, but he did worry about perceptions of impropriety, especially if a woman flirted with him. Thus, like Will, he worked hard to avoid rumors by remaining in public and not being with these women one on one. Will's and Brian's experiences speak to a type of vulnerability that both men and women are susceptible to in the field, albeit in distinct ways: perceptions, rumors, and judgments based on the politics of decency. For David, such jokes and teasing worked to his benefit in the context in which he conducted his fieldwork. He observed that being young, educated, white, tall, and thin were all "marks of privilege" that helped him in the field, not because participants necessarily wanted to sleep with him, but because being perceived as attractive in a given cultural context facilitated interactions with "no strings attached." In other words, when his physical appearance created access for him, he did not feel that anything other than the present interaction was expected of him. In contrast, many of our women participants had to navigate men's attraction *and* expectations. For instance, in coauthor Rebecca's case, many of her men participants expected that conversations and interactions would lead to more. She and other women we interviewed lost relationships or eventually ended them because their participants expected mutual attraction, dates, and/or sex.

Albert, who worked as a teacher at the school where he conducted field-work, described ambiguous and uncomfortable situations when students asked for dates or experimented with sexual boundaries with faculty members. However, he saw this as less about flirtation than pushing boundaries. He gave the example of a girl who came to a meeting with him wearing a slip. She wasn't doing this for him, he felt, but rather to create a provocation. He and other authority figures had similar experiences on several occasions with different girls. He explained the difficulty involved:

> The reason it was such an uncomfortable situation for a lot of faculty members, and I think the reason the girls did it, was it's very difficult to say to a young woman, "You're dressed inappropriately." Because the subsequent parts of those conversations then highlight the fact that a man has been focusing on or paying attention to how these girls are dressing. And so this is what I mean by not so much flirtatious as boundary pushing. There was a lot of attention to the problems of girls' sexuality at the school. And so this was like a little weapon of resistance.

While he did talk to students about these issues, he worried about "the consequences of that because the big problem is [that] I can't control the message, right? So if she then went and complained to a bunch of students about how I was creepy and staring at her . . . " The girls in this case were experimenting with their own embodied power, which placed Albert in a difficult position as their teacher.

Although she generally restricted flirtation to the process of getting men to agree to interviews and not the interview itself, Joan observed that flirting in the field felt like playing a dangerous game: "It was totally nerve wracking because you don't know what their expectations are and how far you are supposed to go." Joan's research in Central America was not on gender or sexuality. But the constant need to pay attention to gender and embodiment illustrates what Harriet pointed out: gender and sexuality shape the entire fieldwork process and are salient even when we do not explicitly set out to study gender (see chap. 1).

The influence flirtation in the field might have on the data we collect calls for reflexivity in ethnographic practice as well as analysis. As Annie noted, flirtation in the field is "forming whatever my findings are going to be."

However, discussions about flirtation, and sex more broadly, are eschewed in much of the methods literature. In thinking about how flirtation shaped her access and data, Annie wondered, "How reflexive do I need to be in field notes of all the gender roles I set today and what their reactions are? What role does that play in my final analysis?" Annie's observation suggests that students are left to wonder how vigilant or reflexive they need to be about these issues. Because flirtation in the field is hard to avoid and often out of the control of the ethnographer herself, it is essential to consider the potential (albeit often unknowable) costs for the data as well as for the mental health and safety of the researcher before entering the field.

BEYOND FLIRTATION: SEX IN THE FIELD

Sex in the field sometimes seems like the dirty little secret no one talks about, perhaps especially in sociology.[33] This is despite the fact that, as Michael Connors Jackman emphasizes, scholars are sexual beings: "They are not passive objects of their informants' affection, but subjects of desire as well."[34] As Liz Grauerholz and colleagues have pointed out, "Attraction is a powerful emotional response that can profoundly influence the research process, just as other intense emotional states do."[35] Although we did not ask about sex specifically, it came up in several interviews. Harriet's comment above alludes to the idea, which other participants also referenced, that cultivating a sexual relationship at your field site is one of the best ways to become embedded and gather good data.[36] This notion, repeated today in perhaps a tongue-in-cheek (but distasteful) manner, has its roots in the sexual violence of the colonial enterprise, of which ethnography is a part. Still, some ethnographers may form romantic relationships with research subjects and as a result become assimilated into the culture, even though securing data during sexual encounters may pose the problem of legitimacy on the researcher's part.[37] This might be even truer for women than for men, since women are more likely to be penalized and ostracized for sexual activity in many contexts, a phenomenon faced with even greater intensity by women of color.[38] Harriet recalled an anthropologist friend directly telling her, "Well, in anthropology before you go into the field, before you get on the plane, your adviser's supposed to take you aside and say, 'Hey, sleep with a native.'" This friend was a man, a little older than Harriet, and this led her to reflect on what she perceived as the underlying assumptions of what he was saying:

"I guess if you're male and you go into the field, sleeping with an informant is actually part of a powerful position, right? But if you're female and you go into the field, then where does that leave you?" The power dynamics inherent in sexual relationships can affect fieldwork and the ethnographic process in multiple ways.

Some participants felt that sex was ethically and even methodologically problematic. Will, for example, said he knows a lot of people, both women and men, who have had relationships with their participants, adding that for many, these became key respondents. However, Will said, the sex is totally excluded from their published analyses. Louise also saw sex in the field as problematic. She spoke specifically about same-sex relationships in the field: "I have seen kind of attitudes of, 'Well, you know, it was mutual.' And I think that it's much easier to argue that when it's a same-sex relationship and it's what [we] tell ourselves that, as researchers, that, 'Oh, there isn't the same kind of power imbalance because it's not a gender power imbalance,' but there's still a power imbalance quite often, I think." Although she understood the value of flirtation and fieldwork crushes, Harriet also asserted that she would never go beyond flirtation. Her personal rule is no sexual intimacy in the field. Fieldwork is full of stress and strain, and "you're in a compressed, heightened emotional state," she said, and as a result, things are sure to go wrong. When they do, you cannot control how the individual or the community is going to respond, and you likely will have cut yourself off from access to a particular part of your field site.

Elena said that while she has personally tried to avoid falling in love or having sexual relationships with participants, she recalls being surprised when students at one of her universities came back from the field with husbands. Still, she observed, intimate friendships, which she does rely on in the field, also demand a lot and lead to expectations that she must meet. Thus while we might see sex as a line we would not cross, there are issues present in other types of relationships in the field that can make them almost as messy as sexual ones.[39]

Indeed, two participants spoke of developing romantic relationships with their participants; both of these relationships became messy and caused tension in the field. Karen, a white researcher, broke up with her partner in order to be with one of her participants in her Occupy study. He left his wife (who was also an Occupier) to be with her. This led to deteriorated trust and access in her field site, especially as her former partner took out his anger on others in the movement. Karen explained:

When Gene and I split up, and he found out about me and Glenn, he did come to the meetings and pop off on everyone and [said,] "All of you knew this. How could you not have told me?" Threatening violence to people, you know, so that was mega uncomfortable and that was the point where I was no longer doing fieldwork and I just knew I had to quit the group as a participant. My personal life became way too distracting for everybody.

Although she is now married to Glenn, at the time of her interview, Karen said the lesson she learned was not to date anyone in your field site.

Fiona, a white woman working in Africa, spent much of our interview talking about the affair she was having with a key informant. She was not worried about the affair damaging her work, although she did think it could damage her lover's career and both of their marriages.

So there's three things: he's my research participant, he's my friend, and he does happen to be my lover now. So it's not an ideal situation, but things happen. So I am hoping that the friendship can be long term. I am well aware that the sexual relationship has to be temporary. As far as the research participant, I am kind of trying to see how I can manage to keep that going too because he is also a really good source of data. So now I find myself thinking, "How do I balance having a relationship with a research participant?" . . . They don't teach this in methods courses, and I hadn't thought this was going to be an issue. To be honest, nobody plans to have an affair when they go off and do their fieldwork.

Though Fiona did not want to end the relationship, it had implications for her work and her sense of self. Before their relationship started, this man had been an excellent participant. However, after the relationship began, he became impatient with her questions related to research. On a personal level, she dealt with pressure for sex without protection that she found difficult to navigate. While the sexual relationship created different problems for her personal and work life, she was reluctant to leave this field site because it was desirable for other reasons. This relationship seemed to become a sort of all-encompassing awkward surplus (see introduction): Fiona was able to collect data for her project through her relationship with this man (even if the relationship itself created barriers for data collection), but she did not want to deal with the effects sex was having on her fieldwork. Instead, this consideration was put to the side as Fiona concentrated on collecting the data that were pertinent to the research questions with which she had entered the field.

For some, sex was an issue not because they dated or had sex with their participants but because they had relationships outside of their field site while doing fieldwork abroad. Even these relationships can have unexpected impacts on our work. Susie spoke of the shame and stigma she felt vis-à-vis other scholars in her discipline because she "went native," marrying a man from the country in the Global South where she did her fieldwork. She sometimes wondered if she was in fact allowed to have a personal life in the field. Similarly, Cathy had a relationship with a Mexican man. When it fell apart, it influenced her ability to trust men. This distrust was exacerbated by the fact that one of her key informants, whom she had known for years, began hitting on her when she told him about her breakup.

Sexual relationships are intimate in ways that overlap with and are distinct from other intimate relationships we build in the field, and they produce different embodied and sexualized interactions in the field. As our limited data suggest, like other embodied interactions in the field, these relationships often become fraught and create tensions that must be navigated. Once we accept that sex may occur in the field, we can begin to integrate this topic into our training and methods, opening up dialogue on the ethics and implications of sexual relationships in the field. These kinds of discussions would certainly have benefited Fiona, who eventually went home after her relationship with her research participant fell apart. She spent weeks thinking about quitting her PhD program altogether. However, she eventually "came clean" with her husband and began therapy, which helped her repair her relationship with him. After some time away from the field, she returned, found a new research location, and finished her research. But the lessons Fiona and others learned from these experiences will remain obscured and hushed, and jocular instructions to "sleep with a native" will continue to circulate, until we acknowledge that researchers, too, are sexual beings and their sexuality in the field, as in their everyday lives, is bound up in a web of power relations.

CONCLUSION

In this chapter we discussed the intertwined issues of access, trust, and building relationships in the field from an embodied perspective. We show why researchers should consider three issues before, during, and after fieldwork: the multiple expectations (from the academy as well as local settings) that shape fieldwork and our narratives of the field, how embodiment and stereotypes of bodies can facilitate and constrain access, and the role and impacts of flirtation and sex in the field. Here we discuss how these issues affect evaluation of data and provide suggestions for writing embodied ethnography.

As we have shown, whether embodiment facilitated or constrained access, most of our research participants worried that their gender and their bodies had a negative impact on their data and projects. For women like Joan whose bodies created access, their data seemed "less valid" due to the way in which they obtained it. For women whose bodies restricted access, their inability to access certain spaces and people made them wonder if they were missing out on the ethnographic intimacy that they needed to conduct good research. One of the reasons it is important for researchers to write embodied ethnographies is to demonstrate that *all* bodies affect research, which might help alleviate concerns about embodiment and "less valid" data. How, then, do we write embodied ethnography?

First, whereas the notion of full integration presents ethnographic relationships as fixed and static, we should write about our relationships in the field as "shifting social relationships that have constantly to be negotiated," not accomplishments that are achieved once we have overcome "barriers" of race, class, gender, nationality, and so on, that separate us from our research participants.[40] Power is an intricate aspect of ethnography that shifts and changes depending on relationships and context. These changes can benefit researchers but can also work to their disadvantage, depending on how race, gender, and other aspects of identity facilitate or bar access throughout their time in the field. These changes and shifts are valuable sources of understanding and should be included as data in our ethnographic vignettes. Indeed, when access is cut off where it existed previously or when formerly forthcoming participants become guarded, these shifts can tell us just as much about our research site and our place in it as does gaining unwavering access and full disclosure.

Second, rather than describe how positionality shaped research in an introduction or a methods appendix, separate from the claims made and vignettes and data used to back them up, ethnographers should incorporate not only themselves but also these embodied interactions in ethnographies. In other words, it is not enough to describe how we felt in a particular interaction or scene; we must also discuss how it felt to be a gendered, raced, classed, sexed, nationalized being in certain interactions. This does *not* mean that all of our ethnographic data must be presented from all of these positions, or that every ethnographic vignette should include reflections on our embodiment. The point here is not to put the researcher at the center of the text but to be honest about how we relate to and are perceived by the subjects we hope to investigate. While reflexivity about positionality and embodiment can be a useful tool for writing about how research affects the researcher, it must also be used to consider how our bodies affect our research and those involved in it. In many interactions, certain aspects of our identities (and others' perceptions and understandings of us) come to the fore, contributing to how our participants and we feel and respond to one another. Even if this is not clear at the time, as we go back through our data and analyze, we should reflect on how our bodies shaped our research and, where pertinent, weave these reflections through our ethnographic vignettes.

To reflect on how your body shaped your research, try reviewing your data and asking what you might have either been blinded to or not had access to based on your embodied characteristics. Similarly, you could share field notes with a peer and ask them to talk about how their own embodiment (distinct from yours) might have shaped the interactions, observations, and interview data that you gathered. Through these exercises, it might become clearer how your positionality shapes both your research and your findings. As Rios has noted, it is important that we write not only about the privileges that our positionality affords us but also about the lack of understanding we may have due to this same positionality.[41]

Third, we need to diversify the ways in which we write about ethnographic relationships and closeness. While intimacy should continue to be included as one of many ways to collect good data, we need to write these other ways into our tales of the field, which could include writing honestly about the barriers we put up between ourselves and our research participants and why, describing the awkward relationships we experience in the field and disclosing the level of closeness with participants we felt was sufficient and safe.

We end this chapter with two excerpts from coauthor Rebecca's dissertation. The first excerpt is the original text that she included in a dissertation chapter. The second excerpt is the revised version of this material, altered as she went through her dissertation with the intent of writing gendered and sexualized interactions into her data. In the second excerpt, Rebecca includes how she came to know Ramón, a key informant, and the emotions and concerns that she had to navigate with men in the field—information that is left out of excerpt 1.

Excerpt 1

After our first meeting Ramón and I spent most of our time together at the police station, chatting as I waited to speak to various supervisors about approving my project. Though the approval never came, the visits gave me time to get to know Ramón and, after texting back and forth for a few weeks, we agreed to meet up one afternoon while he was off duty. We had made multiple plans to meet up before, but Ramón always had to cancel last minute, either because he was called into work or because he had picked up a moving job. When off duty, Ramón spent much of his time moving pieces of furniture or appliances to supplement his income.

The afternoon that he finally became available, he picked me up at an intersection on Sucre Avenue in his moving truck. After I climbed into his truck Ramón told me that he had just gotten back from helping a family move to Barquisimeto, about four hours away from Caracas, and had a few hours left before his shift started. Exhaustion seemed to be weighing down his face and his body, speaking to the long night he had had, but his face lit up when I got into the truck. While I had anticipated that we might grab some coffee or go to the park, Ramón told me that we were going to visit the barrio where he had grown up, since he had recently moved a refrigerator for a family that lived there and wanted to collect his payment. After about 10 minutes of traveling down the interstate we took an exit onto one of the main avenues at the far east end of Caracas. Ramón veered off the main avenue after only a few minutes and we began to ascend up a steep hillside.

Excerpt 2

I met Ramón the first time that I visited the central police station in the Sucre parish. He was a shy community police officer in his late 20s who had previously worked with a municipal police force before joining the police in hopes of better pay but also benefits, especially healthcare since one of his children

Did you have different reactions to the two excerpts? If so, what are the differences? Why do you think you reacted differently to them?

What did you learn about the researcher-participant relationship in the second excerpt that you did not in the first? Is there information in the second excerpt that you think is important for understanding Rebecca's data? If so, what?

Does excerpt 2 provide a more embodied description of data? If so, how?

Rebecca is a white cisgender woman from the United States, and at the time she was conducting this research, she was in her late twenties. If you were conducting this research, how do you think these interactions might have differed? What impacts would this have on access, trust, danger, and intimacy?

suffered from acute asthma and required expensive medication. As I was leaving the police station that day a female officer who I met at the same time as Ramón ran up to me giggling and asked if I was married. I told her no and asked why. After another burst of laughter she answered, "Ramón wanted to know," then turned and briskly walked away.

After our first meeting Ramón and I spent most of our time together at the police station, chatting as I waited to speak to various supervisors about approving my project. Though the approval never came, the visits gave me time to get to know Ramón and, after texting back and forth for a few weeks, we agreed to meet up one afternoon while he was off duty. We had made multiple plans to meet up before, but Ramón always had to cancel last minute, either because he was called into work or because he had picked up a moving job. When off duty, Ramón spent much of his time moving pieces of furniture or appliances to supplement his income. His busy schedule (and initially shy demeanor) ended up working to my advantage. Since we only hung out at his work for the first few months and he had very little spare time flirtation was kept to a minimum and I did not have to consistently turn down offers to go dancing or drinking as I did with many officers, which usually resulted in the end of our relationship.

The afternoon that he finally became available, he picked me up at an intersection on Sucre Avenue in his moving truck. After I climbed into his truck

Ramón told me that he had just gotten back from helping a family move to Barquisimeto, about four hours away from Caracas, and had a few hours left before his shift started. Exhaustion seemed to be weighing down his face and his body, speaking to the long night he had had, but his face lit up when I got into the truck. "At least," I thought, "spending his few free hours with me doesn't seem to strike him as a burden." I then wondered what this time together did mean to him.

THREE

Sexual Harassment in the Field

IN THIS CHAPTER, WE DOCUMENT THE SPECTRUM of our participants' experiences with sexual harassment and sexualization in the field.
Attentive to how context, race, gender performance, and sexual identity
inform unwanted sexual attention in the field, we provide examples of the
behaviors confronted by our participants, from flirtation and come-ons to
attempted assault and, in one case, rape. We also examine the kinds of
resources researchers have for coping with harassment in the field and discuss
how participants ultimately dealt with their experiences. We identify three
common approaches: abandoning the project, modification, and suffering
through. Throughout the chapter, we ask you to consider how your own identifications and fieldwork context might shape the harassment and other
forms of sexualization you might encounter in the field and what resources
you would have to cope.

While much of this book focuses on women's struggles with navigating
harassment and sexualization in the field, we should not think of women as
debilitated by these experiences in all times and places; doing so supports the
belief that women should not conduct work in certain field sites, which
reproduces barriers and ceilings for women researchers. Even in those cases
in which harassment is debilitating for the researcher, the point is not to limit
what kinds of projects women can take on but rather to provide researchers
with the capacity to choose whether they want to continue with a project,
without fear of repercussions if they modify or change their research altogether. Rather than provide a list of restrictions on how, when, and where
women can conduct research, we want you to think about how all researchers
can cope with challenges in healthy ways, how advisers and colleagues can

support students as they navigate these obstacles, and what implications experiences with harassment (and other forms of violence) have for the construction of knowledge.

RANGE OF EXPERIENCES

For purposes of organization, we divide different forms of threats, harassment, and sexualization that researchers face in the field into several categories. However, it is important to keep in mind that the expressions of harassment discussed here are not mutually exclusive. Rather, they are often manifested as interlocking and overlapping. Participants faced unwelcome sexual contact and harassment from key informants and gatekeepers, other research participants, and even nonparticipants.[1] As a case in point, Gina, a white graduate student working on a project for a professor, was hit on by a research participant at a bar in South America. When she went to use the restroom later in the evening, another man attacked her. Though her adviser initially reacted with concern, he chastised her when on another occasion she decided not to attend a dinner with research participants, where she would again be the only woman. Gina had to navigate harassment from participants, violence from others in her field site, and castigation from her adviser when she chose to avoid another potential site of harassment. Thus her research relationships, field site, and the individual who would assess her performance intersected to expose her to a range of harassment and violence.

Participants' evaluations of the severity of the harassment they faced varied. For some, the harassment felt threatening or dangerous to their work and well-being. Some experienced harassment as a one time thing; for others, it felt nearly constant. Participants described harassment in various ways, as debilitating, bothersome, or annoying; a few women reported that harassment did not bother them at all. In the latter cases, experiences of harassment and sexualization were rare, inconsistent, and more easily "absorbed." Context and positionality also minimized harassment's impacts on some participants, meaning that these experiences had little to no effect on their selves or how they evaluated their work.

The purpose of discussing the range of experiences confronted by our participants is not to create a typology or gradation of experiences or to construct a scale of least to most damaging experiences.[2] Instead we seek to illuminate the variety of experiences that exist. All forms of harassment can exact a toll on researchers. Our goal is to validate the incorporation of these experiences into tales of the field. As we discuss below, researchers sometimes write off uncomfortable or even terrifying experiences and relegate them to the "awkward surplus" category when "nothing really happened," that is, when physical assault did not take place. Researchers' delegitimization of their own experiences and their impact on their research have consequences for safety and the construction of ethnographic knowledge, as we show throughout this book. We hope that by incorporating these experiences into ethnographic tales and analyzing them as data, researchers will begin to question the fixations of solitude, danger, and intimacy.

Flirtation and Come-ons

Flirtation and being hit on were very common experiences in the field. Very few women participants characterized the flirtation they experienced as sexual harassment. Instead, they tended to consider it annoying, distracting, and only sometimes threatening to their work or their safety.

Flirtation included random inappropriate questions, as when a man interrupted the interview Cathy was conducting with him to ask, "Do you have a boyfriend?" Rosie felt many men in the festival scene interpreted a simple request to sit down for an interview as a come-on. The women she spoke with did not tend to respond the same way. "Mactivism" characterized the Occupy movement Angie studied, shaping many of her interactions with men in the field. Kista, a queer white woman, drew a distinction between harassment and the "targeted and deliberate and open flirting" and "sexual banter" she experienced in the field. For example, she once mentioned she admired a chaise longue in a participant's home, and the woman responded, "Yeah, that's so I can get you to lay on it." Later in the interview the woman offered Kista water. When she brought it to her there was condensation on the glass, and she said, "This is wet, but don't worry, we lesbians don't mind wetness." Kista found this banter uncomfortable and made that clear to her participant, but she did not feel in danger. Maritza reported that a third of her initial interviewees hit on her in some way and described this interaction with a member of a community organization she was studying: "He said something nasty to me once. We were eating at an event. He was like, 'I am watching you eat chicken, and I am watching your hips because that's where it is all going to go.' And he said that in public." Like many others, she found dealing with interactions like this difficult to balance as she worried that being "mean" could have negative effects on her access. In fact, this instance did affect her access but not because her response to the man's comment was rude. Instead, she decided not to interview him after this interchange. Flirtation and come-ons pose particular challenges for the intimacy we are expected to cultivate with participants. It may be difficult to open up to a close relationship with a participant who sexualizes that relationship. Moreover, the time we spend with participants and the interest we show in their lives may be perceived as a shared desire for sexual intimacy, signaling to the participant that the researcher is not bothered by their actions and words.

As discussed in chapter 2, participants flirted with our men interviewees as well, but the men were more likely to be able to guide these interactions from a position of power. For instance, Will, a white researcher from the Global North, referred to a crush a young woman had on him as "cute"—at first anyway. Moreover, he said, sexual dynamics were not a significant part of his experience, especially compared to other personal security issues he faced in the field. When he did worry about flirtation it was out of concern about abusing the power he had due to his social location.

> It's a bit like, imagine if you're a celebrity, like you're a male celebrity in the States, right? You have a certain power, and it gives you a certain sexual power vis-à-vis some women in some circumstances. And I was a bit of a celebrity going into these super poor neighborhoods. [I was] this super wealthy gringo. I remember I just had to be conscious about how I might have been perceived by young women. . . . It's very easy to abuse power in those circumstances.

In contrast, David, a Latin American participant studying social movements, told us:

> I understand how my gender gives me a lot of privilege. And I know also that sexual harassment is a form of male domination. That being said, as a man, I have experienced sexual harassment almost on a daily basis at these organizations. Hardly a week went by without an incident of someone being a little bit too touchy, someone making too much, a comment that is a little bit too spicy. Someone testing a line.

David pointed out that these sexual advances were made by women as well as men.

Advances went beyond flirtation to include come-ons, propositions, or requests for dates. Sometimes these were bound up in gender expectations in the particular field site. For example, Jackie, a Latina student, said the Latino immigrant men she interviewed routinely asked her and the young woman she worked with to go dancing or come to cookouts and tried to pay for the meals when they interviewed them over lunch or dinner. Amy, a white sociologist, was asked out about ten times while doing fieldwork for her project on marriage education programs, much more than she ever experienced in her everyday life. She characterized these requests as overtures rather than harassment, estimating that 10 to 15 percent of her interactions in the field were sexually tinged in some way. Propositions were more intense in other cases. For example, Jenna, a white researcher, hired a language tutor in the Asian country where she worked who insistently tried to get her to go to a hotel with him when his wife was out of town. When Cristina, a Latina researcher, set up an interview with a security guard at the school where she worked, he chose the location, one with which she was unfamiliar. She described it and her reaction: "I show up, and it's like a sit-down restaurant, and it's after school and I know he should be in his security guard get-up, but he's changed, he's got cologne on. And I'm like [sigh]. It was awkward, but for me, I think because of my background with, dealing with abusive partners in the past, it—it scared me." Here and in other parts of her interview, Cristina pointed out that researchers bring previous experiences with gender violence and harassment with them into the field, which can intensify already annoying or threatening interactions.

Pressure for Sex

Coauthor Rebecca experienced several very intense come-ons, including one from a participant with whom she had to share a hotel room. After traveling all day, they arrived at a hotel in the middle of the night to find that there was only one room left. Though Rebecca considered checking into another hotel, she was reluctant to go searching for one alone, late at night, while in an unfamiliar city. She felt more at ease when the manager said that the room had two beds. She explained what happened that night:

> It was such a long day and super long trip, I was so exhausted by the time it was over with. We got in our beds and literally like two minutes later he got up and was touching my shoulder, trying to wake me up. He whispered into my ear, "I just can't control myself around you, if I don't leave right now, I am not going to be able to stop myself, so I am going to have to go somewhere else. Either we have sex right now or I have to go somewhere else." I was, like, "Well, I guess you are just going to have to find somewhere else to go!" And so he went and found another hotel to stay at, and we finished our trip and we got back to Caracas a few days later. After, we were texting, and he pretty much said, "If we can't be together, if I can't have you, I can't work with you anymore."

Rebecca responded that she could not date him and was sorry they could not remain friends. She noted that this interaction would have been much more difficult to negotiate if she had not been wrapping up her research at the time, making her relationship with this participant less important.

Several women received suggestive or harassing text messages and phone calls. In some cases, the texts were relatively innocuous, though strange or inappropriate in their timing, such as those Daisy, an Asian American researcher, received, asking, "What are you doing?," in the middle of the night. In other cases, they were more threatening. For example, Marina, a Latina researcher, received frequent harassing phone calls from one participant asking for sexual favors over a period of three or four weeks. Michelle also received texts in the middle of the night from men asking her to meet them alone.[3] On a trip with another research participant, Rebecca received a text from him a few minutes after getting into her hotel room, asking if she wanted to come to his room and "warm him up."

While conducting her dissertation research, a European man, who was her gatekeeper to a community she hoped to work with, told Frances, who is Asian American, that he could give her access if she "acted like his girlfriend" or paid him $10,000. When she refused, he stalked her by phone and text for weeks. Frances explained how traumatic this was for her.

> I ended up throwing that phone away, and then recontacting those people I had made [contact with] and giving them my new phone number. For a good part of the entire first week and part of the second week I was really traumatized. I had been a rape victim before. So it brought up all of these emotions that I was not prepared to deal with again. And I just felt completely vulnerable. So I didn't leave my flat in [the city] the first few days.

Like Cristina, Frances connected her response to this man's demand to sexual violence she had experienced in the past. For certain participants, experiences with sexual harassment before starting fieldwork helped them shake off similar encounters in the field. For others, the scars left behind by previous harassment or assault were reopened, making harassment and threats in the field more traumatic. Samantha, a white graduate student, discussed how her own history as a survivor of sexual assault affected her response to the harassment she experienced while conducting preliminary research, referring to the incidents as "triggering" for her. Because she was able to conduct preliminary research and had support from her committee to change her topic, she was able to conduct "fieldwork that was equally intimate and emotional but, so important, not triggering in the same way." This is yet another reason to have open and frank discussions with all students about the possibility of various types of violence in the field, as all researchers, regardless of gender, may have experienced sexual or other forms of violence in the past. Rather than allow students to be blindsided by these occurrences, advisers and professors should prepare them for this possibility and discuss strategies to avoid them when possible and deal with them when they occur.

Complicity

Regularly listening to sexist or other derogatory comments and dealing with discriminatory behaviors were another form of harassment faced by our participants. Researchers also had to stomach racist and homophobic comments. The men who threatened Rosie after she asked them to pipe down one night at a music festival had, before the incident, been talking about the "bitches and hoes they were going to bang over the weekend." When another man tried to get them to stop, they derided him with homophobic slurs. Albert, a white / multiracial man, spoke of colleagues making racist comments about him that he felt he had to brush off because he needed access. He worried, "If I confront these—I don't know if racial microaggressions is the right term, but it's probably pretty close to the right term—it may make future observations more difficult. So I was like, 'Well, I'm just gonna tolerate it.' There are parts of me that it's annoying that I did that, but parts of me that think, 'Well, that's why, that helped me to be able to [do my research].'"

Sometimes the comments and behavior participants witnessed were not directed at them but still created dilemmas in the field. Lenore, a white woman, studied a women's football team whose interactions were characterized by sexual jokes and grabbing and touching of breasts and buttocks. She saw this as part of how the women on the team acted out masculinity and didn't feel threatened by it. However, she knew it would bother her girlfriend if she had known it was happening, and that unsettled her. She also felt uncomfortable for other players who were bothered by it. And because her strategy for dealing with the discomfort was to "step back and remove myself from the situation," she worried that the players might have interpreted her silence as complicity. For others, such as Ronette, a white researcher whose story is told below, the type of sexualized context in which she worked was indirect but nonetheless directed at her. This experience felt like "participating in misogyny" and left emotional scars. Indeed, the dangers we expose ourselves to in the field are varied; they may be physical, emotional, or psychological in character.

The men we interviewed also talked about being implicated in sexism in the field. Participating in sexual jokes is one example of how men were able to build rapport in the field while also unwillingly consenting to the objecti-fication of women. Sergio, a mestizo Latin American, explained how this came into play in his field site in South America: "There is this constant joking about me having relationships with an indigenous woman. . . . And that's like the way in which you created relationships with [participants in this field site] and among them, too, to make sexual jokes all the time. It's very common, and of course, I am like part of the show. . . . And of course, I will play along with them." According to David, there were a lot of sex jokes exchanged within the social movement he studied as well, but even when directed at him he did not feel that these were hostile or objectifying. Instead, he thought of them as an expression of friendship. Will explained it this way: "When I was interviewing a young gang member I'd go in and I'd talk about beer, women, and soccer. That'd be like my holy trinity of ice breakers. I'm a man, I like women, yeah, sex, yeah, I like fútbol . . . yeah, beer, I love drinking, and then, 'Oh, by the way, how many people have you killed?'" For Will, getting close to a research participant was not about allowing himself to be sexualized but rather to some degree engaging in the sexualization of women.

Other men talked about listening to or observing sexist behavior in the field. Claude, a white sociologist who studied a women's sports team, was distressed by the misogyny and homophobia he witnessed. The women he observed were very invested in representing themselves as a heterosexual team and had even kicked lesbians off the team before he started his field-work. Much of the leisure time he spent with the team was at parties where a lot of alcohol was consumed, and Claude often found himself observing situ-ations that were degrading or potentially dangerous to participants, such as a mud wrestling fund-raiser performed in bikinis and micro-shorts. The women often hung out with the men who played the same sport, and as a result he was also privy to the misogynist comments of members of the men's team. He talked about the tensions this created for him as an ethnographer: "What was great about that is that I got to hear these sort of unfiltered com-ments from the men—great but also horrifying because what they had to say was horrifying." Elizabeth, a white sociologist, had a similar experience inter-viewing men in Latin America who engaged in sex tourism. She was repulsed by the men's racism and sexism but also encouraged them, saying, "Tell me more." While women ethnographers are more likely to be the targets of gen-dered comments, men, too, may find themselves confronting barriers to access if they resist or question their participants' discursive frames, especially those related to deep-seated understandings of race and gender that organize society.

Ronette explicitly acknowledged the contradictions entailed in using men's misogyny to her advantage when she worked as a driver for a music festival. (The audience of the music festival itself was the focus of her research.) The trucking team was dominated by men, and sexist and misogynist comments were commonplace. To participate in this was a kind of choiceless decision. She explained, "I consider myself a feminist, and for me to participate in that was really difficult but was also a form of survival." She needed these men to see her as an equal because she had to depend on them for help on the road; all of the drivers depended on each other for loading trucks and dealing with mechanical problems. Ronette went on to say, "I think having to depend on people who are like that, that was the part that was very difficult and is still difficult to reconcile in hindsight. Now I can remove myself from someone who treats women like that and they don't exist for me anymore, whereas in that situation I had to figure out how to collaborate with these people and create an amicable relationship." Ronette eventually found ways to razz the men as well without engaging in misogynist banter, proving that she could "hold her own." For example, when the men started to make her feel uncomfortable, she said, "I would start talking about menstruating and that would really shut them up really quickly." Nevertheless, being exposed to frequent and blatant misogyny exacerbated the loneliness she already felt conducting research on her own.

Sexualizing Researchers' Bodies

Women's bodies often become conversation pieces in the field. Cristina said the whistles, comments, and looks she received from boys at the school where she conducted fieldwork did not really bother her until she started teaching there. When she became a teacher, the comments seemed intended to undermine her authority. And when she later became pregnant, the comments intensified. One boy routinely said things like, "Miss, since you're pregnant, don't you, like, need sex? Don't you want more sex?" Bridgette, a black sociologist, said she still runs into one of the men who worked in the HIV prevention project she studied: "He will come up and say 'Hi.' And he makes little comments like, 'Yeah, I knew right away that was you from behind.'" Karen, who is white, described a time when three men in the Occupy movement proceeded to verbally dissect her.

We are all sitting around or standing around talking. Two of the guys who were regulars, they had brought in a third person who was actually the cousin of one of those two. And I don't remember what started it, but the three of them just started, "Oh, you've got an ass like Beyoncé," and you know, "Your skin is brown. What is your ancestry?" You know, and "Is your nose this? And your hair that?" And you know, just commenting on all of my features. I didn't know what to do. I wanted to maintain the easygoing relationship we had, so I didn't want to get all serious and feminist on them. I don't think they would have really understood without great effort why this might be problematic. I think for them it was also asserting to each other their hetero-sexuality. I didn't want to come down on them and end it in some way, but I didn't want to keep it going either.

Karen's experience brings to light a contradiction between the feminist beliefs of many researchers and what they must do in the field to maintain relationships with their participants. Karen worried that getting "all feminist on them" by rejecting their dissection of her body would make things "serious" and damage the easygoing quality she had spent time cultivating with the group. For the sake of these relationships, she allowed the men to use her body to stake a claim on hegemonic masculinity.

Other participants experienced policing of their bodies. A man in an urban neighborhood in the United States where a Latina participant, Linda, was conducting research called her "dirty" for showing too much skin; she was wearing a skirt and T-shirt. Men stood outside the open window of Asian American student Annie's first floor apartment in rural Latin America while she was making her lunch and called out to her. Nancy, a white sociologist, was mostly bothered rather than threatened during her work in a men's prison, but sometimes, while walking in the hallways, she felt she was "just this person, this woman, for them to consume with their eyeballs." Two correctional officers (COs) who worked at the prison where she was conducting research also policed Nancy's body. She explained that they followed her one day as she was leaving the prison and "trapped" her in a space between two reinforced doors that only opened when a CO hit a button from inside the security control room.

There was a female CO and a male CO. The male CO starts talking, and he is super uncomfortable, and he was, like, "I don't know if you've noticed those male prisoners," and I was, like, "Kind of sort of, what are you talking about?" The female CO was like, "Look, I can see your nipples." She points at my chest. "We know we have difficulty keeping control of the prisoners anyways, and that sort of thing makes a lot of trouble for us. We are supposed to keep you safe, and we are trying to keep ourselves safe, and you need to just not wear shirts like that." I was wearing a high-necked tank top, no sleeves, but it covered me to the collarbone. It was white, and I just had on a normal bra. So I stopped wearing white and bought prison bras—really thickly padded bras—so I never had to talk about my nipples again with the correctional officers.

Social norms and expectations make others feel they have the right to police women's bodies and sexuality. This tendency is not checked when women ethnographers enter the field. If anything, it can become more intense when these women feel compelled to placate gatekeepers and others in order to maintain access.

Physical Harassment and Attacks

Physical harassment and attacks took many forms. Many participants were touched or kissed over the course of their fieldwork. Several elite Central Americans kissed or tried to kiss Joan. An interviewee kissed Cathy on the neck. A man who offered June a ride home tried to kiss her. Jenna's tutor groped her in public. While conducting preliminary research in a natural gas boomtown, Samantha had a man run his fingers through her hair during an interview; this occurred within the first hour of meeting him. As discussed in chapter 1, an interviewee asked to touch the hair of Monira, a conservative Muslim at the time and wearing a hijab. On another occasion, at a research institute where she was employed, Monira cut a conversation short with a young man so she could get back to work. He walked over to her desk, stood over her, and, referring to her headscarf, asked, "Why do you have that thing on your head?" As she started to answer him, he towered over her and uttered, "Because I'm about to rip it off." Only one of the men we interviewed, David, said he felt he faced sexual harassment regularly. Some participants also had to deal with stalking. Frances's story is told above. Michelle experienced the advances of a powerful man in the community where she worked in the Global South. He regularly appeared at the home where she was staying and tried to get her alone, touching her and making "disgusting suggestions." He, too, was a potential key respondent but wanted something in exchange.

Too many of our participants experienced physical threats and sexual assault; one participant was raped. Many of their stories are told more completely elsewhere in this book. Apart from being harassed by that powerful community figure, Michelle escaped from assault at the hands of a European expat. After Jenna accepted a motorcycle ride between her field sites in a South Asian country from a friend of a friend, she found herself in "a situation where I definitely felt unsafe, and it was really hard for me to get out of that situation," which she eventually did by screaming. A man from the community Elena, a Latina associate professor, was studying attempted to break into her house because she had declined to dance with him earlier in the night. A government official in Rwanda attacked Katrina in his office. Lori, a white researcher, had her buttocks grabbed at least five times when she was simply walking down the street in the Latin American city where she worked. Notably, few of our participants told their advisers about these experiences. Lori explained that one act of sexual assault is experienced as multiple forms of violation, increasing one's sense of vulnerability. She had been working out while in the field and, as a result, "felt stronger." "I was more athletic than I had been since I was like fifteen or something," she explained. "So my body in a lot of ways was getting stronger." However, after being groped in public, she said, "It made me realize that actually when I am in this situation, I still feel helpless. There was a little bit of a struggle between feeling more powerful but knowing that when it really matters, ... the fact that I am a woman puts me in this position where I have less power." According to Lori, this was another aspect of the violation that she endured: the strength she felt she had achieved was taken away from her.

The ways in which race and gender intersect produce different threats for researchers.[4] This was true of the street harassment targeted at Lena, an Asian American graduate student, by European neo-Nazis. Cristina likewise faced gendered threats at the school where she worked, and these were exacerbated by the racism of white teachers who failed to come to her aid. (Her story is told more fully in the next chapter.) Their experiences show that race must be taken into account in order to understand harassment in the field.

Two men also reported experiencing sexualized threats in the field. David attended an event with an organization he was working with and ended up having to share a hotel room with seven men he didn't know. Five of them got very drunk and high and started talking about raping him. David was terrified. He explained:

> It was like two in the morning. And I was like, "How the fuck am I getting out of here?" ... I had no idea who they were, but at the same time, you know, are these guys just joking? Or is this ... ? I could not tell. I didn't want to fight them and lose access. So I solved [it by saying], "You guys are making too much noise." And I walked very fast towards the door. And that was the

end of it. I stayed a couple of hours outside the room, pretended to be talking to other people.

Clark, a white trans man, conducted some of his fieldwork in a gay bar. He suffered a terrifying transphobic experience when a leader in the gay community came in with a group of friends. Clark described what happened next.

> He asks me loudly, "Were you born a man?" And this is a really busy bar. It's a busy night. This is not a huge bar, so you know, there's three bartenders, we all know each other, maybe two bar backs.... And so I was like, "Oh, you know that's not what, that's a really weird, that's a strange question to ask. What kind of question is that? You know, I gotta get back to work." And he sort of grabs me again, and he's like, "No, really. Were you born a man?" And his friend is like, "Aw, look at him. He's totally a dude. What are you talking about?" So I was not interested in reproducing a transphobic kind of narrative, so I was like, "Listen, I really gotta—I have to get back to work." And he, he was like, "I don't think you were born a man." And I was like, "Okay, whatever. I gotta get back to work." So I get out of his grab, and I get back to my thing. So, within a week, the other bartenders started asking me. And again, this is not, this is one of those spaces where to be trans would be very, very unsafe, and so I was like, "That's a weird question. Why are you asking this?" And this went on for a few days, and then one evening, I went up to—this bar had two levels. It was sort of a slow night. The lower bar had a smattering of people. The upper bar, the bartender was super drunk, and there were a couple of patrons who were also pretty drunk, and otherwise it was pretty empty. So I'm running upstairs doing some restocking, so I'm grabbing, you know, some liquor back stock and stuff like that, and the bartender grabs my arms and pins them behind my back, and he's like, "So what's in your pants?" And I was like, "Ha ha." You know, "Really funny. I really, you know, we've got a lot of stuff to do. Just, you know, I need to get back to work." Then the guys, the patrons of the bar start undoing my pants.

Clark managed to get away, and he quit his job at the bar, choosing to abandon it as a research site. However, this did not end the activist's aggression against him; he later emailed Clark and threatened to out him as trans.

Men and women alike may face a variety of dangers in the field, especially if they are working in settings such as conflict or postconflict zones or gang-dominated neighborhoods. But the dangers of the field are always filtered through our particular positionalities, as should be clear from the examples above. For women, routine events in the field are more likely to present sexual as well as other physical risks. Joan worried each time she got into a car with an elite Central American. June, a white sociologist, received warnings about places she should not go in Mexico, and Elena said of being attacked on the street at night in Mexico, "That's when I learned women aren't free to walk alone." Safety, in this sense, is gendered.

The expectation that good ethnographers will face danger in the field led some women to ignore signals and their instincts about participants, thus placing themselves in harm's way. One of Samantha's advisers encouraged her to continue to work in her field site even though she was uncomfortable with the sexual dynamics. Samantha reflected, "If you do dangerous ethnography, somehow there is this reverence for you." According to Michelle:

> Whenever I talk to women going into the field I really tell them to listen to their gut feeling. Because that's the other thing we all did [referring to a group of women with whom she has discussed these issues] was ignore signals that we had gut reactions to, try to put up with it because they didn't actually do anything and we need this data. I did this also with the person who attacked me. I met him as somebody who said he was gonna help me, introduce me to people in the field, and give me contacts, and all of that is why I was in contact with him. And [I] had a bad feeling about it and then totally ignored it because I was like, "You're just being wimpy, you need to do the research." So what I try to tell women who haven't been to the field is you need to trust that. . . . Every single time and woman I know [who] felt those things, it escalated and something happened.

As Sofía, a Latina researcher, observed, the sociological ethnographer continues to be conceptualized on some level as an omnipotent, distant, and ultimately dehumanized intellectual, a conceptualization that does not serve anyone well in the field. This concept of the intrepid ethnographer led the women we interviewed to disregard their safety. Samantha felt that more honest conversations about risk taking in the field are necessary. For example, she noted that one of her professors who worked in a dangerous zone never went to the field alone and never went at night. However, Samantha only found out about this after she had conducted her own preliminary fieldwork. Being aware of the measures mentors and colleagues take to remain safe in the field would allow students to consider these options viable. By remaining silent about her self-care strategy, Samantha's professor contributed to the mystique surrounding dangerous ethnography, making it less likely that Samantha would consider certain strategies while planning and conducting her research.

Men are not exempt from the pressures associated with "good fieldwork," even if they experience these pressures in other ways. David still knows the individuals who threatened him that night. The men talk about having threatened him with rape as if it was a joke. Yet, despite how terrified he was at the moment, David still wants to protect this organization and these men: "I feel bad because, and that's why I tell you [to] keep these things private and be very careful about how you want to share this, because this organization does an amazing job, you know?" He now chalks it up to a couple of guys who got drunk and started acting stupid, suggesting that he has internalized the notion that the researcher holds more power than his participants and must therefore not only seek to understand them, but withhold judgment, regardless of the severity of their behavior.

"Nothing really happened"

Like several other participants (including Michelle and, in a sense, David), Cathy used the phrase "Nothing happened" when she described the outcome of a risky experience in the field. In fact, certain participants told us they had hesitated to contact us about taking part in the study because "nothing actually happened" (i.e., they were not raped).[5] Framing come-ons, unwelcome flirtation and touching, troubling text messages, or even assault that does not entail rape in this way downplays the significance of these experiences, justifying them as necessary costs we incur in the field. As other scholars have shown, such minimization is a common response to unwelcome sexualized encounters.[6] For example, 23 percent of the 1,092 women surveyed by Melanie Harned labeled unwanted sexual experiences as "pressure," "coercion," and "misunderstandings" instead of sexual assault or abuse.[7] But as we discuss in chapter 5, this labeling can prevent us from analyzing the significance of these experiences as part of the fieldwork process. These experiences— whether labeled harassment, assault, violence, awkward interactions, unwelcome advances, or something else—must be taken seriously, not only for thinking about the protection of researchers,[8] but because of their relevance for collecting data. All varieties of sexual threats and harassment affect the researcher and the research. Though writing about rape, Sarah Deer's reflection on sexuality and identity sheds light on why sexualized threats can be so unsettling.

> If our sexuality is part of that which defines who and what each of us is, then it is at the very core of our self-identity. I think this is because the very nature of sexuality represents the best of humanity—the creation of new life, or the sharing of deep mutual affection and attraction. When this manifestation of

our humanity is violated, it has life-changing ramifications for one's feelings about self, others, justice, and trust. In consequence, rape damages something critical to our being and personhood.[9]

Of course, the trauma of rape is more egregious than the damage incurred by threats, objectification, and come-ons. Ultimately, however, all of these displays of power are connected and can violate the trust that researchers have in others as well as damage how they perceive themselves.

Context

Sexual harassment and sexualization, of course, occur in everyday life and across contexts; however, context matters for understanding how they occur and how they are perceived by those involved. Furthermore, these experiences can be more intense in the field for a variety of reasons; for example, one may be working in a cultural context different from the one they were socialized into or may be far from home and support networks. Participants talked about how sexualization in the context in which they were doing their research sometimes made it difficult to carry on with their fieldwork. For some, sexual harassment or unwanted attention saturated their field sites. For example, Samantha and Mary both did fieldwork in natural gas boomtowns, where men vastly outnumbered women. For Samantha, the unwanted sexual attention and contact was so all-encompassing that she abandoned her project after a month of preliminary research. Mary finished her dissertation work but reflected that she had no backstage, no place to retreat from her role as researcher. Others talked about how it was impossible to go out at night in the countries or neighborhoods where they did their research. A white anthropologist, Susie, for instance, said that in Madagascar she could not go out at night and could not go dancing without being groped. She felt she acquiesced to, rather than coped with, this situation. In Central America, Tammy, a white sociologist, felt a constant male gaze in the field and was often subject to "kissy noises" or comments in the street. She spoke of the effects of street harassment.

> It's disturbing. I feel, sometimes I feel afraid, because I don't know what to say or I don't know what to do. There's a lot of conflicting opinions: Should you ignore them, should you say something back? But I feel like it, kind of, like I feel forced to be quiet. I guess I feel like my space is being invaded and not just like my physical space but my emotional space. I just want to enjoy—sorry,

I might get kind of emotional—I just want to enjoy being here and do my work, but I constantly have to try to manage my emotions and not get angry [crying] at these men because, I mean, if I get angry, maybe something worse will happen, or if I respond in a way that the man doesn't like—I feel like I am constantly managing my emotions, just try to blow it off or take it lightly. But it's exhausting.

These attributes of the context of research can exacerbate the sense of isolation many women feel in the field.

It is clear that cultural differences played a role in some of the situations faced by our participants. However, the colonialist discourses that continue to structure ethnographic methods reproduce silence on this issue, sustaining the notion that ethnographers are somehow above the communities they study even as they immerse themselves in them and are therefore immune to conflicts and power dynamics. Although it is not a sufficient explanation for all harassment, lack of familiarity with cultural codes (and insufficient preparation to deal with them) affected women's experiences in the field. Virginia, a white archaeologist working in South Asia, talked about how it can be difficult to read the signs of a come-on in another linguistic or cultural context. The father of a family June knew in Mexico was the fare collector on a bus she took regularly. She would speak to him whenever she saw him. One day, he was getting off work and offered her a ride, which she accepted. When he dropped her off, he tried to kiss her. She later felt she had inadvertently encouraged the man by talking to him, although she was only trying to build relationships in the community, as any good researcher would do. Experiences such as these drive home why teaching methods courses without accounting for how gender and sexuality shape researchers' experiences in the field falls short in preparing women students for what lies ahead.

Women should not be blamed for harassment related to differences in cultural codes when it does occur. Nor should it be assumed that conflicting cultural codes are only a problem for those working outside of their own country. Sexual harassment must be recognized as a pervasive problem across cultural contexts. For example, both June, who worked in Mexico, and Brittany, a white woman who worked in the U.S. South, felt that simply smiling at men could suggest interest. Furthermore, all researchers—regardless of whether they are working in their own country or another—should contemplate the ways colonialist assumptions continue to shape assumptions of what we will encounter in the field as well as potential cultural or regional differences and the misunderstandings they might produce.

Considering your embodiment and the context in which you are interested in conducting research, what kinds of dangers do you think might arise in the field?

How might your body be read differently in this context, in comparison to how it is read in the environments in which you are normally embedded? Are there steps you can take to prepare yourself for these differences?

Sexual stereotypes also complicated life in the field. Many participants working in Latin America encountered the stereotype that U.S. women are naive but sexually available. Susie felt being married to a Malagasy man made harassment and propositions worse because it made her seem like more of a romantic possibility to others. Jenna noted that in South Asia there is also a stereotype that Western tourists are "easy." As a result, she did not feel like she could turn to women for help when her tutor was coming on to her or when she faced other harassment or dangerous situations. She thought other women would blame her, because they, too, saw Western women as sexually loose. Norms and expectations of behavior are infused with gendered meanings in any context, often intersecting with views on race and nationality to create specific challenges for differently situated researchers.

COPING STRATEGIES

In her interview, Elizabeth spoke about how having experienced sexual harassment in her everyday life gave her "skills" to navigate harassment in the field. However, she and others noted that harassment in the field was distinct from harassment in other areas of their lives. Elizabeth explained, "I guess the difference is that in the rest of my life I might be more likely to be like, 'Fuck you,' or 'See you around,' whereas in the research situation it's like, 'Haha, tell me more.'" Similarly, Bridgette said:

> I think in general I am kind of used to sexual harassment. . . . I think the difference is that I have to talk to these people and I actually need something from

them, so you kind of have to deal with it. . . . You kind of laugh it off or you still try to use it to your advantage to say, "Okay, this person is interested in talking to me, I'm maybe a little uncomfortable, but I am going to try to use it to have a conversation with them, you know, to build a rapport in the community."

Frances reported feeling like she was "at the mercy" of her research participants: "I mean, they were, in a sense, doing me a huge favor by agreeing to do this interview." She added that beyond needing "something" from her research participants, she felt indebted to them: "I wasn't paying them any money, you know? And so I felt like it was my obligation to try and make them feel comfortable." Concerns about making participants feel comfortable because they are doing researchers "a huge favor" might place researchers in the contradictory position of brushing off sexual harassment while at the same time trying to make harassers feel comfortable and at ease.

Despite feeling restricted in how they could respond, our participants used a variety of strategies to deal with different types of harassment in the field. These included strategies recommended by other qualitative researchers: wearing a ring or talking about a boyfriend or husband (either real or invented) to signal that they were unavailable, dressing conservatively, meeting in public places, and ignoring comments and come-ons.[10] Sometimes these worked, usually they failed, and in certain cases they were counterproductive.

In fact, some participants found that these strategies just led to more questions. Mary, for example, wore her wedding ring in the field but found it was incomprehensible to people in the conservative midwestern town where she worked that she would be living apart from her husband for so long. In Venezuela, police officers used the fact that Rebecca's then-boyfriend was in the United States as a way to hit on her, telling her they would "protect her" and "show her a good time" since her partner had "left her all alone." Nor did talking about how much he loved his girlfriend help David avoid come-ons from women. He chose to leave a "fascinating" potential research participant out of his project for this reason. "I would love to interview her," he said, but "I can't because I know if I get in a closed room with her, she will cross the line. You know, because her personality, a lot of it depends on this very overt sexuality, you know? Like talking to men, and she is very touchy."

Michelle rejected the advice she received to invent a husband and children. She explained:

I don't feel it's ethical to lie to the people in your field research site, and so I didn't want to tell them that. I feel like I'd just be wrapped in a web of lies. . . .

With the men it would have helped to a certain extent, except ultimately they would be like, "But your husband's not here, what kind of a marriage is that, what kind of wife are you, you're not with your husband and children, you're clearly not a good wife or mother so you must be up to no good. Therefore you're even more like somebody that we should target because you're not a respectable woman."

Others similarly were reluctant to deceive their participants, even if there was a chance they would avoid harassment as a result (though, again, the consensus is that these strategies are not very effective). Frances was angered when friends suggested she wear a ring. She felt it was not only inauthentic but also clearly demonstrated the gendered inequality of fieldwork. The "unfairness" that she would have to lie to research participants about a fake husband in an attempt to stay safe smacked of male privilege, not to mention heteronormativity.

Perhaps the most frequently mentioned strategy to avoid harassment was altering one's dress or physical appearance to appear more conservative and thus, it was hoped, less of a target. "Conservative," "baggy," "chaste," "no makeup," "drab," "hair pulled back," "serious," "desexualized," "defeminized"—these were the terms our participants used to describe how they regulated their appearance in the field. A minority of participants felt this strategy helped a bit. Most thought it was a colossal failure. As Nancy observed, as a woman doing research in the prison system who was not an employee of the corrections department, "I could have gotten hit on wearing a knapsack, even a burka." Despite adding padded bras to her research repertoire, Nancy continued to deal with harassment throughout her project. Tammy likewise reflected:

> You know, I used to blame myself. I used to think, "Well, I just need to wear loose clothing and never wear short skirts and never wear tank tops." And I did that for a while, and then I felt like, "It doesn't even matter what I am wearing. I am still getting the same kind of nonsense from men, regardless! And so why am I going to just control everything about me even before something happens?"

It seems that simple strategies like wearing a ring or altering one's dress *may* provide researchers with an illusory sense of control over what happens to them in the field, and these may be worthwhile tactics in that regard. Taking action, regardless of whether it is successful, can be empowering. But Tammy suggests these strategies might also contribute to researchers blaming themselves when things do go wrong: "I should have worn my hair up. I should

Considering your own positionality and self-presentation, what strategies might you be able to utilize in the field to cope with sexual harassment, sexualization, and sexual violence? Taking into account our participants' experiences with common tips and strategies, how useful do you think some of these strategies will be for you?

Do you believe that it is disingenuous or unethical to be anything less than completely honest with research participants? Why or why not?

have worn a looser top." This is part and parcel of cultural expectations that women and girls police and be held accountable for their own sexuality as well as that of men.

Our participants discussed different approaches to turning men down. Many women talked about trying to let men who came on to them down gently. June explained, "I did sort of have a sense that if I didn't navigate this in the right way—like I couldn't offend them, you know? Then they wouldn't be as helpful. But I still felt like . . . it was okay for me to reject their advances. I just had to do it carefully." Our participants' worries about turning down men's advances were related to concerns about ongoing access. As we have seen, however, the "soft letdown" approach can be counterproductive. Indeed, some participants felt a more direct approach was better. For instance, Virginia said her body language and verbal responses are more assertive now than they were when she was just starting out. She said, "I'm not afraid to be aggressive in telling people to back off or whatever. My body language has changed in the way that I respond to even just initial kinds of suggestive things. I think it is much stronger than when I was younger. So I feel like it doesn't progress as far." And she has developed a repertoire of phrases that are effective in her South Asian field site, such as, "Would you want your sister to go out with a strange man?"

Participants also talked about laughing off men's come-ons, ignoring them, or avoiding particular situations altogether. As we discuss in chapter 4, isolation was another coping strategy. Decisions about technology are also relevant here. Bridgette gave people her email address rather than her phone number if she wanted to maintain contact, because she felt giving people your number is sometimes seen as "a sexual thing." And Brittany did some of her interviews one-on-one via Skype in order to avoid having to deal with men performing masculinity in front of their buddies.

Hiding was an extreme form of avoidance engaged by some participants. For instance, when the man who held a powerful position in the village where Michelle worked was harassing her, she began to hide whenever he came around. Others also went to extremes to avoid being noticed. Ogling was so intense in the boomtown she was studying that Mary found a way to hide from view when she was assigned to the drive-through at the fast-food restaurant where she worked as part of her field research.

A few participants talked about avoiding research with men, period. Tammy, for instance, has chosen research topics for which the majority of the people she observes or interviews are women. Of course, this still does not protect her from the street harassment she described. Monira, who as a veiled Muslim woman was harassed on several occasions by young men, said, "If there is a lesson I've learned from those experiences, it's been to avoid [laughs] research with younger men. I'm actually deterred from conducting that type of research now." Similarly, as a trans man, Clark spoke about how he has chosen research topics and sites where he knew the possibility of violence or trans/homophobia would be limited. His considerations were directly influenced by concerns for his own safety.

Other men also engaged in strategies of avoidance, for various reasons. Will talked about finding ways to avoid a young girl who had a crush on him. Claude desperately tried to avoid parties that the women athletes he studied wanted him to attend. Neither Will nor Claude was trying to avoid danger. Rather, they sought to avoid uncomfortable situations in which they might unintentionally abuse their position of power in the field. Claude described one such situation at the parties he attended.

> They would line the newbies [rookie players] up on this little ledge and they would walk me [and other men] through and I would have to go through all of these introductions, and it was these players who I knew really well [who] were trying to lick whipped cream off my neck.... One of the women said— she was wearing a g-string—and she would say, "My name is Muffy, please pet my muff." And she would take the man's hand and put it on her crotch. So I am trying to not do these things.

Claude's fieldwork was very challenging in this respect. He explained, "Having been a professional activist organizing against men's violence, to be in these situations where I was seeing lots of microaggressions and macroaggressions and feeling pressure not to intervene when I would have in my own life really was a challenge and it made me feel like a bad feminist." He described one incident when he did choose to intervene.

> Another thing the newbie players had to do, they had these little candy necklaces that were candy discs on an elastic string, so it would fit really tight on their necks, and they couldn't leave the party until the men at the party had eaten all the candy off the players' necklaces, right? So, they are drunk, they have had alcohol poured on them all night. . . . The house where the parties were was the house where all the male players lived together. It's set back in the woods. So I see these three newbie players back in the woods and I poked my head around a tree and asked if they were okay and they were eating the candy off of their own necklaces so the men wouldn't have to do it. And they were terrified that I was going to tell on them. I actually said, "Don't worry about it," and I stood guard to make sure nobody else saw them so they could eat all the candy off and so then they could come back to the party without having to be groped and molested, essentially, by the men at the party against their will.

While in most cases, actively resisting the misogyny he witnessed would have curtailed his access, in this situation Claude was able to do more than cope.

In the end, experiencing harassment in the field is not a question of strategies to prevent it or stop it. As Bridgette said, "I have strategies to deal with it, but that doesn't mean it's going to go away or stop. The best that I really hope for is maintaining my safety." This, and the fact that tips and strategies failed for so many of the women we interviewed, requires that we rethink how we discuss these issues in methods classes (when they are discussed at all). Perhaps we might have to admit that the best we can do is prepare students for sexualized interactions and sexual harassment rather than simply give them tips that, as Tammy noted, can make the researcher feel responsible for the harassment. This requires that methods classes address head-on the social structures (within the academy as well as the field site) that produce inequality and violence in the field. But it also means discussing coping mechanisms and how to build support networks (both in and outside the field) rather than just focus on prevention.

Creating professional distance was an approach that worked for some participants like Sofía, who had a background in clinical therapy that helped her create boundaries and protect herself. She frequently referred to the rules that she was obligated to follow as a professional and made clear to participants what these were. Creating professional distance was particularly important for women researchers dealing with men. Sofía said part of presenting herself as a professional vis-à-vis men involved "desexualizing" herself—pulling her hair back and wearing glasses and a jacket, for example. Several participants made the trappings of the researcher—notebook, pen, recorder—more visible in order to make it abundantly clear that theirs was a professional endeavor and nothing more. And Mary observed that while her interviews with women often became quite emotional, she tried to maintain stricter professional boundaries with men, perhaps unconsciously at times. Susie agreed, noting that mannerisms, dress, and other factors all come into play. Phoebe, a white sociologist, had to learn not to touch people in the field. Frances pointed out how race, age, and gender intersected for her in the field as a young Asian American woman. She was already accustomed to Asian fetishes and anticipated that they might play a role in her fieldwork, so she tried to deflect this by being professional. Nevertheless, she noted, "the unwanted attention was still there." Thus while professional distance was an important part of women participants' tool kit, it was not always sufficient to end harassment in the field. It can, however, help manage harassment and cope with the costs it entails.

Our men participants also spoke of recurring to professionalism when navigating certain interactions in the field. For instance, Albert recurred to school rules to deal with girls wearing skimpy clothes. And Scott, a white education scholar, applied strategies he had learned as a teacher in his research with young people. For example, in one-on-one interview situations, he would sit in front of an open door. He felt it was especially important to be clear with women students about the scope of his research and his role as a researcher, as he did not want to create a situation in which he might be perceived as sexually inappropriate. Again, though, these men were coming at these interchanges from a position of authority—as current or former teachers.

Talking about professional ethics specifically was one way that participants were able to shut down advances. After one of her participants brought her flowers and kissed her (see chap. 2), Harriet, a white woman, spoke to him the following day, saying, "You know, I'm very flattered. But I can't pursue this. It's really unethical for me to do that. As a sociologist I can't get involved with any of my informants. It's just how it is." She saw this as "an easy way to sort of close that down." Likewise, when Frances's gatekeeper asked her for $10,000 for help finding participants and then said he would reduce his price if she had sex with him, she also invoked ethics procedures. She recalled thinking during the interaction, "I'm not going to have sex with you. And I'm pretty sure I can't give you $10,000." However, during the meeting itself, Frances felt too scared to say anything that might anger him. Instead she told us, "I resorted to a rational explanation about university ethics / IRB procedures and tried to end the meeting as fast as I could and get away. I don't know what took over my brain, but it was just like this total rational explanation. Because I was scared. But I didn't want to show him that I was scared, because I wanted to get out of there."

When research participants hit on Louise, a white queer researcher who conducted research with LGBT immigrants, she would share her opinions about researchers abusing their power.

> I would try to start a conversation [with people] who I felt might have been developing some kind of attachment, saying, "Oh, you know, I think it's terrible when researchers abuse their power in the field." And, "I think for me I've got to try and be very responsible and I hope you feel very safe around me. I would never even consider abusing your trust or repeating anything that you say."

Disciplinary ethics and professional boundaries can be useful tools for deflecting unwanted attention from research participants, even if this tool does not always end it.

Several participants talked about the importance of establishing local support networks. For Phoebe, being able to talk to her Brazilian roommate was critical to helping her confirm that her gatekeeper was out of bounds. Lena, too, talked about how building friendships in your field site is important. For a few participants, older men played a sort of grandfatherly role, protecting them from the advances of other men or helping to find research contacts. Elena recommended staying with local families and creating a network of fictive kin, although another participant, Jenna, cautioned that this is not always the best option, having lived with a family where alcoholism and domestic violence were a problem. Several participants talked about going through men's wives to get access to their husbands or at least, as Michelle discussed, getting to know the wives well enough to avoid the generation of gossip about the researcher's intentions.

What appeared to be the most effective strategies recommended by our participants fly in the face of the notion of the solitary, intrepid researcher: hiring research assistants and conducting collaborative research. For some, the decision to hire assistants came after facing dangerous situations in the field. This was the case for Elena, who now hires women from the local community as research assistants. Not only do they help with her work, but they connect her to the community in ways that she believes help with access and may also serve as a protective mechanism. Frances, who was already working with research assistants, began to have them accompany her on interviews after her gatekeeper propositioned her. Michelle began to hire local women as research assistants after realizing that her efforts to talk to men on her own came across as "seeking lovers or something." Spending time with women was more intelligible to people in her field site and seemed to convince them she was actually doing research.

Other participants modified their research by creating alliances with women in the field. Phoebe, for example, worked harder to build relationships with women in her field site after being propositioned by her gatekeeper. Cathy contrasted her research experiences in two different field sites, one where a local woman facilitated access for her and accompanied her on her interviews and one where she had no such assistance. She explained:

> [In the first site] I was basically always accompanied by a local woman. [She] would even accompany me to my interviews and would be there during the interviews. That's just kind of how it worked out in terms of access because in the towns I was working it would have been just too weird for me as this outsider American woman trying to just chat it up with people. But most of my time was spent in [my other field site], and I didn't have anyone like that . . . and that's where I had the most angst around sexual attention.

Cathy did not have the money to hire research assistants, but the woman who volunteered to help her provides a nice illustration of why it is worth doing. Although methods texts and classes tend to focus on the value of local research assistants in terms of facilitating access, they should make clear that this strategy can also provide a sense of safety and peace of mind in the field.

A few participants had engaged in collaborative research, which served as a protective mechanism. For example, Bridgette was working on a collaborative research project on HIV prevention that entailed going to clubs to recruit for interviews. She and her collaborators worked in pairs for safety reasons, anticipating potential harassment or violence. Men still hit on them, but Bridgette said that she and her research partner were able to discuss and even joke about it later. And Gina observed that working with another researcher can serve as a "benchmark for safety" in the field. Indeed, June, who has completed her dissertation, now has collaborators and describes this as enormously useful. She does not have to go on interviews alone and can also bounce feelings off someone else when things go awry, asking, "Did you feel uncomfortable in that situation? Because I did." Or, "How [could] we deal with this differently?" Of course, collaboration can present other risks for researchers, as in the case of a collaboration between a student and an abusive mentor. (And Eva Moreno was assaulted by her research assistant, who was a man.)[11] As with any other project, we encourage researchers to consider carrying out a risk assessment, taking power imbalances into account, before agreeing to collaborate.

Participants also talked about a range of strategies that did not necessarily involve addressing harassment or unwanted attention head-on but helped them take care of themselves in the field. These included keeping a journal, going to therapy, watching movies, eating candy, eating well, exercising, meditating, taking breaks or going on vacation, and deciding not to live in their research site. Perhaps the most common coping strategy was to seek out contact with friends and family. Prioritizing emotional well-being and physical safety over "getting good data" was absolutely essential for many participants, perhaps especially in retrospect.

SUFFERING THROUGH, MODIFICATION, AND ABANDONMENT

The coping strategies we have discussed so far were often utilized as researchers suffered through harassment to finish their projects. Often, the trials faced by participants reached an extreme before they took steps to change the situation, usually out of concern for ongoing access. For instance, Michelle suffered for a long time before she finally asked her host family for help.

> I didn't want to tell anyone in the village because I didn't want to create problems, particularly because this was a person of higher position in status and I was worried that he could retaliate against my family members if I were to create any problems for him. But eventually, it was just getting worse and worse, and I started thinking that this person could actually try to rape me and if that happened and I told people after, that then ... they would be like,

"Well, we never heard anything about this." And they wouldn't take it seriously, or they would think I brought it on or did something. So I realized it wasn't in my best interest to keep it a secret because that put me in more danger.

When she did tell her host mother, the woman did not take her seriously at first. But when she saw Michelle was crying, the family began to do "whatever they could to make sure I was never alone with him," even telling him in a joking way that "his position could be jeopardized if he were to consider pursuing something."

Many of those who soldiered on despite the harassment did so in part by repressing experiences. We discuss this practice in greater detail in chapter 5. There we draw on Joan Fujimura's concept of awkward surplus to discuss how researchers might set aside experiences that are not consonant with their image of what the research endeavor is "supposed" to be, based on what they have been taught in classes and told by their mentors. In part, this sort of reaction is related to a fear that unintelligible experiences—those that do not "make sense" as part of the research project—will "taint the data." But it is also a survival mechanism. Downplaying the seriousness of interactions that feel unsafe or threatening, or forcing oneself to forget them altogether, can allow the researcher to continue working. However, as we discuss in chapter 5, ignoring uncomfortable experiences has important implications for the construction of ethnographic knowledge as well as for researchers' well-being. It also has implications for mentorship. If mentors, women and men alike, treat their own previous sexualized interactions in the field as awkward surplus, they will be less likely to introduce the topic to their students and also less likely to take seriously or even know about the problematic situations confronted by their students.

There are two other strategies researchers used when confronted with ongoing harassment and sexualization: abandoning a project or modifying it. These strategies are particularly important to consider because, as was true of coauthor Rebecca, researchers can become so focused on getting the data that they may not even realize these options are available. Others may feel ashamed when they decide to abandon or modify a project. Indeed, participants talked about "suffering through" because they were afraid to lose access or to come back and say they failed, because they were convinced it might get better, or because they thought the harassment was their own fault. In this section, we discuss these two alternatives to "sticking it out," as some researchers were encouraged to do.

Abandoning the project was a more frequent response than we expected. Abandonment could be temporary. Lena left the city in which she was conducting preliminary fieldwork and considered abandoning her project entirely after experiencing racially motivated sexual harassment in Europe. She eventually decided to modify the project, from an ethnographic to an interview-based one, and returned to the same city for a "limited period of time." Conversely, Maritza took a year off from interviewing research participants, focusing instead on the ethnographic component of her project, after the men she tried to schedule interviews with attempted to turn these requests into dates. When she went back to interviewing, she had secured funding that allowed her to pay her interviewees for their time. This time, only one man hit on Maritza during an interview. "What changed?," she said. "I believe offering compensation changed men's expectations of the interaction. Men no longer felt entitled because they were doing me a favor by participating in the interview." Maritza also changed her recruitment tactics: "I posted flyers in coffee shops, on Craigslist, and stopped asking men that I had just met for interviews. This removed the element of men feeling flattered because a young woman approached them." By abandoning part of her project for a time, Maritza was able to obtain economic support, which changed the dynamics of her interviews. The extra time also allowed her to rethink her approach to recruiting participants.

Cathy reported that she "just shut down" and stopped conducting fieldwork for periods of time. These periods were followed by feelings of guilt that eventually led to her going back into the field, but she did so begrudgingly. Some of the men temporarily halted their fieldwork (or portions of it) in response to other types of danger. Will stayed out of one of the neighborhoods he was working in for a while after receiving a death threat. Brian, a white man, described a frightening experience when people in an area in conflict with a mining company thought he was a spy for their adversary and warned him, "People might want to hang you and your family." Brian and his family left town, and he did not go back until he found another way to develop access. Another option was to never return to sites that were dangerous. Elena, for example, generally avoids the part of Mexico where a man tried to enter her house and assault her many years ago. Michelle avoids the city where an expat attacked her. Frances ended up dropping a whole component of her study after a gatekeeper propositioned her. In contrast, when men in his field site tried to pick fights with him, Sergio did not feel he needed to end his research there, but he did feel that he had to prove his masculinity in order to continue. He described his thought process when this happened.

> What is the best way to preserve my physical safety [and] to preserve the environment of my research site? I don't want to get into a fight with someone there, because later you don't know how that's going to turn out. And also, I feel like I need to preserve my masculinity. Like, I need, I don't know, this is the first time I am thinking about this, but probably I need to show that I am also capable of retaliating or fighting and showing that I am a man. I won't get into a fight, but I will diffuse it or make jokes and try to just stand up in front of this person who is trying to get into a fight with me.

Sergio felt his field site required that he show he was not afraid in these situations, lest he lose respect. When asked if this need was manifested differently in the field than in his everyday life, he said it was different in the field at first because it was more constant. Once people knew him, though, there were fewer tests of masculinity through physical altercations. Sergio also modified his project in the interest of safety, leaving out potential research sites that he considered too dangerous.

Some participants abandoned projects before they were even off the ground. It only took one visit to a trans sex-work site at the encouragement of an activist friend for Sofía to realize it wasn't for her. She did not feel safe and decided against including the site in her project. Louise eliminated Uganda as a potential field site because of fears about the country's antigay policy and the consequences conducting research there could have had for her and her participants. She worried that her mere presence in neighborhoods might "implicate others" and decided that it was not worth the risk to potential research participants and interlocutors. Some time after being harassed while conducting preliminary dissertation research, Jenna came to the decision to speak to two of her women advisers about the unease she felt at her field site. She told them in general terms about what she had experienced. Both advisers were responsive and worked closely with her to change the site and the focus of her dissertation as well as put her in touch with their connections who had experience in the region. Jenna reported that she ultimately had more professional and personal success finding local connections from this network and felt safe during the entirety of her dissertation fieldwork.

Others, though, decided to abandon their projects after more time had been invested. This was the case for Karina, whose story is told in chapter 2. It was also true of Adela, a multiracial researcher who ended her project on online gaming after being harassed by another player. After men responded to her requests for interviews with innuendos and overtures, Lisa first avoided doing interviews in her study of men's cycling culture but eventually ended the project altogether because the "rampant masculinity" created too many issues with access. Gina quit the project she had been working on with a professor after he chastised her for not wanting to go into the field alone after she was harassed and assaulted. This had costs for her career, as they had agreed that she would be able to use the data gathered in the project for her dissertation. Clark eliminated an ethnographic component of his project after he was assaulted in the bar where he worked. Claude dropped his first attempt at dissertation research after four months. He had been studying emotion management among first responders to violence in a police crisis unit, but he said the culture "was so overtly masculinist and antifeminist and I thought, 'I don't know if I can survive this project myself.'" Frances abandoned qualitative research for several years after being stalked and propositioned in her field site. "The whole experience itself left me kind of feeling like 'uck' about qualitative research," she said.

More participants ultimately responded to dangerous situations by modifying their projects, which can be seen above in our discussion of coping strategies: they chose to bring friends with them into the field, dropped particular research sites, or did not attend events when they felt unsafe or debilitated. Like Maritza, some researchers did not set up interviews with people they had originally planned to interview because they hit on them or just put off "bad vibes." Based on her earlier experience in Madagascar, Susie modified her dissertation work from the beginning by interacting with men between the ages of twenty and forty in a very formal manner. Compared to the older men she worked with, she kept relationships with younger men as professional as possible. She recognized that she might have sacrificed some closeness as a result but felt it was worthwhile in order to avoid the types of issues she had experienced in the past. After a man told her four or five times over the course of an interview that he knew how to make a woman "go cuckoo for Cocopuffs," Amy simply stopped the recording and left. Angie generally ended the conversation if men in the Occupy movement she was studying began hitting on her. Other researchers chose to eliminate men from their research altogether. Choosing to modify projects and eliminate sites and participants made some of our participants worry that others might critique the validity of their research. However, modifications can protect researchers' physical and mental health, which undoubtedly leads to better research.

CONCLUSION

In this chapter we have documented the range of harassment confronted by our participants during their fieldwork, as well as how they coped with it. In contrast to the message some mentors sent to participants, harassment and sexualization cannot be understood as just one more challenge to be faced in the field. Harassment in the field can force researchers to relive previous trauma they experienced, can lead to the termination of projects (which can have an irreparable effect on their careers when they do not have the support of their committee and mentors), and can force them to rely on unhealthy coping mechanisms. Indeed, though we have not discussed these in depth here, researchers may turn to mechanisms that have long-term consequences for their health and well-being. Rather than suffer through harassment in isolation, we encourage researchers to violate the expectations that researchers must go it alone, whether that means seeking out collaborative research or building support networks before entering the field.

Although certain forms of harassment and violence are undoubtedly more traumatic, come-ons, pressure for sex, and misogynist comments also leave scars, which must be dealt with in the field and after. As we have shown, researchers are already prone to writing off uncomfortable or even terrifying experiences when "nothing really happened" to get through fieldwork. They do not need encouragement from others to ignore or overlook these experiences. All forms of harassment, violence, and sexualization need to be taken seriously by colleagues, mentors, and peers, so that students feel supported in modifying or even abandoning research projects. Few of the men we interviewed felt they were ever in danger of sexual abuse. However, some men will face harassment, sexual assault, or other forms of violence in the field. Thus all researchers should learn beforehand that changes and modifications made in the interest of safety are nothing to be ashamed of. If changes are part and parcel of the research process, those made in response to gendered experiences should be recognized as inherent to this process. Finally, for those who decide to suffer through, we hope this chapter has provided some options for healthy coping mechanisms and that reading about others' experiences will make them feel less alone.

We have briefly discussed the various costs associated with harassment. Some participants had to begin a new dissertation project from scratch. Others became complicit participants in sexist and / or racist discourses and practices. And at some point in time, almost all of our participants were made to feel that they were not in control of their own bodies. The following chapter zooms in on this issue to demonstrate that harassment and sexualization have costs for individual researchers as well as the knowledge they produce.

FOUR

The Costs

OBJECTIFICATION, SEXUAL HARASSMENT, and abuse are part of the fabric of women's socialization, and violence against women, and the expectation that women endure it, is normalized at a young age.[1] Though normalized, sexual harassment has long-term effects on women's emotional well-being, shapes their interactional strategies, and restricts their ability to feel safe in public places and thrive in educational and work settings.[2] Like sexual harassment in other areas of women's lives, harassment and advances in the field have myriad consequences. So do the socialization processes we undergo in academia that teach us how to understand and respond to harassment. In this chapter, we focus on two types of costs—emotional and occupational—incurred in the ethnographic field and in the field of academia. The "curious policing of socially correct feeling within the fieldwork community" has kept researchers from discussing the emotional and embodied costs of fieldwork.[3] We seek to better prepare researchers to anticipate these costs and destabilize this policing.

The emotional costs reported by our participants include self-blame and self-doubt, a debilitating split between self-image and objectification by others, and isolation. Harassment also has consequences for ethnographers' work, including reduced efficacy, concerns about access, reduced mobility, and changes to or abandonment of projects when harassment becomes too severe. While on the surface these costs can be understood as the result of experiencing harassment in the field, they are indirectly produced by several intersecting factors: socialization that teaches women to blame themselves when they are harassed or assaulted and requires that they deflect attention from gender at work; gender expectations in our particular field sites; gender expectations in the academy that cultivate silence about harassment; and the ethnographic standards and fixations we discuss in chapter 1. That is, broader gender expectations are both reflected in and reinforced by academic fields that still implicitly envision the ideal ethnographer as "neutral," that is, a white cis man. As a result, when harassed in the field, women "fail" as both researchers and women. They recognize that they are not meeting the standards of "good ethnography"; nor are they "correctly" managing their sexuality and men's desires, as heteronormativity demands.[4] Women frequently attribute these failures to their own actions and bodies, blaming themselves for harassment, aggression, and assault. Our findings show this can happen even when women ethnographers are well aware of the structural roots of harassment.

Over the course of this chapter, we address an often-overlooked issue: the way in which participants' power and positionalities affect the researcher. We also show that gender expectations and fieldwork experiences can make ethnographers complicit in the reproduction of gender hierarchies. We challenge readers to think about how gendered and racialized expectations will affect them in the field and to critically analyze experiences they might have as the product of social and institutional structures. At the end of the chapter we discuss strategies that can help researchers navigate these costs without suggesting that they can be avoided.

EMOTIONAL COSTS FOR INDIVIDUAL ETHNOGRAPHERS

Our interviewees are smart, educated, and critically minded. They understand the structural character of oppression—including its manifestations in the form of harassment and objectification. In other words, they do not view harassment and objectification as individual experiences brought on by women's actions or men's biological urges. Instead they understand these and other forms of gender violence as patterned forms of social control and exercises of domination sanctioned by patriarchal social institutions that reproduce gender inequality and violence against women. Indeed, some of our participants even set out to study the dynamics of gender oppression, sexual harassment, and objectification. Many identified themselves as feminist scholars and had feminist mentors. Their discussion of the emotional implications of unwanted sexual attention in the field and their responses to that attention were striking, however, in their similarity to the explanations many women recur to after experiencing harassment in their everyday lives. This suggests that academia is not that different from other workplaces in terms of the discourses available to women. Furthermore, it suggests that gender expectations and the three fixations may neutralize or cancel out the critical, analytic perspectives some of us learn in graduate school, at least when it comes to understanding our own experiences. In this section, we address three themes that emerged as participants discussed the emotional costs of unwelcome sexualization in the field: feelings of self-blame, self-doubt, and shame; an alienating split between how they understood themselves and how they were objectified by others; and isolation both as a consequence of harassment and as a strategy to avoid it. These consequences led the women we interviewed to question their skills and the quality of their research and even to change the course of their research projects.

Self-Blame

While IRB procedures and many methods texts encourage researchers to consider the risks and harm to which they might expose their research participants, the women we interviewed reported being unprepared to anticipate how their projects might harm them as researchers, not only physically, but also psychologically and emotionally. Self-blame and self-doubt were perhaps the most common emotional responses they reported. For example, when Elena, who is now an associate professor, was a graduate student, she chose to live alone in the rural Mexican community where she conducted her fieldwork. When some men tried to break into her house after she refused an invitation to dance at a village party, she blamed herself for not understanding the social expectations for women there, despite her own Latina background.

> I made the decision to live by myself, and I should have known better. But . . . I was coming from a university, a university in America, as a student. So, you know, I was kind of used to having that same kind of freedom that I had. And then women in rural communities in Mexico, they are really constrained. There are gendered expectations that I didn't know about and wasn't aware of because no one told me about them.

Elena blamed herself for not anticipating gender expectations in the context where she was working, even though her training and mentorship had not prepared her to anticipate them.

Participants conducting research in the United States also blamed themselves for the unwelcome sexualized experiences they faced in the field.

Frequently, these experiences were overlaid by other factors, including race and ethnicity. In Monira's case, religion also structured her experiences. When a man she interviewed touched her and asked provocative questions about her hijab, her initial reaction was to feel she had done something wrong.

Even when they understood the structural aspects of what they were experiencing, participants found it difficult to avoid self-blame. This response is unsurprising when we consider that women are not only raised to police their own sexuality and bodies but to anticipate and maneuver men's sexuality and desires.[5] However, in some cases, it was others in the field who suggested to our participants that they were responsible for the harassment or advances they experienced. For example, a white graduate student, Phoebe, was made fun of by her roommate for not anticipating her gatekeeper's pursuit of her during her fieldwork in Brazil. Self-blame was exacerbated by comments made by advisers, mentors, and peers. When Phoebe told her adviser about her gatekeeper's constant advances, he told her to "suck it up"—meaning that she should be strong and tolerate it. Others said things like, "Oh, that's what you get for spending so much time with him." These responses naturalized the sexual harassment that Phoebe experienced, suggesting it was obvious that a man would respond the way Phoebe's gatekeeper did.[6] From this perspective, Phoebe should have assumed she would be harassed as she attempted to build the intimate relationships with her research participants that ethnographers often glorify. Interestingly, the implicit message here is that sexual harassment is an "obvious" part of fieldwork, yet it is something that no one brought up, nor was it discussed before Phoebe entered the field. The same was true for many other participants. The implicit understanding that harassment is so obvious that it should be anticipated justifies and perpetuates the silence of peers and mentors on issues of gender and sexuality; it also places the blame on women for not anticipating what they are told only after the fact. Although Phoebe recognized that what happened was not her fault, she talked about how hard she had to work to keep from internalizing these messages. After a government official attempted to assault Karina, a white researcher, in his office, she also blamed herself for not adequately "policing" her body: "I knew so much of it had to do with the fact that I was a woman, [but] I'd blame myself about stupid things, by which I mean maybe I should have worn my hair back tightly, or maybe I should have worn nicer shoes, quote-unquote stupid things like that." Others similarly second-guessed themselves: I shouldn't have worn that dress; I shouldn't have smiled so much. But, as we discuss in chapter 3, even when women tried to change their clothing and behavior, many still experienced harassment and assault.

Some women identified a contradiction between the routine demands of fieldwork and the ability to protect oneself. They nonetheless blamed *themselves,* rather than this contradiction, for their experiences. Jenna, a white graduate student from North America who was working in South Asia, described finding herself in a dangerous situation after accepting a motorcycle ride between two of her field sites from a friend of a friend. She talked about how she regretted going places she should not have gone and trusting people she should not have trusted, even though these types of decisions go with the terrain of ethnographic fieldwork.

> I was like, "Oh, that was stupid of me to get on a motorcycle with a man I don't know." Everyone says you shouldn't do that. But then looking back on it, when we're in the field things like this happen all the time. And that's the reality of it. You're actually not in a very safe place to begin with, so all of those split-second decisions that you make—I mean especially like in places like [this country in South Asia] where there's not good public transportation, where there are no lights at night—you sort of just have to make a split-second decision about whether or not you're going to trust someone. And so a lot of the things about personal safety that we're told are our own responsibility. I feel like it's just compromised to begin with.

Although some interviewees were cognitively aware that they were not to blame for the harassment, this knowledge did not keep them from feeling responsible, a feeling that resulted in emotional burdens they carried during and after their fieldwork. These experiences demonstrate how effective gender socialization is at "keeping women in their place," even when women are critical of it.[7] Far from exempt from this process, ethnographic research can place women in situations where sexual harassment is perhaps more likely than in their daily lives. Methods courses, mentors, and the standards by which accolades are distributed can actually provide incentives for remaining quiet, communicating to researchers that "sucking it up" and persevering is what leads to "good" data.

Understanding Self-Blame

Three intersecting gender processes lead women to blame themselves for harassment in the field. First, the socialization women undergo as they take on and form their identities teaches them to blame themselves when they have

Why do you think some women blamed themselves for the harassment they experienced?

Evaluate the responses of Phoebe's mentor and roommate when she told them about her experiences. In what other ways could they have responded? Would these alternative responses have been more or less helpful to Phoebe?

negative sexual experiences. Family, peers, religion, media, and other forces of socialization continue to teach women that they are responsible for protecting their bodies from harm and, thus, liable when their bodies are threatened. What to wear, how to talk, how to move, and what spaces to enter all become daily decisions that women must make "correctly" to avoid negative sexual experiences. Because these are a woman's decisions, according to this logic, when she faces uncomfortable, threatening, or harmful experiences, it is because she has chosen poorly and has failed to anticipate men's dominance, aggression, and desire, attributes that are considered natural. Just as in other aspects of life, this socialization informs how women interpret and respond to what happens in the field.

Second, there are gender relations in any ethnographic field that women must negotiate. When entering the field, ethnographers anticipate that there may be customs, rituals, language, norms, and expectations that will take time to learn. As discussed in chapters 2 and 3, many of these are gendered in character. These challenges are perhaps especially salient when conducting research abroad. Among other issues, participants mentioned more rigid divisions between the public and private spheres, perceptions of Western women as easy, and the politics of respectability as factors that could easily lead to missteps, misunderstandings, and unwelcome advances or harassment. In addition, when the women we interviewed discovered they were unprepared for or caught off guard by local gender expectations, they often blamed themselves for not knowing about them beforehand. As Elena said, she "should have known better" than to live alone in her field site. Although this self-blame contributes to feelings of incompetence at the individual level, we insist that these feelings are socially produced through gender norms at home, in the field, and in academia. The colonial heritage of ethnography is evident here: students are encouraged (but unprepared) to enter spaces where their bodies and actions do not conform to local systems, with the universalizing assumption that researchers hold power over participants (originally because of their ties to colonial administration).

Third, the expectations and norms associated with participation in academia—and ethnography in particular—reinforce the individualization of experiences of harassment. Dana Britton has observed, "the contexts in which women experience gender at work have implications for the ways they understand its role and relevance."[8] Interactions with peers and mentors can teach women that harassment and unwanted attention are an accepted part of being in the academy. As we pointed out in chapter 1, graduate school often teaches silence on these issues.[9] And the assumption of the neutral ethnographer blinds us to anticipating and discussing how research might go differently when conducted by a person who does not embody "neutrality." Failing to recognize the three intersecting processes means that students are not trained to understand their harassment as a structural problem. Nor are they given the tools to fight against the impulse to blame themselves when facing harassment in the field.

The costs of the implicit assumptions about the race, gender, and class of the "good ethnographer," as well as the academic status of the researcher, are nowhere more apparent than in Mercedes's story. After her research study had ended, Mercedes, a Latina sociologist, was asked out for coffee by one of her participants, a veteran. She was recently divorced and was lonely. She found this man interesting, so she agreed to join him. They went out for coffee twice. In retrospect, she says, she found him a little "off" at times and regrets "not listening" to herself. After their second coffee date, he invited her to his house, ostensibly to watch a documentary. Mercedes found this a strange invitation, but she knew he lived with his brother and sister-in-law and their baby, so she did not think she was engaging in anything risky by agreeing to go. When she arrived, however, he was alone. His demeanor was cold. He did not greet her and avoided eye contact. Rather than a documentary, he was watching combat footage. "Right then I should have known, but I didn't listen to myself, that something was not right," Mercedes reflected. He raped her, later calling it an "accident," and telling her, "This was your choice, you know. You're the one that brought yourself here."

At the time of our interview, in addition to suffering the physical consequences of the assault, Mercedes was questioning her own responsibility and the potential consequences of the assault for her career. She questioned why she stuck around despite the red flags. "I'm a recovering people pleaser [laughs]. [I'm] getting over it and working on it," she reflected. "I chose not looking bad or seeming mean . . . instead of my own safety and my own red flags that I felt inside. And so I stuck around. Also [I hoped] I was wrong because I was interested in this person in some ways." Like many rape victims, she knew logically that the rape was not her fault but could not avoid feeling ashamed and responsible for what had been done to her.

Connected layers of social control silenced Mercedes. She was very worried about the consequences of having been raped for the project she was working on and for her academic reputation. She felt she had overstepped a professional boundary by going out with a participant, even though her work at this particular site had concluded by the time of their first date. In addition, she did not want people in the rapist's community to know what had happened so as to avoid any possible implications for the project. She worried what the community members she had come to know and respect would think of *her* if they knew what had happened. And she worried that people at her university would think of her as a Latina who couldn't get her life together. The sociology wiki served as a controlling mechanism in this context, as she imagined her rape being discussed. She explained:

> That's the first thing that popped in my head, and so it's awful and I feel like . . . as academics we're overly concerned with how people think of us, but . . . I don't want to lose my credibility. I already have a hard time with credibility. Like, I already have a hard time convincing people that I know what I'm doing. I've been asked several times, "Oh, so when are you going to get your PhD? When are you finishing?" I'm like, "I already finished. I actually work here." [Laughs] I think I'm not the only woman who's encountered that, but I feel like my credentials and my abilities are questioned [as a] Latina [and] because of my working-class background, which in some ways . . . makes it [so] I didn't have as good a high school [education] as others did, but I already have so many levels of trying to show that I can do this. And I feel like [this] is what came into my head: I'm going to be pathologized— like a pathology of this young Latina who can't get her life together.

Mercedes's case shows how the prevailing norms of what makes a good woman, a good ethnographer, and a good scholar more generally can prevent women, and perhaps women of color in particular, from seeking support when they most need it. Patriarchal and racist norms—both inside and outside academia—inform our expectations of what makes a good ethnographer and a good woman and intersect to shape how women respond to harassment, violence, and the emotional consequences they suffer as a result.

Self-Doubt

Participants doubted their skills as ethnographers when they experienced harassment. Several recalled feeling that they should have known how to deal with the issues they confronted, despite the fact that they received no training or mentorship in this regard. Rosie, the white sociology student who faced sexual threats during her fieldwork on music festivals, felt "out of control of the situation," like a "bad researcher" who "wasn't able to handle this in the way that I needed to." Frances, the Asian American sociologist who was studying immigration, lamented that she had failed to notice the red flags in her relationship with the gatekeeper who eventually tried to get her to exchange sex or money for access to his community. She connected this experience to the pressures of gaining ethnographic access: trying to gain entrée to the community, she felt, led her to ignore her instincts about this man. Nevertheless, she, too, blamed herself for what had happened. "Maybe it was something I wore or maybe something I did?," she wondered.

Marina, a Latina, described how, after receiving harassing phone calls from a survey respondent to whom she had given her phone number, she blamed herself for not having the "proper" skills. This sense of guilt was overlaid with concerns about whether she had acted "appropriately": "I keep going back to it, and I thought, you know, was it something I said during the interview? Did I sit too close to him? What was it about our interaction that led him to think it was okay for him to do that?" Marina's gender socialization clearly interacted with her methodological socialization and training (or lack thereof). In all of these cases, the individual considered herself responsible for what happened and for not knowing how to respond; participants' training in and assumptions of what ethnographic research should look like discouraged them from evaluating the systemic character of their experiences. Marina was conscious of this: "I know that's a totally inappropriate way to view this episode, but I think [I feel that way] because we're kind of socialized into thinking that this is our fault and that there are so many things we can do to avoid it."

Lena, the Asian American sociology student who was stalked by neo-Nazis in Europe, recalled feeling, "irrationally, like it says something about me that I am this target of harassment when other people look stronger or more capable of handling themselves." The costs of research that Lena incurred cannot be understood if we look only at her field site. Instead, we must take into account how race and gender structured the overlapping social worlds in which she was embedded: gender socialization, methodological training, graduate school culture, and the field. It was one of Lena's graduate school peers who exacerbated her self-doubt by telling her, "You know, if you look scared, you will get harassed." This gets to the crux of why so many participants were reluctant to talk about their experiences with others in their departments.

In addition to doubting their capabilities as researchers when sexualized interactions took place, many women expressed doubts about the strategies they engaged to try to avoid them. Rosie felt she was cheating somehow when she began to bring men friends along when she went into the field. Her worries about turning down invitations or creating protective barriers arose because these actions transgress the ethnographic trilogy, an evaluative benchmark: danger, solitude, and intimacy. Bringing people into our field sites flies in the face of intimacy in particular. For instance, in order to do research that is truly "illuminating," Wacquant advocates "carnal ethnography," which involves long-term intensive work and deep involvement with participants' lives in order to achieve "social competency" in their worlds.[10] Be vulnerable. Never say no. Break down barriers and boundaries. All of these methodological mantras express the importance of ethnographic intimacy, encouraging researchers to become as close as possible to their participants. They also contradict what many women are told to do to keep themselves safe in their everyday lives. In other words, researchers are asked to do precisely those things that women are shamed for doing after they experience sexualized violence. Transgressing the intimacy standard (by saying no or bringing another "outsider" into your field site) contributes to self-doubt, as women worry that they cannot do research the "right" way and stay safe at the same time.

The men we interviewed reported fewer experiences of harassment or sexualization in the field. Those who did experience sexualization did not tend to have the debilitating feelings of vulnerability, self-blame, and self-doubt that the women described (though some men did have harrowing experiences). Brian, a white sociology student, described several moments in which he worried that botched interactions with sexual undertones might have put his research in Central America at risk. On one occasion he took a trip with a small group of men and women from one of the organizations he was studying. One of the men in the group got upset because Brian might have to share a hotel room with the two women (which was not his decision). Brian worried that he had destroyed his whole project because the man who was upset was a prominent leader, but he was also frustrated at the way his intentions had been misinterpreted. While events like this created anxiety for Brian, they did not make him feel like a failure. Because men are less likely to learn that they are responsible for others' actions as they grow up, Brian's socialization likely shielded him from the self-doubt and self-blame so many of our women respondents experienced.

Furthermore, men had different options and strategies to draw on when they received unwanted attention. A case in point is Will's experience of two of his research participants propositioning him when he was conducting research in Latin America. While he described being shocked and annoyed, Will did not feel he was in danger during these encounters, nor was he particularly concerned that they would keep him from completing his research. Apart from the fact that he was much larger than the women he was working with, Will noted, patriarchal norms structured these encounters in such a way that they were notdetrimental to his research relationships. When one member of the organization where he was doing participant observation undressed in front of him a couple of months into his fieldwork, it did not cause him extreme anxiety. "By then I had friends there," he explained. "We all liked each other. You know, I would say I was a friend of hers before this happened, right? And I knew everybody else, and I was well liked at the organization." Will benefited from having had time to build alliances in the organization before this encounter occurred. Because, as he noted, men are often expected to make the first move (a norm that holds across various cultures and contexts), he had the time to build relationships with others that he could lean on in the event this interaction did damage his relationship with one contact. Contrast this experience to that of Michelle, who was afraid to tell her host family about the community leader who was harassing her because it might create problems for them.[11]

Although he experienced various types of threats in his fieldwork (a death threat; entering violent neighborhoods as an obvious outsider), Will did not feel vulnerable to sexual violence. Nor did he blame himself for the threats he encountered. He simply saw them as part of doing research in dangerous environments. In other words, Will attributed these threats to his environment rather than to his individual choices or shortcomings. Moreover, these

Given your own positionality and research plans, what types of power could you foresee having over your research participants? What types of power could you foresee they will have over you?

If you experience sexual harassment or physical threats or danger in the field, would this cause you to question your competence as a researcher? Why or why not? Are there other experiences that might make you question your competence as a researcher? What are they, and why do you think they would elicit this kind of response?

are forms of violence that could earn Will academic capital, which is not true of sexual violence. When he was concerned about the politics of gender in his research, these concerns arose from the position of power he inhabited. Will noted that he held the empowered position in the relationships with those who objectified him.[12] For example, Will talked about working with poor young adults at one site: "I had to be a little bit conscious about the way I presented myself when I was interviewing some of the young girls there. Because I was this very exotic, wealthy, powerful, white, blond, blue-eyed Martian who turned up on their doorsteps, who was showing interest in their lives. . . . I just had to be a little bit careful because I was actually in a position of power in those circumstances."

Because of his gender and appearance, Will benefited from what Lena referred to as the "alpha male pose" ethnographers are expected to adopt. While men may be objects of sexual desire in the field, they are usually in a position of relative power. Furthermore, at least in Will's case, his experiences did not leave him feeling less efficacious. Will observed that while no ethnographer has total control over how research participants construct them, he benefited from the way in which his participants understood him: he was a "rich," authoritative foreigner and, thus, economically and symbolically powerful relative to his participants. Although this experience does not reflect that of all men ethnographers, it stands in marked contrast to the debilitating experiences of many of the women we interviewed, even when they, too, understood harassment as a product of the structures and institutions in which they were operating.

Split in the Field

The range of emotional costs women reported as a result of unwanted sexual attention, harassment, and assault in the field included feelings of fear, vulnerability, irritability, and hopelessness, as well as short and long bouts of depression.[13] Considerations of how to cope with emotional costs takes us to the third major theme of this section: the "split" women experienced between the demure, feminine self they felt they had to present in the field and the efficacious self they felt themselves to be in other parts of their lives. By "self," we are not only referring to the ideas that we have about who we are, but also to the embodied practices and forms of self-presentation that are the foundation of our identities. Our "selves" are constituted by institutional arrangements and interactional orders. Women's embodiment in the field and how they alter bodily practices and performances in order to do their work also alters their sense of identity, self-efficacy, and psychological well-being. Policing their own bodies in order to conform to gender expectations—changing movements, tone of voice, form of dress and speech, and body language—destabilized researchers' sense of self. It is unsurprising that consenting to their own domination challenged women's identities. For some, performing this consent on a regular basis disempowered them as women and as researchers.

Virginia, a white woman and the one archaeologist in our sample, spoke of how the experience of being treated in a way that you are not used to can "challenge who you are and how you see yourself." It took her about ten years in her field site to feel comfortable being herself, wearing what she wanted and not lying about her relationship status, for example. Having to do those things, she observed, is "really, really hard emotional work." Being required to lie about something as basic as romantic attachments in order to avoid being harassed in the field (which usually doesn't work anyway) requires being untrue to yourself and to the people around you—essentially, living a lie. Ultimately, she decided it wasn't worth it. Others agreed that because fieldwork was such a long-term process, it was important to be themselves (i.e., authentic or genuine) in the field. Of course, even the participants who made this decision could not control how others defined them.

Sexual and gender identities can produce similar "splits" in the field for some men. Clark never outed himself as a trans man while conducting research with gay men in South America. Similarly, Antonio La Pastina hid his identity as a gay man while conducting research in rural Brazil.[14] Although he had worked to claim his sexual identity "after almost thirty years of denial," La Pastina chose to hide it while in the field, telling research participants that he had a wife back in the United States.[15] He reflected on the personal histories of gays and lesbians who grow up learning to "pass" as straight. For them, fieldwork can become "an extension of the repressive environment many of us grew up in."[16] For La Pastina, the absence of honest relationships, "coupled with my anxiety about having to be back in the closet, pushed me many times to the borders of a depressive state."[17]

Fieldwork for La Pastina required that he construct a false "straight self" in the field. For many of the women we interviewed, presenting a feminine self in the field meant remaining silent when others objectified them. Sometimes it even meant playing into this dynamic. Thus, a split occurred as researchers complied with sexual objectification by others in the field, which often led them to question if they were efficacious subjects outside of it, resulting in contradictions in self-evaluation before, during, and after fieldwork. Often, this split came up when our participants talked about access. For example, Annie, an Asian American student conducting research with former combatants in Latin America, felt she had to be nonthreatening and therefore could not respond as she normally would to harassing behavior in the field. She could not become angry or aggressive, as she might at home, and this felt like a "self-enforced weakness" to her. "It's extremely debilitating," she said. Behaving in a demure, nonthreatening way felt inauthentic to her, as if she was being forced to not be her true self. Nancy, a white woman conducting research on the criminal justice system in North America, noted that maintaining these two selves was draining and exhausting; she had to engage in constant self-surveillance in the field. Fieldwork is draining and exhausting for many—if not all—researchers, regardless of sex and gender. Nevertheless, gendered and sexual impression management for women (and some men), as several participants describe below, can entail feeling completely out of control.

Maritza, a Latina whose research takes place in a major U.S. city, talked about what facing daily cat-calls did to her psyche.

> I can't go out, without, like, it happens almost every day. And I know that it's not about me, but it's just reached a point where I want to be invisible. Like this summer, it reached that point where I was like, "I am not going to let my hair down, I am going to put it up in a bun because I know that my hair is what gets attention." So my hair became tangled in a knot, and it took me more than two days to untangle it. And when I noticed a group of men

walking by, I would just look down, and that's not healthy for anyone and it's not good for me as a woman because if I am trying to be in academia and we think about self-presentation, that's not who I am. I never walk looking down at the floor and trying to become invisible. So it's just these very little things, like these microaggressions, that really got to me this summer.

For coauthor Rebecca, not having more control over how people perceived her in the field was surprising and disempowering and unsettled her identity in ways she had never considered before her research. It was a "total inversion of what I thought research was going to do for me, identity-wise." Although instances of objectification were destabilizing and could be deeply troubling, participants described laughing them off, in effect acquiescing to them as part of fieldwork. But the effects of these experiences on one's sense of efficacy in the field and beyond can be long-lasting. Indeed, several participants, including Rebecca, noted that this can be a long-term burden, altering their ability to trust men not just in the field, but in other aspects of their lives. Similarly, Hoang writes about the "embodied costs of conducting the kind of ethnography that does not conform with feminist expectations."[18] She discusses the acts of submission and role playing in which she engaged as part of her fieldwork on sex work in Vietnam. In her case, these were voluntary acts, but they still had costs for her understanding of self and "blurred the boundaries of my real life." Acquiescence, even in the name of fieldwork, can feel like self-abuse, and it leaves psychic scars.

Sometimes the ways in which race, nationality, and power intersected encouraged acquiescence and constrained participants' ability to respond when faced with unwanted sexualized interactions in the field. Several participants mentioned that they held back from responding forcefully and remained silent about their experiences because they were concerned about reinforcing stereotypes about their participants.[19] For example, Marina described her qualms about telling her white feminist adviser about the harassment she faced working with Latino men at an informal street corner market: "I didn't want to make these men look, you know, a certain way. And they are already a kind of stigmatized population, you know?" Similarly, Leanne Johansson faced harassment from her gatekeepers during her fieldwork in Central Africa.[20] She observes that she was paralyzed by the expectation that a good ethnographer engages in reflexive self-critique about power and ethnocentric assumptions. Insofar as this commitment to reflexivity about power in the field implicitly takes a gender-neutral ethnographer as its starting point, it also may encourage differently situated ethnographers to put the interests of their harassers above their own.

Experiences like these can mean returning from the field with decreased self-confidence and then having to perform in spaces where aplomb and assertiveness are highly valued: networking with peers and mentors, going on job interviews, and giving conference presentations. Thus, doubts about one's ability as a researcher can go on to have a negative impact on one's ability to network, build academic capital, or perhaps even secure a job. These effects of fieldwork can be exacerbated by the "chilly climate" of academia in which patterns of inequitable treatment accumulate, inhibiting "women's confidence, self-esteem, and accomplishment."[21] In short, disempowering research experiences and the scars they leave not only affect women in the field but their career trajectories as well; just as researchers carry the gender and race inequalities of academia to the field, inequalities in the social worlds we research can exacerbate these same race and gender hierarchies in academia.

For participants who experienced sexual assault in the field, the impact on sense of self and independence bled into other aspects of their lives. Elena described being scared to go out, especially at night, and having to be "very, very careful all the time." Lena felt anger and hopelessness at realizing it was unlikely she would be able to defend herself if the stalking she experienced evolved into something even more serious. Although she eventually returned to the field after her initial exploratory trip, she went through what she referred to as anticipatory depression beforehand. Gina described how her sense of self-possession was destroyed after her assault: "In the immediate aftermath I felt like I had been reduced to a fourteen-year-old girl. I didn't want to see any men, I didn't want to go out, and I was covering myself as much as possible, and I was like, 'I feel like this body is a liability, I need to be really careful.'" Not only did she abandon the project she was working on, but the experience made her more cautious: she spends a great deal of energy making sure she is as safe as possible in the field.

Allowing others to define fundamental aspects of your self in order to get the job done has additional costs. Joan, a white sociologist, recalled engaging men's flirtation as a means of fostering access while conducting research on political elites in Central America when she was a graduate student years ago. She felt that playing up her appearance and the idea of a harmless cute girl may have helped set men at ease, but in retrospect, she reflected:

Being talked to as a child every day, I don't think [that is] super great for your self-esteem as an adult. Yeah, my feelings about it now are . . . partly annoyed at myself for the lack of faith in my own abilities, and also I think that I completely overestimated [the] amount of power being an attractive female gives you. I don't think it gives you very much at all. I think I misunderstood that! [Laughs wryly.]

Karina similarly suspected her appearance may have facilitated her access to government executives in Rwanda, where she conducted her fieldwork, and yet to achieve access on this basis affected her self-perception. She explained, "They really wanted to talk to me because I was this sweet little girl. 'Come into my office, let me tell you, oh, you're so cute for asking these questions.' So it was a benefit in a way that made me feel terrible [laughs] but that worked for my research. . . . It's really condescending but at the same time gave me a lot of access." Women who use their appearance or sexuality to gain access in the field have to deal with the fact that this access depends on adhering to their role as a subordinate. This can wreak havoc on a person's sense of self.

Of course, all ethnographers must manage their presentation of self. Richard Tewksbury and Patricia Gagné have examined the difficulties of competing field and professional identities.[22] Reuben May has written about the challenges of conducting research—particularly research about race—with white participants as a black man.[23] And much has been written about the challenges of doing research with populations that hold racist or homophobic beliefs. For example, Kathleen Blee writes of the obstacles to gaining rapport and building relationships with white supremacists, whose views she abhorred.[24] Bernadette Barton describes the toll homophobia took on her, as a researcher and a lesbian, when she conducted research with Christian fundamentalists in the Bible Belt.[25] Among our own participants, Elizabeth, a white sociologist, found her identification as an antiracist challenged by the requirements of her fieldwork, as when the North American tourists she interviewed said racist things and she was compelled to encourage them to tell her more. Similarly, Claude, a white man who is an avowed feminist, spoke about the difficulty of witnessing misogyny and listening to misogynist comments by the college athletes who were the subject of his research (see chap. 3). Although he did not suffer the direct consequences of that behavior, it affected his emotional well-being and understanding of self.

What can make negotiating presentation of self in the field unique for women was summed up by Cathy, who observed that ethnography often requires researchers to act in ways that contradict how many women learn to act in the public sphere—that is, to be open and inviting as opposed to on guard and closed off to potentially compromising or dangerous situations. Being open and inviting is considered a basic part of the research process but can also be used to justify women's experiences of harassment and sexualization. Harassment and sexualization, then, are peculiar "challenges" in that individual researchers may be blamed when they experience them. To the degree that these interactions—and how peers and mentors respond to them—alter our identities and sense of self, they go beyond other challenges of self-presentation in the field.

Many of our participants were feminists and could analyze their experiences through a feminist lens, but there were times when that perspective was simply not enough. Feminism might help us reconceptualize the social world and our place in it, but it does so after we have come to know ourselves and the world through patriarchal, racist, heteronormative socialization (as well as other systems of power). It does not undo this socialization. It does not take away the exhaustion or added stress of conducting research in a world that is organized on these inequalities. In fact, identifying as a feminist can create unresolvable tensions for researchers in the field. In many cases, researchers cannot react to sexual advances and discrimination in a way that aligns with their principles. Sometimes they find they must conform to and reproduce stereotypes and inequalities in order to do their work. It is precisely those feminist and antiracist actions aimed at destabilizing stereotypes and challenging inequalities that participants often felt they could not take in the field.

Isolation

Isolation, the fourth consistent theme that arose in our discussions with participants, was both an emotional cost and a self-imposed strategy to avoid harassment. Samantha, a white sociology student, for example, said she "dreaded" leaving the place where she was living in the fracking community where she did research because she did not want to face the unwelcome attention she knew she would receive at her field site. She found herself becoming more timid and withdrawn as time went on. Annie noted that there were a couple of days when she simply refused to leave her house: "And it's so hot there, like 90 degrees, 100 percent humidity, and I didn't open the windows because it was a first floor apartment and men would just stand at the window while I was cooking my lunch and call at me. I just kept the windows shut and sweated and was angry."

The isolation of the field that results from unwelcome sexual attention can be compounded by other identifications. Janet, a black sociologist, explained the effects of not being able to be herself when she was conducting research on a very conservative Black Muslim group in the United States: "With this Muslim group it was [the intersection of] gender and religion, and I had to remind myself, 'Oh wait, okay, I can't be my typical [self] or wear everything I want to wear.' You have to learn the scene and what's appropriate." Even though Janet knew she needed to adapt to the norms of the group she was working with, doing so left her feeling uncomfortable at times. She did not expect this to be as emotionally difficult as it was, and she eventually learned the importance of placing limits on and borders around her field relationships. While this tactic seems antithetical to the way many of us learn how to do ethnography, it allowed Janet to protect her sense of self in the field and manage the costs she experienced.

Cristina, a Latina sociologist who conducted participant observation as a teacher for her dissertation, felt she did not have the support of many of the white teachers at the school, who she observed acting and speaking in racist ways toward students and other teachers on several occasions. Cristina described how these feelings of alienation affected her ability to respond when threatened by a troubled student.

> We had a couple boys who were [in the institution where I was working] for assaulting their partners. And one of the boys, he was a white male student. He was in a classroom the second year that I was substituting, and I would often go in there, and he was very mean to me. He called me a bitch. I know I heard him saying things about me behind my back, and I turned around and I'm like, "I heard what you said. You need to stop talking about me. That's really disrespectful." . . . And he was like, "I wasn't talking about you." And I'm like, "I'm sure I heard you." . . . He would see me, and he would just roll his eyes at me. He just would whisper to other students about me. He just, like, hated me.

Cristina described writing up referrals on the student, observing that his behavior was more troublesome to her than that of other boys who said sexually inappropriate things. Eventually, he left the school, and a white teacher who often contributed to racial animosity among the staff approached Cristina and said, "Well, you know, he didn't really like you. I know he didn't like you because, well, you know, he beat up his girlfriend. Like, to a pulp." Cristina said the white teacher continued, "You know, he doesn't like women, but, you know, there were also some racial things there. Like, that you were Hispanic." Cristina's response was one of shock and silence. She sputtered as she described her reaction.

> And I'm like, why do—like, that—why wouldn't you, like, do something? Why wouldn't you intervene? Why wouldn't you come to my aid? Especially if you know he hates women, and apparently he hates, like, Hispanics, Hispanic women, maybe—maybe that's what his ex—his girlfriend was. Maybe she was a Hispanic woman, you know? And I just felt really kind of betrayed in that moment.

She contrasted this woman's failure to warn her to another experience in which a student was targeting her. A black teacher warned her that she was worried the student was going to try to assault her. Speaking again of the white teacher, Cristina recalled her feelings: "Wow, you just don't have my back, and I think *you* hate me, too. You know?" As a woman working with the same students, the white teacher had an opportunity to provide support and show solidarity with Cristina when she was in danger. Her racism not only put Cristina in a dangerous position but also deepened the isolation Cristina felt in the field. Not only did she face possible assault by a student, but she felt betrayed by those in her field site who could have provided an important network of support.

In Karina's view, fieldwork can be more isolating for women than it is for men: "I couldn't have a life. It's not like I could go out as a single female in downtown and meet people, whereas I had male friends doing research in other places in Africa and they were having the time of their lives because there's this big expat community, they would go out. . . . So I think that makes a really big difference, too." She recognized that both men and women can feel lonely in the field, but given the gender norms in some contexts, these problems can be more severe for women. Beyond the normal isolation or loneliness that we might expect ethnographers to experience, our respondents emphasized that the loneliness they encountered in the field was compounded by what was often a "choiceless decision" to self-isolate as a result of gender dynamics.[26] Like gender, sexual identity can also exacerbate loneliness. For example, La Pastina could not be honest with his research participants about his sexual identity because of the homophobic culture where he worked. As a result, he felt unable to construct close relationships in the field, compounding his isolation.[27] In the colonial tradition, public spaces were historically marked as "male" and "straight," and being able to appear in public required these attributes. Although these barriers have been challenged over time, they continue to regulate movement and restrict the right to be present in many places.

Self-isolation was a go-to strategy for many participants, but it should be noted that it is not a positive one. Not only does it reinforce the loneliness of fieldwork, but, as Elena noted, it can actually compound the dangers women encounter in the field. She observes of her experience in Mexico, "I could have been killed and no one would have known." Isolation can also continue to shape women's strategies when dealing with men once they are out of the field. It took over a year for Rebecca to be able to interact with men without immediately worrying about harassment or sexualization. As Harriet, a white sociologist studying organizations, noted, "Those fears that you pick up, or those attenuations you pick up in the field, they persist with you outside the field. They persist with you when you come home." Here again we must consider how these emotional responses contribute to the reproduction of gender hierarchies when women return from the field and must present themselves as competent and confident researchers, students, and professors in order to compete for academic resources.

Experiences in the field can also trigger an impulse to isolate due to posttraumatic stress or previous experiences of racism, homophobia, and misogyny. As described in chapter 3, Frances is a survivor of rape, and her experiences with the gatekeeper who wanted to exchange access for sex and money and then stalked her on the phone for weeks reignited her sense of vulnerability such that she was unable to leave her apartment for several days. Cristina similarly described how her experiences of racism as a child informed her emotional response to racial and sexual harassment in the field. She also linked her reaction to abusive relationships in her teen years.

> I had two really abusive relationships in high school ... and maybe even like that kind of—some of those feelings came up for me.... Maybe just some of that cruelty was so similar to the meanness that I had experienced when I was younger myself and in a relationship with this horrible guy. That really emotionally was hard for me. And I'm like, "You knew that this person was violent."

She added that racist interactions in graduate school also contributed to her feelings of isolation; she lacked a substantial network of peers she trusted enough to go to for help when racism and sexism occurred in her fieldwork.

Some women did not report any perceived emotional costs, even though their fieldwork was sexualized. Typically, they attributed their ability to shake off the harassment and continue with their work. For example, for Bridgette, a bi black woman researching gay-affirming churches, dressing in a certain way, in part to avoid being hit on, while conducting fieldwork was not effective, but she did not internalize this as something she was doing wrong: "I typically don't blame myself, partially because of this knowledge of how sexual harassment works. It has nothing to do with you in particular, it's just the fact that you are a woman. No matter what I am wearing, I will be hit on. No matter how I speak, I will be hit on." For Bridgette and others, understanding fieldwork as yet another aspect of life in which interactions are shaped by sex and gender provided some emotional protection. Remembering the structural character of gender and racism may not eliminate problems or frustrations about sex-, gender-, and race-related obstacles in the field, but it can sometimes keep researchers from doubting their skills and blaming themselves.

GETTING WORK DONE?

Harassment and unwelcome sexual attention in the field interfered in various ways with women's ability to do fieldwork. Destabilization of self-efficacy often made it difficult to carry out fieldwork day to day. In order to fund her research, Ronette, a white graduate student who drove a truck for a music festival associated with her research, was the only woman among about thirty drivers. She articulated the costs of lost efficacy well, observing that even though the men were not the subject of her research, the emotional isolation she felt dealing daily with their misogyny "made it hard to keep working" and remain clear-headed when she tried to transition from truck driver to researcher. Phoebe noted that warding off the sexual advances of her gate-keeper took time and attention away from the work she was doing in the field. Not only did it interfere with the progress of her fieldwork, but it angered her because she felt the work she was doing was really important and navigating her gatekeeper's behavior tainted it and ultimately put it at risk.

Concerns about losing access to their participants was by far the most common reason that women put up with harassment or unwanted attention in the field, and, indeed, putting a stop to harassment sometimes did entail the loss or restriction of access. But harassment and other unwelcome sexual attention also affected women's mobility—the freedom to move around and accomplish what they needed to do. For example, Cathy routinely avoided following up with respondents in one field site because doing so was so often misinterpreted. The diminished confidence that women felt was undoubt-edly tied to the restrictions placed on their bodies. Indeed, restrictions on our bodies are also restrictions on the selves we can construct. Contrast this with one of our men participants, Bob, who said he felt more confident as his time in the field went on. Clearly, not all men feel this way and not all women ethnographers feel less efficacious as their fieldwork proceeds, but the point remains that harassment and constant objectification in the field can destroy a person's sense of self and alter how they approach their projects.

Dealing with harassment in the field is disconcerting because unlike a standard workplace, there is no human resources office to go to for recourse. As Maritza reflected after describing men hitting on at her at organizational meetings and in churches, "I shouldn't have to deal with this when I am working." For Cristina, it got to the point that men were simply obstacles to getting work done: "I never thought of men as helpers in the field, just more of [a] hindrance."

Concerns about access shaped participants' responses to harassment in the field in various ways. After Michelle finally talked to her host family about being harassed by her village gatekeeper, there were consequences for her work.

> It was really a shame because actually I met this person because he came forward as someone who was going to be very helpful, [someone] who had access to a lot of information, knew everything that was going on that I was researching, knew everyone involved. And when we first met he took me around to meet those people, to see those things, to learn about that. And then the inappropriateness slipped in. And it became clear that, I think for him, it would have been an exchange. You know? So I had to basically cut myself off from any access to all of that.

For Michelle, getting some respite from the unwelcome advances of this man meant sacrificing access. For Rosie, the threats she received on the night she decided to stay in her car caused her to become much more careful about her personal safety, but it also made her more suspicious of her later participants; she became less invested in her interviews and missed opportunities for participant observation because of her safety concerns. Over time, she said, she lost the will to build rapport.

Karina noted that multiple forms of harassment affected her work in different ways. In the prisons she visited in Rwanda, she might be whistled at while walking in, which affected her comfort level when sitting down for one-on-one interviews because "there's already this uncomfortable power dynamic whereby I recognized my privilege but simultaneously felt unsafe and uncomfortable because of the catcalls and objectification." In addition, after the government official grabbed her and tried to kiss her, she immediately pushed him off and left his office. Later, though, she feared the potential ramifications: "From that point on I was, I was very afraid to meet government officials. Especially, you know, while one on one. Almost all my meetings were one on one. And obviously there is no recourse to action if something happens. And not only that, if they decide they don't like me they can put a hit out for me, you know? [Laughs] So it was terrifying." Given that the Rwandan government was extremely authoritarian and officials were known to have arrested and incarcerated foreign researchers, especially women, in the past, her fears in this situation were quite real.

Some men also had concerns about access as a result of sexualized interactions in the field. However, in their case, this did not seem to carry the same baggage of self-doubt and self-blame that it did for many women. Clark, who is gay and trans, said being hit on while conducting research on LGBTQ issues in the United States and the Global South was "sort of expected" but did not have emotional consequences. Still, it sometimes had consequences for his research.

> There were points where a guy took me around the city and we're hanging out for a while and then he was like, "Oh, do you wanna come back to my place? You know, we can eat food or something." So we went back to his place and he definitely sort of leaned on me and started trying to kiss me and I was like, "Oh, you know, thank you, but I am just not in the mood." So, yeah, that happened consistently, and there were [times when] guys were really interested to chat and then we would chat and then they'd be like, "So you wanna hook up?" And I would say, "No, I'm really sorry. I'm actually, like I said, not really looking for a hook-up." And then they wouldn't want to chat anymore, which is fine. You know, they're welcome to chat as long as they want and then stop.

In these instances Clark benefited from his identity as a white man. Still, while Clark was open about his gay identity in the field, he only occasionally revealed that he was trans, perhaps due to apprehensions about his ability to do research safely. This fear was most likely informed by the time a group of men at the gay bar where he was working and conducting research attempted to undress him to see if he had been born a man. He decided to stop working where the attack occurred and discontinued this area of research. (See chap. 3.)

Self-efficacy, access, mobility, and being able to bring a project to completion are all essential to being not only a successful ethnographer but also a successful scholar; all of these attributes and achievements are at risk when ethnographers are harassed in the field. Gender, race, nationality, sexuality, and other aspects of our positionalities intersect with contextual factors to create opportunities and constraints in the field that are not the same for everyone. Although individual ethnographers are required to negotiate these in case-specific ways in the context of daily life in the field, it is paramount that we also recognize the institutional factors in the academy that compound these experiences. Deciding to alter a research project, say no to opportunities that feel unsafe, or leave a field site altogether affect not only the researcher's self but also how their peers and mentors evaluate them as a scholar. When the women we interviewed considered changing their projects because of gendered and sexualized experiences, they frequently worried this was a poor reflection on their skills as an ethnographer. They worried about being labeled inconsistent, uncommitted, or lacking the "persistence" necessary to be a "good" researcher.[28] Self-presentation and impression management are just as important in the university as in the field site. The women we interviewed were acutely aware of this and factored it into their decisions, even decisions about whether to report sexual violence. Ethnographic training can and must do better at acknowledging these realities and preparing ethnographers for them, such that women are not implicitly or explicitly blamed or accused of messing up when they are harassed or assaulted in the field. This acknowledgment will make it more likely that researchers can consider changing projects as a legitimate possibility. A researcher who modifies her project to protect herself and minimize the costs we have discussed in this chapter should not be considered a failure or an unskilled ethnographer. Keep in mind that all qualitative researchers modify and alter projects as they unfold for a variety of reasons. Change should not be made taboo in research but acknowledged as part of the qualitative process.

NAVIGATING COSTS

In chapter 3 and throughout this chapter we have discussed a few strategies women relied on to mitigate, or at least navigate, the costs of research. Here we discuss other tools researchers can use to cope with these costs, recognizing that many will be unable to avoid them. This is true for ethnographers taking on "dangerous" research but also for those working on topics that might appear safe. Despite the extensive literature on qualitative research, the various debates on techniques and approaches, and the classes on qualitative interviewing and observations offered in multiple disciplines, few researchers are prepared to deal with the costs we have discussed in this chapter before beginning research. We hope that some of the tools presented here can be used to fill this lacuna in methods classes.

In reflecting on her own experiences in the field, Elena suggested that living with other people and letting people know where she was going would have helped her manage these costs. She also recommended establishing strong networks with local universities or nongovernmental organizations, creating a network of people to rely on if things go wrong. Elena noted that in her recent work she has incorporated these as strategies in the field, but they were not included in her doctoral training. Beyond institutional support, if you are conducting research in an area where there are other researchers who could provide support, contact them and organize times to visit while you are in the field.

While academics are often encouraged to cut themselves off from other researchers—either to meet the standard of solitary ethnography or to "guard" their data and project from being scooped—being in contact with other researchers who are geographically available can provide vital support. Cultivating these networks and connections is also one step toward making research a more collaborative endeavor. Another strategy is to establish a way to communicate with researchers from your own department or university. For example, some of our participants established groups of their peers to check in with via Skype, regularly or in case of an emergency, while they were in the field. Setting up networks of people—inside and outside universities— to provide support is one step qualitative researchers can take to manage costs.

While we address this issue more fully in chapter 6, it is worth noting here that the material costs of doing research are inextricably tied to the emotional, physical, and emotional costs associated with fieldwork. For example, if Ronette had received funding for her research, she would not have had to rely on driving a truck for the organization she was studying. Ronette's lack of material support placed her in a position where she had to take on additional emotional costs. Encouraging students to engage in collaborative research can help reduce all types of costs associated with research.

The strategies suggested in the literature on sexual harassment and field research may or may not help you avoid these costs.[29] As shown in chapter 3, many of the commonly mentioned strategies, such as wearing a ring, dressing conservatively, or mentioning husbands and boyfriends, failed to help most of our participants avoid sexual harassment and the costs it entails. Nevertheless, reading others' accounts of harassment before going into the field may prepare researchers to think about harassment at a structural and institutional level before these experiences occur.[30] Thus, we suggest reading work on sexual harassment—its causes, consequences, and dynamics—before going into the field.[31] Reading literature on research as an embodied process can also provide ways for all researchers to think about the emotions they experience in the field.[32] More seasoned professors should talk to their students about their own experiences with harassment and danger in the field. Displays of emotion may be considered unprofessional and a mark of incompetence among field researchers,[33] but reproducing the deception of detached neutrality passes emotional costs on to other researchers, who are then sent into the field unprepared for "the broad range of emotions at play in fieldwork."[34] These shocks could be substantially mitigated by more forthcoming discussions about the emotional as well as the psychological and physical costs of fieldwork.

The costs that researchers incur are not only the product of the places where they are carrying out projects; they also result from interactions with peers and mentors, which further solidified our participants' feelings of self-doubt, self-blame, and decreased efficacy. While graduate students may be limited in their ability to correct mentors, research experiences and disciplinary structures must be examined sociologically in order to challenge the construction of sexualized experiences in the field as the fault of women researchers.

FIVE

Constructing Knowledge

THE PRIVILEGING OF THE MIND and the erasure of the body in knowledge production is a defining marker of Western intellectual culture.[1] A broad range of feminist epistemologists, including Dorothy Smith, Sandra Harding, Patricia Hill Collins, Susan Bordo, Donna Haraway, Genevieve Lloyd, Linda Martín, and Nancy Tuana, have underscored the relevance of embodied experience, standpoint, and positionality to knowledge creation, critiquing the dualisms of mind and body and reason and emotion.[2] And yet throughout this book we have shown that qualitative researchers are often still encouraged to write as if their data and findings were the result of a cerebral endeavor alone, leaving aside the embodied component of knowledge production. As seen in the previous chapter, this has important consequences for ethnographers and their ability to carry out their work.

In this chapter we show that these dualisms, and their connections to the three ethnographic fixations (solitude, danger, and intimacy), have implications for the construction of knowledge. They encourage researchers to edit gender and sexuality, and the ways they are mutually constituted by other categories of identification that are manifest in and on the body, out of their fieldwork discussions and publications, thus contributing to a disembodied presentation of research. Although experiences are structured differently according to a researcher's positionality, the ethnographic fixations encourage researchers to adhere to narratives of fieldwork that exclude the researcher's body and social location. These homogenized narratives conceal the multiple paths ethnographers take to collect their data, thus reproducing the fixations.

Here we draw on Joan Fujimura's concept of awkward surplus to understand why interactions that bring sex, gender, and the body to the fore often become residual data or are ignored altogether. We argue that despite the fact that calls for reflexivity have become more common, they have paradoxically resulted in only superficial acknowledgment of the effects embodiment has on fieldwork. Both of these tendencies are linked to the androcentric, colonialist, racist, and positivist norms that undergird ethnographic methodology and produce the fixations we analyze in this book. Because all ethnographic work is shaped by researchers' gender, sexuality, race, and other corporal characteristics, a more open discussion of how these dynamics contribute to the production of ethnographic knowledge would lead to better, more complex and nuanced ethnographies. We therefore end this chapter with a discussion of how to integrate "surplus" data into analysis and writing.

AWKWARD SURPLUS

Where do stories of flirtation, uninvited physical contact, or sexual propositions fit into ethnographic analyses of migrant populations, social movements, or sports and leisure activities? For our participants, it was difficult to determine what to do with this "data" and whether it should be considered data at all. This confusion is compounded by the fact that only a few participants went into the field anticipating uncomfortable or threatening sexualized interactions. Most were blindsided by their experiences and as a result tried to ignore or set them aside. Borrowing Fujimura's term for the data scientists misrecognize because they do not fit their preestablished categories of analysis, we refer to these experiences as awkward surplus.[3] Writing about geneticists who study sex development and determination, Fujimura explains that they "used their own sociohistorically located normative definitions of sex in their experimental designs and frames, thereby setting the stage for reproducing their own taken-for-granted categories of sex."[4] Fujimura notes that certain findings could have led researchers to new insights, but these were not recognized as data: "New signals read through old frames can be discounted: in their conclusions researchers decided to ignore data that contradicted their initial assumptions."[5] Though writing about the "hard" sciences, Fujimura's analysis is appropriate for the social sciences as well. Indeed, this process is precisely what occurred with the researchers we interviewed. The "old frames" used by researchers flagged embodied data as unimportant and thus information to be discounted and discarded. Shaped by androcentric, racist, and colonialist epistemic assumptions, those old frames separate mind and body, privileging the former over the latter. The old frames matter not only because they incorrectly portray the relationship between knowledge and the body but also because they certify some as capable of producing knowledge while delegitimizing others' role in this process. White men from the Global North are the embodiment of the rational, objective mind while women, people of color, and people from the Global South are associated with the untrustworthy, emotional, and irrational body.[6] The bodies of nonwhite women, in particular, have historically been treated as transgressive and unrestrained.[7] Because embodied experiences are not considered or categorized as data, these "other" experiences are dismissed, reproducing androcentric and racist / ethnocentric ideologies that delegitimize the value of these experiences, turning that knowledge into epiphenomenal emotionality.

Coauthor Patricia described several experiences that she set aside as she proceeded through her fieldwork and later analyzed her data, including an occasion in which she found herself walking down a dirt road in the pitch-black night with a group of men—activists she had just met. As they walked, the men joked about "exchanging" her with another woman. Occurrences like this were uncomfortable, objectifying, and mildly frightening, but they were easily set aside as irrelevant to the fieldwork at hand. When asked during her interview what strategies she used to cope with instances of unwanted sexual attention (which, for her, often were racialized or inflected by views on her religion), Monira, a Muslim American graduate student, told us, "I've dealt with it by pushing it out of my mind. Actually when I read [laughs] the invitation to this research question, I thought to myself, 'Hmm, have I ever actually experienced anything like that?' And then suddenly I remembered that one incident. But all these other things I've actually remembered during the course of this interview, I had forgotten about them as well. I just pushed them out of my mind." Monira's reflections speak to the power of the "socio-historically located normative definitions" of fieldwork, which mark these interactions as ones that should be set aside. In this way, these definitions reproduce taken-for-granted understandings of what does or does not count as data, or at least "good" data. While qualitative researchers are trained to be attuned to interactions and dialogue and to mentally record as much as possible, many of the women we interviewed did the opposite with sexualized interactions. These interactions were pushed to the side, forgotten, effectively erased from their fieldwork.

Because women face sexual harassment in their daily lives as well, when they experience it while conducting research they sometimes chalk it up to "just being a woman." In other words, women viewed such experiences from the perspective of either researcher or woman, marking sexual harassment as part of "life," not "work," and reproducing the dichotomy that Dorothy Smith and other feminist theorists have long critiqued. When we asked Bridgette, an African American researcher, if she thought there was anything to be done about sexual harassment in the field, she said, "It's kind of unavoidable. And that's the thing, too. Yeah, I have strategies to deal with it, but that doesn't mean it's going to go away or stop."

Bridgette, who had conducted research in nightclubs, notes that "putting up" with harassment during research is also inflected by gendered racial stereotypes.

> Participating in the black community, there's kind of stereotypes about how black women are sexually, as being promiscuous and being open to being hit on and that kind thing. And, you know, so if someone in the club . . . might grab my arm to try to talk to me or be insistent on getting my phone number or something like that, I am just like, "No, leave me alone." I think that the stereotypes about black women have influenced that. To make people feel a little more comfortable about doing that. And the kind of, you know, making comments about my butt. That probably won't happen in other communities, so those types of things are, I guess, unique to my experience as a black woman.

The gender stereotypes and expectations that shape our societies and field sites, always inflected by race, class, and other factors, thus create different justifications for leaving these experiences out of our research.

In addition to socialization and experiences in specific field sites, perceived expectations of the academic field led some participants to try to brush off harassment and treat it as awkward surplus. Marina, a Latina graduate student, explained that expectations she had of herself as an ethnographer contributed to her confusion about how to react to the harassing phone calls she received from a day laborer who was a research participant.

> I was very troubled by this episode, and I was very troubled by, kind of, my reaction to it. And really confused about how to respond, because I thought, you know, I'm an ethnographer and I should be able to navigate these spaces and set boundaries, and if I'm in a dangerous situation I should be able to get out of it easily. And, you know, have this really thick skin. And then I was going through this experience with this guy and I felt really vulnerable. And in a way that I hadn't anticipated or expected. And I didn't know who to talk to. I didn't feel like it was something that I could talk to [my adviser] about because she would probably just brush it off and be like, "Hey, it happens everywhere."

By playing out the interaction between herself and her adviser in her head, Marina anticipated the response she would receive within the academic world if she talked about the phone calls: sexual harassment "just happens," and women have to "brush it off."

Marina's comments point to another reason sexualized interactions might be left out as awkward surplus: they seem to suggest that one is inept at conducting research. This then led some to edit out these interactions for the sake of "professionalism." Like several other participants, Marina assumed she should already know how to deal with these kinds of situations. To talk about them openly would suggest that she was unprofessional and unskilled. Experiences that are awkward and uncomfortable, then, might be set aside in order to present oneself as a competent ethnographer, continuing the cycle of silence that leaves students unprepared to navigate certain encounters. As Phoebe remarked, "No one gets excited about an ethnographer who has awkward, strange relationships with the communities they are trying to work in" (see chap. 1). Such expectations elide the fact that ethnographers do not exist above or outside the power relations that constitute their field sites. More to the point, if we assume when we go into the field that our relationships with research participants must be close, warm, and intimate, these expectations filter relationships that do not have these characteristics out of our analyses and ethnographic narratives. Awkward experiences, then, become awkward surplus.

Marina's confusion was also related in part to the sexualized content of interactions on the street corners where she conducted her research: "[These street corners are] masculine spaces, . . . I mean almost always exclusively male. But also what happens on these corners, when a woman passes by, the way that women are treated, talked about. And so you kind of put yourself in a situation where these things happen." The threatening character of the phone calls was difficult for Marina to disentangle from the masculinized environment she had put herself into, as she phrased it. Again, interactions are placed in the category of the personal rather than considered relevant to the work at hand. Relegated to the personal, these interactions appear irrelevant to research. When written about at all, they are consigned to the methodological appendix.

As discussed in chapter 4, the complicated ways in which gender intersects with race and nationality in the field, and filters through concerns about the privilege and power of the ethnographer, also reproduce women's silence when it comes to sexual harassment. One of the members of a feminist collective writing on these issues was sexually assaulted by the white brother of the owner of the boardinghouse where she stayed while doing fieldwork in Cuba. She provides this poignant account.

> The kinds of [micro]aggressions we experience due to our contradictory racial-class-sex-citizenship positions do not vanish when we return home. Being a black woman got me assaulted, and in this case my internalized ideas about being an activist anthropologist kept me quiet about it. I maintained my silence out of fear that talking about my assault would potentially over-shadow the research or cause harm to its perpetrator.[8]

Leanne Johannson also writes about how she was limited by ethnographic expectations when she experienced unwanted sexualized interactions in the field.

> I felt paralyzed by my desire to be a 'good anthropologist,' one who actively deconstructs her own authority in an attempt to minimize the power she exerts over social situations. Thus, I hesitated to respond from within my own ethnocentric conceptions of gender relations and definitions of 'harassment.' ... What is more, sexual dangers were a product not only of how people per-ceived me, but also of how I felt about my own identities in the context. I was uncomfortable with my whiteness and foreignness, which I felt automatically placed me in a position of power. I was also uncomfortable with my identity as a researcher and the exploitative potential embedded within it.[9]

To the extent that ethnography is taught as a race- and gender-blind approach, even the norms of activist or reflexive ethnography can encourage consigning experiences of harassment to awkward surplus.

Today most ethnographers, not only activists, are trained to think about how they may be exercising power over their participants, imposing their own worldview, and exercising privilege and exploitation by their very pres-ence. Researchers are expected to be reflexive about these power differentials, with the goal of minimizing them and keeping researchers accountable to participants. These are very legitimate concerns, reflecting the colonialist past and present of ethnography. However, as Johannson points out, the "reflexive turn"—in anthropology, perhaps best epitomized by James Clifford and George Marcus—continues to assume a male-bodied researcher.[10] And yet privilege and power dynamics in the field depend on the researcher's posi-tionality vis-à-vis the field they are studying. The notion that a woman researcher would not be subject to the (racialized) gender norms of her field site to some extent reflects the nineteenth-century assumptions of the naturalist ethnographer standing outside of or above the field he or she studies.[11] In reality, however, we are deeply embedded in power relations in our field sites, and race and gender norms in them can create privilege and authority for some and subjugation and vulnerability for others.

When participants did bring up experiences of harassment to faculty members, the (implicit and explicit) responses they received often encouraged them to put these experiences into the "awkward surplus" category. Participants recalled advisers telling them to "suck it up" or laughing at their stories, as if they were just one more awkward moment or uncomfortable situation *all* ethnographers experience in the field. For example, as described in chapter 3, although Gina's adviser initially reacted with concern when she told him about the harassment and assault she experienced, he later chastised her for being unprofessional when she backed out of a dinner engagement that would have entailed again spending time alone with a group of men. While he demonstrated empathy after the assault, his later response discouraged Gina from using the assault to guide and inform future interactions with men. Encounters like these reinforce the belief that harassment and sexualized interactions are par for the course but not pertinent to the work at hand, and they communicate that these interactions should not inform researchers' decisions in the field.

Describing others' reactions to her decision to write about having been raped in the field, Mingwei Huang explains that some of her professors could only understand this decision as "careerism," unable to grasp why including this event in her research would be important: "One professor, who was puzzled about why I would write about rape, asked me if 'it was in fashion,' as if there was little merit, intellectual or otherwise, to sharing such an experience." Another "well-meaning professor" encouraged her to publish her "work" first and write an essay about the experience after she was an established academic; this kind of advice confirms women's concerns that writing about gendered experiences poses risks for their career trajectories. As Huang notes, the pressure to put these experiences aside as we write our tales of the field not only perpetuates silence around them but also "provides yet another example (if indeed we needed one) that academe has not escaped the insidiousness of rape culture."[12] Here expectations within the academic field and in our field sites reinforce each other. One study found that one in ten women graduate students at major research universities reported being sexually harassed by faculty.[13] The increasing proportion of adjunct or nontenured faculty members makes it even less likely that those who have been harassed will come forward, as doing so may end careers; historically this has been true of assistant professors as well.[14] As is true of other careers, the (verbal and non-verbal) advice many women receive when they are harassed within academia is similar to the advice they receive about field research. Silence—shuffling these experiences into the awkward surplus category (here the surplus consists of experiences that "don't fit" within our academic narratives)—is preferable to the questions, doubts, and reprisals that women face when they "complain."[15] As Eva Moreno has pointed out, the relevance of gender is often elided in academia, making women reluctant to draw attention to the ways our experiences are gendered, lest they damage our scholarly reputations.[16] It is not the case that these experiences are always unknowingly or subconsciously set aside by women. Messages received from mentors and peers, communicating that these experiences are either unimportant or even potentially damaging to one's career, actively encourage researchers to view them as awkward surplus. For some researchers, though, experiences of harassment were so extreme and constant that they could not be ignored. This was the experience of coauthor Rebecca. Sexual advances permeated her fieldwork with Venezuelan police. With almost all of her key relationships characterized by some degree of sexual harassment or sexualization, avoidance was not an option.

And yet, despite experiencing extreme and dangerous situations, many participants were reluctant to talk about their experiences with their committees and advisers.[17] Their apprehensions went beyond fearing that their advisers would laugh it off or tell them to "suck it up." Michelle,[18] who conducts research outside of the United States and had been assaulted while conducting research, explained at length:

> I've had conversations with a few female researchers about this and every single one has had serious sexual harassment in the field if not outright physical attacks. And most of them have not reported it to anyone. . . . We all discussed how we felt like we couldn't do anything because we wouldn't be taken seriously as researchers and we had to come back with the same good data that all our male peers came back with. . . . I haven't talked to my committee members about the extent of the sexual harassment and how that curtailed . . . my access, . . . primarily because I feel like, on some level, people sort of act like they're on board with that but then ultimately just think that you're not really a good researcher. I know some of [the women I talked to] were in very dangerous situations, . . . their lives could have even been in danger and they continued. They didn't take themselves out of their research settings because they felt they had to get the data. And they didn't report it,

or they didn't even necessarily speak up to these people, just like I didn't, for fear of making a scene in the community and losing access. And ultimately we all talked about feeling that we just didn't want to cause a scene.[19] And by not causing a scene we put ourselves in more danger. And discussing this, we realized the double standard, because if a man were to feel threatened in the field, . . . likely he could get into a physical altercation with somebody and the next day would not be blamed for that. [And people would] say, "Oh, he's just a little hot-headed."

While her comments are insightful, Michelle's assertion that there would be no consequences for an ethnographer who is a man and had a fight in the field is debatable. Indeed, it was disputed by some of the men we interviewed, as evidenced by several examples we provide in other chapters.

Nevertheless, Michelle's reflection correctly summarizes the dilemmas faced by women who are harassed in their field sites. She seems to suggest that admitting to any sexualized experiences in the field will be understood by peers as polluting the data, and taking steps to protect one's self in the field is perceived as a weakness or inability on the part of the researcher to do the job at hand. As we discussed in chapter 1, this reflects both the androcentrism of the field (which can also harm men by placing value on the "hardiness" and "courage" of the researcher and asking men to live up to hegemonic standards of masculinity in the field) and the underlying commitment to positivist notions of validity, even among ethnographers. Because the cis white masculine body is still taken as the standard and data collection and quality are still measured against their experience, most men—particularly white men—are not expected to examine how their sex and sexuality enter into their field experiences; it is women's situatedness (always marked by other social statuses) that brings this to the fore.

The lack of attention paid to men's bodies in research relative to women's bodies was evident during a conversation Rebecca had about her fieldwork on police officers in Venezuela with a scholar from a prestigious university at a conference. During the conversation, she mentioned that she had been in touch with other women researching police and had found that they experienced similar challenges. The scholar responded that he was skeptical of women conducting research on police officers since he thought officers would alter their behavior around women, regardless of how much time they spent in the field. According to this man, there would always be a wall between the woman researcher and the police that might keep them from getting "real" data, indicating the belief that there is such a thing, as opposed to differently situated researchers who gather different data depending on their own location vis-à-vis the milieu they study. Unsurprisingly, this scholar demonstrated no reflexivity regarding how police officers might alter their behavior around researchers who are men. Interactions like this one contribute to women's concerns about writing embodied ethnography, leading them to erase their presence in their own writings.

This interaction also speaks to how superficial attention to embodiment can blind researchers to important aspects of their research. The scholar with whom Rebecca had this conversation made at least two faulty assumptions, each of which has implications for knowledge production. First, he assumed that his own body and masculine presentation of self would not affect the data he collected (i.e., how officers interact with one another), implicitly asserting that the body of a (cis) man is a more neutral instrument. Second, he assumed that the police officers who were being studied were all men. The first assumption justifies leaving the body out of ethnographic data and suggests that men are more neutral producers of knowledge. The second reproduces a long-held assumption in the social sciences: what men do "counts"— here, men police officers—more than what women do and thus are the default subjects of study. The onus of thinking about how sex and gender play into fieldwork, then, is not placed equally on *all* ethnographers.

Connected to this delegitimization of women's data is the fear that advisers, committees, and peers will say women just do not belong in particular field sites. During her interview, Marina talked about the concerns of the research team that hired her to do interviews with men about sexual activity.

> In the case of . . . this study, I think I came in a little hesitant, maybe concerned, because the team was really worried about bringing on more women. They had had some issues with one of the interviewers who they had trained and hired to do interviews with men. Apparently she was just having a really hard time, she was struggling through the survey, and there were a lot of questions that she didn't feel comfortable asking. There's a lot of language [in the questions] about penetration, anal, and so she wasn't comfortable asking certain questions. And I think the team's response was, "Okay, maybe we shouldn't hire any more women because this may be a problem for women."

Purported concern about the difficulties women might face in certain field sites operates to reproduce gender discrimination in academia. This concern also reinscribes men as neutral observers, presuming that their bodies are not affected by and do not have an impact on the field.

Like gender, the meanings assigned to a researcher's race by colleagues and readers can either lend credibility to a study or generate suspicion around it. White academic gatekeepers often seem to expect scholars of color to do more to justify their particular embodiment and its effects on their fieldwork and then turn around and punish them for it by questioning the validity of their work. Victor Rios notes that encouragement to leave out researchers' positionalities in ethnography is supported by publishing outlets.[20] After *Contexts*—a magazine published by the American Sociological Association— released a forum titled "How to Do Ethnography Right," Rios wrote a searing critique of the complete absence of race in the forum's articles. In a later piece he expanded on that comment, writing, "It's not surprising that *Contexts* would hold back on discussing race, reflexivity, and privilege, as it is representative of the current state of the discipline of sociology that continues aggressively to push a color-blind and power-blind agenda; let's just not talk about race and maybe true knowledge will emerge."[21]

No ethnography can provide a full panorama of the research context and the researcher's positionality in it; however, "disembodied" ethnography provides a narrower glimpse into the world of researchers and participants, resulting in a less rich, and ultimately less complete, image of this world. Ignoring embodiment, linked as it is to structural inequalities, leaves out information that is crucial to the production of knowledge.[22] While ethnographers should not aim to tell the reader everything about their positionality in a given research context, they should strive to provide the fullest account. Below we discuss how superficial attention to embodiment leads to narrower glimpses of the social world and argue for a deeper engagement with the researcher's body in our work.

WHY SUPERFICIAL ATTENTION TO EMBODIMENT IS BAD FOR THE PRODUCTION OF KNOWLEDGE

Despite an emphasis in ethnographic methodology texts on reflexivity and positionality, our continued fixation on solitude, danger, and intimacy leads to only superficial attention to the effects of the researcher's embodiment in the field. As Kristine Kilanski observes, it is "as if the body, once acknowledged, can then be written out of the work."[23] According to a Latina participant, Maritza, this emphasis has influenced our theories but has not saturated our practice: "It's interesting because we will talk about race, class, gender, and positionality in a general sense … I feel like on some level we realize that all those factors influence the construction of knowledge, but we recognize that in theory, and we don't do a good [job] of connecting that to the practice of doing ethnography." This perfunctory approach to positionality has important costs for researchers and the production of ethnographic knowledge. When we write about race, class, and gender in the field as obstacles over which we must prevail,[24] or which we must set aside or completely ignore, we miss "the opportunity to reflect on how being a gender [and/or race, class, etc.] outsider impacts the actual process of field research."[25]

Relegating uncomfortable interactions to the category of awkward surplus proved to be a useful tool in the field that allowed ethnographers to push through and get the job done. While putting aside this surplus data allows researchers to cope with fieldwork—whether by modifying their projects or pushing on—it also keeps them from consciously integrating what these experiences tell us about the field and how they structure fieldwork in their research presentations and writings. For example, in retrospect, experiences with sexual harassment or other forms of danger often shape *the ethnographer's* trust in her respondents as well as how she chooses to interact with them in the future. As Patricia said, "I never really admitted to myself until now [how] the level of discomfort I experienced [with the activists] shaped the rest of my research. I think I repressed that a little bit within me. I definitely made decisions, but it was like, 'I am not going back to that community.' But I didn't admit to myself I felt so uncomfortable and unsafe there." Similarly, Bianca Williams writes, "I was drafting the dissertation and trying to make sense of my own personal experiences in the field while analyzing the data from my participants. I wasn't ready to really dig into the ways certain gendered and sexualized forms of harassment had influenced which individuals and communities I ended up engaging (or not), and the spaces I made my research home (or not). To be honest, I probably haven't completed that processing, and probably will choose not to. Thinking about all of it and sharing it is exhausting."[26]

Allowing these interactions to be set aside meant that for Williams and some of our participants certain research opportunities were unconsciously avoided: less time was spent with particular participants, and research sites were removed in favor of others that felt safer. These decisions do not make the work less valid, but not talking and writing openly about them limits our collective understanding of how ethnographic knowledge is constructed.

Superficial attention continues to privilege the "neutral" body that we have discussed throughout the book. Sonya Sharma, Sheryl Reimer-Kirkham, and Marie Cochrane argue that leaving the researcher's body out of our work "can grossly miss the richness and depth of an encounter with a participant, and can put the researcher at risk of aligning with his or her position of privilege."[27] Qualitative research has the capacity, they write, to "bring the lived experience of the marginalized to the forefront," but this capacity is constrained when the researcher does not engage with her own experiences and positionality in the research process.[28]

Disembodied research not only reproduces privilege in the field site, but within academia as well, where certain kinds of knowledge production and the bodies involved in this process are recognized with acclaim. As Dorothy Smith wrote in 1974, "The first difficulty is that how sociology is thought—its methods, conceptual schemes, and theories—has been based on and built up within, the male social universe," a universe, we would add, that also privileges white, heterosexual, and cis bodies.[29] Indeed, marginalizing (in)formative experiences can come from the contradiction faced by feminist researchers: they are taught to be reflexive, but they also feel pressure to do work that is judged as valid by their peers, including many who do not share their epistemological assumptions. For many women ethnographers, this involves the atomizing experience of allowing themselves to be objectified by research participants while simultaneously suppressing that experience.

For these reasons, methodological training must recognize that *all* bodies are instruments of research and all research projects are shaped by the embodiment of the ethnographer. Clark, a white trans man, articulated how his race and gender shaped his research and afforded him access when he studied LGBTQ issues.

> Much of my [earlier] research was really about trans women of color and issues of sex work and profiling. . . . You know, they can just kind of be killed, die, suffer, and, and then, "That's not something that we need to worry about." So I am also trans, but I am not a trans woman of color. In some ways it's almost laughable to include me in [the same category]. I mean, I have friends who were literally kicked out of a country because they were black. [One was] a black woman. [They were] doing research in an area, and they were kicked out of a country, and their grantors, who are major national grantors, said, "Oh, well, that sucks for you. If you can't get back into the country, you're gonna have to pay us back." . . . If anything, I sort of exemplify the privilege. . . . I mean, I'm white, fairly gender normative, and depending on the space, I'm not actively read as trans.

Clark points out that embodiment, and the structures of privilege in which his own body is embedded, is relevant to who gets access to doing research at all (as opposed to being the objects of research). Whereas the scholar Rebecca spoke with assumed that data gathered by women studying the police would inherently be "worse" than that produced by men, Barbara Sutton points out that *any* researcher's embodiment enables their access to particular sites and insights and necessarily shapes the data they gather.[30] As Nancy, a white graduate student, points out, if a man had done her project on men in prison, it still would have been gendered, but gender would have been less likely to come to the fore in the analysis. "It wouldn't have been neutral if a dude had done these interviews," she said, in the same way that research with police is not "neutral" just because a man conducts it. She explained, "Gender would have had an effect on the things that they would be willing to talk to him about and the way they would have spoken to him. . . . It would have been a very different project, but I don't think it would have been a less gendered project." Certainly, men's fieldwork is gendered, too. Will, a white gender scholar who works with gang members in South America, is attuned to this reality. He spoke about how he used camaraderie to his advantage in interviews with men: "I used my sort of man-on-man flirting, you know, like, 'Hey bro, we're best mates. Beer, women, fútbol.'"

Like Nancy and Will, most of our participants believed men's projects are gendered, but some felt that men do not seem to notice it (or at least do not draw attention to it in their written work) because of their socially dominant position. For example, Maritza noted a gendered gap in urban ethnography as it relates to masculinity: "There is a huge gap that isn't theorized because all these men studying urban ethnography, they are studying men's spaces. All these things about gangs, it's about male gangs, it's about gender. They don't call it gender. They only call it gender when it's about women."

Of course, men may also be propositioned during fieldwork, and they may also face danger in the field. To the extent that they involve displays of manhood and homosocial violence, threats to men's safety in the field are also gendered. Superficial attention to embodiment, then, can also place men in danger. As discussed in chapter 3, David, a Latin American PhD student, was threatened with gang rape by some men during his fieldwork on social movements. In thinking about this harrowing experience in retrospect, David was ambivalent about his relationship to the men involved while simultaneously blaming himself for trusting them. He said:

> When that happened, I realized I don't know these people, I don't know who they are. Actually later, I ended up knowing a lot about them, but even if you

interview [someone], you don't know if they actually told you the truth, you don't know who they are. I trusted, I was in this space, and I was scared, very, very scared. . . . Would I do that in my real life? I would not.

Like many of our women participants, David drew a distinction between the risks he was willing to take for the data and the risks he would take when he was not working as an ethnographer. He continued his musings on trust, noting the conflicted feelings a researcher can have after a frightening incident like the one he experienced. He explained that he felt guilty for not trusting these particular participants afterwards.

And I realized, man, I just, I trusted too much. And at the same time . . . you feel guilty because these are people who are fighting the good fight. You can disagree with them politically or whatever. But they are doing a lot of good stuff. Or they are doing the stuff that you are not doing. I am staying comfortable with my middle-class life. I will never be hungry and stuff, and these guys, they have everything to lose, they are risking everything to help others, you know? And I think badly about them because, you know, I don't trust them because I had a bad experience [and] I will never really know if they were actually intending harm or not. I just judged them guilty, I didn't presume them innocent. . . . And I did not trust them anymore because of this.

David's comments speak to the embodied character of field research: men's fieldwork can also be fraught with danger due to power dynamics played out via gender and sexual violence, which has consequences for researchers and their relationships.

For men as for women, not telling advisers and others about the dangers they encountered can have a gendered dimension. Lena's story about a colleague illustrates this point. When Lena asked him how his research was going in the conflict zone where he was working, he told her:

It was horrible. I had to hire bodyguards. They burned down a village when I was there and people were getting shot, so I was afraid to talk to [people] because that would identify them. And I said, "Well, did you tell—did you tell your adviser?" And he said, "No. I just—I told him it didn't work out." "Why didn't you tell him? I mean, he's not [sigh]—he's not unreasonable. He'll understand that you were in danger."

Lena reflected on this interaction: "I think it's this idea that he was supposed to be intrepid and go into this site that he already knew about and that things would be okay, and instead what he painted to his adviser was, 'Oh, this just simply didn't work out,' . . . instead of telling him, 'I was physically in danger. Other people were physically in danger as a result of talking to me.'"

Lena said the adviser responded by implying that the student had wasted several years in the field. In this case, the student may have feared that if he diverged from the narrative of the courageous and hardy researcher, he might have been criticized more harshly.[31] Like some women we interviewed, he might have been told that he should have just "sucked it up" to get the data. Such concerns would be understandable given the ongoing influence of the three fixations. In this instance, the ethnographer was violating tenets of both intrepid ethnography and courageous masculinity, two deeply inter-twined ideals. Despite these consequences, the pervasive expectation that a good ethnographer goes into the field intrepidly makes it difficult to reveal what we eventually come to understand as failures.

Participants pointed out that in order to change how these issues are handled within academia, men must understand how research is gendered and become allies of their women colleagues. Too often women described advisers and peers who dismissed their experiences, blamed them for what had happened, or mansplained their experiences to them. If ethnographers are to embrace an embodied approach it cannot only be women calling for attention to bodies in research. Men must also acknowledge that the opportunities and constraints they encounter in the field are gendered, raced, and so on. Mary added that men should talk about their experiences of vulnerability and fears in the field so that women do not feel like they are coming up short in comparison. Furthermore, as Ruth Behar has argued, writing vulnerability into our ethnographic accounts can serve as an alternative form of validity.[32] By writing about their personal experiences as part of the fieldwork narrative, Behar suggests, researchers expose ethnography as "a mode of knowing" that depends on "emotional involvement with their material." If we are to understand what is observed, "what happens within the observer must be made known."[33]

We need not view a researcher's gender or sex as polluting. Indeed, there are ways that we can think about different positionalities as contributing to the research process. Mary, whose fieldwork was conducted in a natural gas boom-town in the rural United States, talked about the long and difficult process of deciding not to enter certain spaces dominated by men because of the potential danger they posed to her. She described thinking through all the implications and angles and eventually coming to peace with her decision. Then, just as she was leaving the field, a man ethnographer entered the same site and automatically entered those spaces. Although this researcher might have considered how and why he gained entry to the site, his body did not disrupt gendered expectations within the space that he hoped to observe. While he might have reflected on how his body structured his research, he easily could have overlooked this crucial fact as he moved on to cultivating research relationships. This made Mary angry, but it also made her think that perhaps her own fieldwork was made better because gendered safety concerns pushed her to engage in such a deeply reflexive practice. As Sharma, Reimer-Kirkham, and Cochrane have written, the researcher's body can reflect and connect to the "complexity and variations of selves and personal histories.... This complexity becomes part of the 'thick description' sought after by qualitative researchers."[34] Mary's positionality in her field site forced her to reflect on this complexity, complexity that would not have been as readily apparent to a man in the same space.

Mary's case demonstrates how, as Elizabeth Hordge-Freeman has written, a researcher's positionality can be used as an advantage in fieldwork, but only if it is acknowledged and engaged.[35] She writes, "Taming subjectivity may be promoted in mainstream sociology as a way to achieve (the illusion) of objectivity, but there are ways in which developing and manipulating [the researcher's] subjectivity can provide tremendous insight into the very phenomenon that we study."[36] Hordge-Freeman also argues that paying attention to our interlocking identifications can provide unique opportunities for researchers to engage in activism while in the field, opportunities we miss as we try to "tame" our subjectivities in the pursuit of objectivity or validity.[37] Building on the work of W. E. B. Du Bois, Gladys Mitchell-Walthour and Hordge-Freeman argue that racial positionality in research can provide black researchers with a unique perspective that white researchers do not have access to, given the "second-sight" and "heightened awareness and discovery" produced by racial marginalization.[38] The "color-blind" and "power-blind" agenda in sociology that Rios refers to prohibits researchers from talking about how their positionality and subjectivity can be powerful tools in the field.

Far from making our research better, the erasure and ignorance of embodiment, subjectivity, and positionality harms the production of ethnographic knowledge as well as those who produce it. Furthermore, when we leave these essential elements of knowledge construction out of our work, we limit our readers' information about our process, evidence, and findings. Ironically, ethnographic standards encourage us to erase our bodies from our writing to evidence objectivity and neutrality, yet, in our view, these same standards weaken the validity of our research by constraining others' ability to interpret and evaluate it.

Many sociologists, even ethnographers, still seem to cling to the notion that the same data would be collected by any researcher. It is as if there were not multiple stories to be told in the same field site, as if our bodies were not instruments of research that affect the stories to which we have access and those we are interested in telling. Women's presence can allow for the gathering of data men may not have access to, and their presence might "destabilize" situations dominated by men, teaching us new things about those contexts. But these possibilities are not acknowledged when we focus on singular models and values for what makes ethnography "good."

So how do we integrate data into our writing that at first glance we might consider surplus or extraneous? First, we must consider how to remain attentive to leaving embodied data in our fieldnotes and our analysis. Although researchers have been encouraged to keep "venting journals" or some kind of document separate from "real" fieldnotes where they can write about how they feel (about interactions with participants, the emotions they feel at the end of a day in the field, etc.) as they conduct research, we encourage researchers to integrate these observations into their fieldnotes. It is harder to separate our bodies from our data when the two are integrated in the texts we produce while conducting research. Second, while researchers are trained to write in extensive detail about settings, participants, and observations, they are less often taught to write about their feelings and responses to them. As Karen Throsby and Debra Gimlin have written, "Even those moments where the researchers' bodies and practices *are* evident are profoundly difficult to write into publications—despite a feminist commitment to reflexivity—in part as a result of the desire not to engage in self-revelation on a personal issue, and in part because it is not always clear what the utility of that revelation would be."[39] When you sit down to write notes about the observations you have made or the interviews you have conducted, it might be useful to ask yourself some of the following questions and to include your answers to them in your notes.

- Did I feel comfortable and at ease during the observations or interviews? What might have produced these feelings?
- Did anything make me feel uncomfortable or concerned for my safety? What? Why might I have responded in this way?
- Were any comments made about my body or my appearance? How did these make me feel? How did I react? How did others react?

- How did I feel after my observations or interviews were over?
- Did I experience any interactions, emotions, or responses during the day that I would feel uncomfortable sharing with my friends, family, or academic peers and mentors? Why would sharing these make me uncomfortable? Have I left these out of my notes?

As you engage in analysis, do not leave these data to the side or relegate them to the "methods" category. Instead, include them in your coding and memos; think about them as insight into the structures of your research site. Just like your observational or interview data, your reactions to participants and their reactions to you can tell you a lot about how gender, race, sexuality, and other social structures operate in your research site.

As you transform your data and analysis into a book, article, policy paper, or class assignment, use your embodiment to set up scenes, explain the research decisions you made, and contour your findings. Take, for example, Jennifer Randles's research with low-income men of color. Randles writes about how being a pregnant middle-class white woman allowed her to gather her data.

> Despite significant social differences between respondents and me, my pregnant embodiment evoked memories of their transition to parenthood and the meanings they attached to parental responsibility. This provided an important window into how disadvantaged fathers narratively construct their paternal identities.... It ultimately created a unique kind of rapport, one that allowed me to negotiate a key aspect of insider status with otherwise socially dissimilar individuals.[40]

Randles's pregnant body was a part of her findings and conclusions and thus a key element of her production of knowledge.[41]

> My pregnancy was an embodied state—and an analytic text—onto which fathers projected their own parenting successes, challenges, and aspirations. It encouraged respondents to disclose important messages about why they were good fathers and the need to challenge stereotypes that they were lesser parents because of their race, class, or gender.[42]

Randles could have left her body out of her analysis and findings, but doing so would have erased this process of knowledge production.

Similarly, Maree Burns reflected that during some of her interviews with women who binged and compensated (by fasting, vomiting, etc.), she felt "fat" and "greedy" if she had eaten a large meal beforehand.[43] Burns, who dealt with bulimia as a youth, wrote about one interview, "At the time I shifted uncomfortably in my seat, trying to reduce the pressure on my stomach from my slightly too-tight waistband."[44] Burns's integration of her responses to this setting and her interviews provides powerfully detailed description of how social norms that regulate the feminine body are produced and reproduced through women's interactions with one another. If social categories and classifications are "a map of the power relations of the particular time period and also have the power to normatively govern the ways humans act and feel," then including our own actions and feelings as data can provide insight into these power relations and how they operate.[45]

We end this chapter with an example from Rachel, a white graduate student who took a qualitative methods class with Patricia while we were working on this book. For her class project, Rachel was conducting observations of probation revocation hearings at a Superior Court. During these observations, she experienced a highly sexualized environment. Although Rachel had written about her experience with harassment, she chose not to include these reflections in the field notes she turned in to Patricia, marking the experience as awkward surplus. After a class discussion about sexual harassment during fieldwork, Rachel went back and included the field notes she had initially excised in her final paper. They contained the following excerpt.

> After I told [the bailiff] I was there to observe, he told me to sit on the end of the bench right next to the door. I didn't understand why he was so specific in where he wanted me to sit because the courtroom was virtually empty. . . . I turn my head to the right to see a large group, anywhere from eight to eleven, in-custody male defendants. As soon as I start trying to identify their respective ages and races, I notice that almost all of the men are staring back at me. I become increasingly conscious of my surroundings in this moment because whistles, kissy noises, and "hey babies" are coupled with the stares from these men. I immediately turn my head back to focus on the front of the courtroom but the comments continue. I hear the men snickering to one another, and now I'm worried about what they are saying. My face is definitely turning bright red because I feel flushed, sort of like I have a fever. . . . I am following what is going on in the courtroom but I make sure to keep my head still and not look to the back right of the courtroom. I have this feeling that if I look over there again, I would be feeding into the men's behavior and I didn't want to give them that satisfaction. I made sure to make my blazer and scarf cover my chest; I think this was a product of being self-conscious about my womanly body. Additionally, this reaction could be because of the multiple sexual harassment altercations I have dealt with [in my life], which have always

revolved around my larger chest. So, I spent the entire two hours in the court trying to cover my chest, trying to make sure I didn't look at the large group of male defendants to my right, and attempting to take good ethnographic fieldnotes.

After the class discussion of sexual harassment, Rachel decided that the notes should have been included in her analysis because they "speak to the environment of this courtroom as well as my mental state throughout my time there." She did not believe the experience biased her observations and felt she still had been able to gather good field notes. Nevertheless, she also reflected, "I might have been more distracted than I was willing to admit due to the sexual harassment." She continued, "I would have stayed in the court longer to observe more cases, . . . but I felt so uncomfortable after this experience that I needed to leave." Including this experience in her field notes, she felt, was a truer portrayal of the experience and also opened up the opportunity to be reflexive about how it may or may not have shaped her findings. Doing so also helped her think about resources she could turn to in order to cope with such scenarios in the future.

SIX

Moving Forward

IF EFFORTS TO REDUCE SEXUAL VIOLENCE are to succeed in academia, we must deconstruct the foundations of knowledge production in the social sciences and move beyond the restrictive categories and rules that limit how we study the social world. Doing so requires nothing short of the transformation of existing social relations and hierarchies in academia. In this concluding chapter, we argue for systemic change at multiple scales to move us toward institutional and cultural transformation. We begin with implications and recommendations for researchers, mentors, and methods professors, including suggestions on how to teach, conduct, and write embodied research.[1] We give substantial attention to mentors here, both because this is a defining relationship for students in graduate school and because those in positions of power (relative to students) must be advocates for change. We then move on to suggestions for change at the institutional level, addressing the disciplines writ large. Change, we argue, must occur across these scales. If we are ever to move beyond ethnographic fixations, we must replace them with alternative standards of evaluation that recognize diverse methodological pathways. We also situate this work in the current historical moment, during which many institutions are examining the ways in which their complicity has allowed sexual harassment to flourish.

METHODS AND MENTORSHIP

As we have argued, the failure of ethnographic traditions to grapple with the ways that sex, gender, and the body shape research is exacerbated by the continued fixation on solitude, danger, and intimacy and reinforced by a disembodied approach to writing. The delegitimation of sexualized and gendered interactions as constitutive of fieldwork and data has promoted a "fiction of a genderless self," contributing to a disembodied presentation of research and further obscuring the fact that the white cis man's body remains the default in research.[2] Indeed, it is unsurprising that a collection of articles published by the sociology journal *Contexts* in 2016 about how to do ethnography right failed to include any information about researchers' race or gender.[3] As Victor Rios wrote in response to the lack of attention to race and privilege in the collection, "The truth is that there is no one right way to do ethnography, but there are many wrong ways to do ethnography."[4] Disembodied ethnography, we argue, is one of the wrong ways to do ethnography. However, as we have shown throughout this book, there is a multiplicity of ways that "good" fieldwork is carried out. If our narratives and evaluations of ethnography are to support and reflect this diversity, as a community of scholars we must be more reflexive about the norms—like intimacy and danger—we pass on to the next generation. Below we place these two fixations under scrutiny and suggest how to change methods conversations to better prepare researchers for fieldwork and acknowledge the multiple and diverse tales of the field that can be told.

Moving Beyond Danger

The glorification of dangerous ethnographies not only puts researchers at risk but also reproduces the exoticization of the lives of those who have been marginalized, leading to knowledge that has more to do with the researcher than the lives of those they study.[5] As we have shown, the praise given to dangerous research encourages researchers to prioritize getting the data over the safety of participants and themselves. To demystify the fetishization of danger, we must elevate epistemological approaches that decenter the hardy male body and the intrepid researcher. Such approaches include the "mindful ethics" proposed by Gloria González-López and Valeria Bentz and Jeremy Shapiro; Anima Adjepong's "invading ethnography"; Ruth Behar's vulnerable observer; and the various versions of reflexive social science proposed by Sandra Harding, Donna Haraway, Pierre Bourdieu, and Michael Burawoy.[6]

Rather than encourage ethnographers to engage in dangerous research, we should consider ways to gather data that do not put them at risk or at least minimize potential risks. From the beginning, mentors should encourage students to mitigate and avoid danger whenever possible rather than encourage them to stick with it no matter what. By bringing these issues into the open, professors can help students build risk assessments before they enter the field, a practice that should continue throughout our careers. This practice is perhaps even more important for those who do not have the resources to conduct preliminary research, a strategy we discuss below. As Leanne Johansson writes, risk assessment does not require "a systematic identification of all possible risks and action plans, but getting students to think through risk as a product of positionality."[7] Establishing this as a practice will benefit even the most seasoned ethnographers. As we have shown, even seemingly safe topics like social movements, education, and recreational activities can become dangerous field sites. Thus we cannot relegate discussions of danger and risk assessment to students doing fieldwork in war zones, gang territory, and police stations. Indeed, when we designate certain spaces as dangerous and others as safe a priori, we participate in the exoticization of these spaces, reproducing class, ethnic, and racial assumptions about the safety and nonviolent character of places like schools, the office, and civil society. Such an approach also reproduces the ideal of the neutral researcher, ignoring how environments that are safe for straight cis white men may be unsafe for women, people of color, and LGBTQIA+ people.

Although much of this book has explored women's experiences with violence in the field, we must also be careful not to gender danger. It is important to keep in mind that men are more likely than women to be victims of certain types of crime and violence. Indeed, in the United States, men are more likely to be victims of all forms of violence other than sexual assault and rape.[8] We remind readers of this for two reasons. First, men must also be able to speak openly about threats and risks they face in the field and be empowered to change or modify research projects without being criticized for not meeting the hegemonic standards of masculinity upheld by ethnography. Second, concerns about danger and risk cannot be made a "woman's issue." In other words, mentors and peers concerned about danger in the field must be careful to not reproduce "vulnerability to violence" as synonymous with femininity.[9] As Kristine Kilanski and others have noted, fear is a patriarchal instrument that has historically limited women's movements and access to public spaces,[10] with the "shadow of rape" looming over women's interactions.[11] Associating women alone with vulnerability only further delegitimizes women researchers. Nor should we assume that women are more likely to be victimized in their field sites and thus must be cared for and watched over in ways that men do not require. Throughout the book we have acknowledged that men also face danger in the field, danger that is often exacerbated by hegemonic masculinity and expressive of homosocial violence. Although pointing out the threats men face in the field could serve to place them at the center of analysis, acknowledging these threats and dangers is important in order to avoid relegating embodiment in the field to a women's issue, thus marginalizing it. Work by cis white men must also be attentive to embodiment in the field, to acknowledge how embodied dangers shape their work, as well as to interrogate how their embodied privilege might blind them to certain types of data.

Though we agree that safety training for qualitative researchers in general is inadequate—at least partly due to the colonialist gaze and the ensuing exaltation of dangerous research that we have critiqued—counter to Elizabeth Kenyon and Sheila Hawker, we are not advocating for a "mandatory . . . professional code of practice for those entering fieldwork settings."[12] Additional safety codes and regulations are unlikely to protect researchers. In fact, what we have shown is that research experiences are dependent on one's positionality. Institutions would be hard pressed to establish regulations that anticipate this diversity. While changes do need to be made in academia, coming up with rigid rules and guidelines for how to do research will not help, since these rules and guidelines would most likely eschew the different ways in which research takes place. Moreover, administrative rules and regulations can become forms of bureaucratic harassment that exacerbate rather than alleviate gender inequality in the workplace.[13]

In contrast, we are calling for a more honest and continuously evolving discussion of issues related to embodiment that should be considered before entering the field. Students should know that all field sites present potential dangers and forms of harassment, and they should feel empowered to make decisions that prioritize their safety and sanity. Mentors and instructors should help students develop on-site and off-site support networks and should remind them of the importance of self-care in the field (see chap. 3). Mentors can encourage students to be aware of the diverse challenges they might confront in the field, and they should also support the decision to say no when these challenges are too costly. As we have discussed, modification is part and parcel of the research process. Changing a project to avoid sexual harassment and other forms of violence does not negatively affect the quality of research or reflect poorly on research skills. Indeed, it can be quite difficult to turn down research opportunities that might result in data but also put the researcher in danger. Saying no to the allure of these opportunities is a mark of strength, not weakness, and should be encouraged rather than shamed. However, recognizing that not all mentors will take us up on the advice in this conclusion, we call on peers to also engage in all these forms of support. Moreover, these steps remain important beyond the student years. Experienced researchers also need support networks to remind them to resist the ethnographic fixations, establish networks of support, and engage in self-care.

For students to feel that saying no is an option, sexuality, harassment, and violence must be addressed in methods syllabi and texts. Indeed, it is essential to counteract the silence surrounding these issues, silence that communicates that harassment and violence are not proper subjects to discuss in relation to methods. Students should know that they have the support of peers and faculty members if they choose to modify or abandon projects, but few will expect this kind of support if it is not explicitly discussed. Just by bringing these issues to students' attention before they enter the field, we reduce the likelihood that they will be blindsided by harassment and violence (as so many of the women we interviewed were). Indeed, when some of the students we interviewed finally told committee members about their experiences, their advisers suggested that they modify their projects or leave the field entirely. However, as Michelle noted, because she had never discussed these issues with her committee before entering the field, she did not know how her adviser would react. Of course, for these conversations to take place, committee members themselves must feel their own careers and work will not be delegitimized when they discuss harassment and violence they may have experienced in the field. In short, support for these conversations is important not only for students; it is critical for all.

Whenever possible, students should conduct preliminary research before beginning a project. Preliminary research provides the opportunity to reflect on how a project might be modified before committing to a particular research design and gives us the chance to abandon a project early on if we decide it is not worth the personal sacrifices carrying it out would entail. Preliminary research allows time to discuss issues encountered with peers and mentors, making it more likely that the researcher will have developed coping mechanisms and safety strategies to rely on during their time in the field. Like other university resources, the time and the funding necessary to conduct preliminary research are shrinking. This is yet another reason we encourage qualitative researchers to consider collaborative projects in which resources can be pooled and shared. While not all researchers work on topics or in locations that would allow them to collaborate with others, removing the stigma from collaborative research might make it less likely that those doing individual research think they must "go it alone," suffering through fieldwork in silence.

Collaborative research in and of itself is not a panacea. Until androcentric, racist, colonialist, and heteronormative academic institutions are transformed, collaborations may put researchers in positions where they are harassed and assaulted by those with whom they collaborate. This is particularly a concern where researchers end up collaborating with those who hold more structurally advantageous positions. Maya Berry and colleagues rightly critique collaborative research as a "reformist solution" to "structural antagonisms" that disempower and delegitimize those who are "othered" in academic settings.[14] Scholars who do engage in collaborative research should learn as much as possible about potential collaborators before agreeing to work with them. And just as we advocate for research-participant relationships, we recommend coming up with procedures and boundaries that guide collaborative research.[15] Nevertheless, this does not detract from the value of collaborative research, nor does it mean that we should not advocate for it as we work toward the transformation of academic institutions.

Furthermore, avoiding potential research participants and sites need not be viewed as methodological transgressions. Though some of our participants reported feeling that taking measures to protect themselves was a form of cheating, these decisions can be important data for understanding the gendered politics of their research site. Indeed, it is likely that Rosie's threatening encounter, which led her to hide out in her car, was one other women in field sites similar to hers have experienced. However, because Rosie (and many other participants) internalized the call to "dive into the stream of [social] action to the greatest possible depth"[16]—as if this stream were not intersected by racial, gender, and other dynamics—she viewed this choice as detrimental to her project and a shameful part of her history as a researcher. If we recognize these experiences as data we can use gendered and sexualized interactions to understand how power is structured and distributed in the social worlds we study. As the experiences of Rosie and others demonstrate, these possibilities are not acknowledged when we fetishize danger and focus on singular models and values for what makes ethnography "good."

We appreciate—and know from experience—that fieldwork requires persistence, commitment, and pushing though awkward and uncomfortable situations. However, we ask that researchers reflect on why the history of ethnography discourages them from putting safety before getting good data.[17] As an academic community, we must also be more honest about when danger does not lead to successful ethnographic fieldwork. As some of the projects discussed in this book show, danger often prevents data collection and can end projects. When researchers choose to engage in dangerous research, we should encourage them to discard masculine bravado and write about the suffering, contradictions, and ethical dilemmas they face in the field. Discussing these experiences can begin to crack the armor of the idealized "hardy" ethnographer and work to draw back the curtain that is integral to the fetishization of dangerous research.

Going Beyond Intimacy

Students preparing to enter the field are encouraged to think about the responsibilities of the ethnographer to research participants but are taught little about the ethnographer's responsibility to the self. Nearly all of the women we interviewed said they had thought a great deal about power before entering the field—the power they might exert over research participants, the damage they could do to the communities where they worked, and how they might unintentionally take advantage of those involved in their studies. This approach to methods turns a blind eye to the body and power dynamics in contexts where researchers do not inhabit dominant positions. While recognizing that intimacy can be advantageous, we need to present it as one of many ways by which to build strong relationships with research participants. Until intimacy is dislodged as a knee-jerk evaluative benchmark of good qualitative work, we will continue to send students into the field who are not attuned to the multifaceted nature of power.

Discussions in methods classes should not only highlight the ways in which intimacy can protect our research subjects, or even (as Judith Stacey points out) the ways that it can harm them.[18] These discussions must also prepare students for the ways in which misunderstandings of intimacy could endanger researchers themselves. Moreover, intimacy cannot be perceived only from the standpoint of the researcher but also must be understood according to the preexisting cultural categories and gender roles through which participants filter and interpret our actions. As several of our participants pointed out, actively seeking time with people in the field, showing interest in their life histories and everyday activities, and breaking down formal barriers between them and us can mean something very different to our participants than it does to us; attempts at ethnographic intimacy may come at the cost of unwelcome advances, harassment, and even assault.

While intimacy tends to conjure up thoughts of compassion, care, and respect, similar to everyday life, intimacy in the field may open researchers up to violence, abuse, and mistreatment. As Berry and her colleagues note, dominant strands of anthropology inscribe researchers' bodies into new colonial narratives that assume that "rapport or intimacy with those with whom we are aligned necessarily results in more horizontal relations."[19] However, as we have shown throughout this book, intimacy often leads to power inequalities in fieldwork relationships, which do not empower women or democratize the research. Intimacy can also create motivations for research participants to be less, not more, honest with us. For example, participants may hide unflattering details about themselves in an effort to maintain closeness with the researcher.

Lack of education about the downsides of ethnographic intimacy had a negative effect on women's ability to respond to sexual harassment and violence in the field. It also left participants like Maritza, a Latina sociologist, unprepared to deal with the emotional labor that intimacy entails: "One of the things that I wish people had told me is that intimacy involves developing empathy. And that means, if you work with people who are discriminated against or are undergoing very difficult circumstances, [you] absorb some of their feelings and that is going to be really tough. My advisers didn't talk about emotions." She felt this failure to talk about emotions in the field was itself gendered. Maritza also observed that the struggles and contradictions of fieldwork often were not discussed in ethnographic texts, which she feels present a sanitized version of what it means to do fieldwork. Mary, a white graduate student, seemed to agree. She laughed as she observed that carrying out fieldwork was "really nothing anyone ever writes about." This suggested to her that even a methodological appendix is "a narrative piece rather than a reality of the field," indicating what an author chooses to represent and how more than a comprehensive telling of their experiences in the field.

Our participants expressed doubt about the value of intimacy for other reasons as well. Mary, for example, suggested that researchers might exaggerate the extent of intimacy they achieved or feel they achieved greater intimacy than they in fact have.

I think . . . you can falsely feel intimacy. And I think it's really dangerous to feel that you've established intimacy with someone because there are a lot of people who are really good at sharing a lot of personal details and shutting off at the end. They spelled it out to you, you were their temporary counselor, and after that that's the end of the interaction.

Along similar lines, others questioned whether intimacy was as important as we make it out to be, noting, for example, that for some projects we can get great data from a one-off interview, even with someone we have never met. Lisa, a white sociologist, suggested that the obsession with intimacy is a type of navel gazing: "When we use intimacy as a measure [of the quality of research] we're measuring us. We're not measuring the study. And I think that that's unfortunate." As with any principle of ethnographic research, we must be flexible in our understanding of when intimacy is called for. As our participants indicated, it is possible that intimacy is sometimes the route to the data we are looking for, but at other times it may be that some distance is necessary either to protect the researcher or the researched or for clarity of vision.

Furthermore, some participants spoke of the emotional, financial, and other expectations that come with close friendships in the field, some of which can be difficult to satisfy. For example, based on previous experiences in the field, Susie, a white anthropologist, realized that she needed physical distance for her own emotional well-being. She argued, "There's this ideal of intimacy but I . . . learned that there's a range and . . . maybe you don't necessarily need to have this idealized version of it to have good research." And as Marina, a Latina graduate student, noted in her interview, intimacy sometimes creates problems of access. After becoming "really close" with some of the women in her study on informal economies, she found that "once we crossed the line they didn't want to talk to me about their work. . . . They wanted to talk to me about their husbands and their personal lives and their children and anything else other than their work." According to Marina:

I can't even have those conversations with them because it would be really insulting to them, I think. . . . It violates the friendship because it becomes like an instrumental thing. . . . I did go in wanting to have that relationship with them because I felt that somehow I was going to be able to understand, you know, their social world. So I needed to have this intimacy with them. But once I was able to have that really close relationship, then that was kind of off the table. I could no longer talk about those things with them. And so in some ways I think that hurt my research project.

Of course, intimacy should continue to be one of many ways through which we collect good data. But we must recognize intimacy not only as a path to knowledge but also as a double-edged sword. We must draw a distinction between access and intimacy in the field and evaluate relationships based on other criteria, such as the trust and rapport researchers achieve with participants. When intimacy—which implies the breaking down of barriers and boundaries—is the goal, these other aspects of our research relationships—which often hinge on the respect of boundaries—can be overlooked.

Rather than emphasize one type of relationship as the key to illuminating data, we should begin to discuss what kinds of relationships lead to different, and equally good, types of data. For example, after being propositioned by most of the police officers she was studying for her dissertation fieldwork in Latin America, many of Rebecca's research relationships necessarily became defined by their punctuated or short-term nature. She explained:

> I got to a point with my research where I could kind of tell when things with men were gonna get to a point where they would no longer deal with me because it was clear I wasn't going to sleep with them or date them, or I would have to turn them down so blatantly that they would no longer deal with me.... I only had ... anywhere between a one-and-a-half- to three-month window for the most part.

Because spending consistent time with her participants resulted in the end of these relationships, Rebecca began taking time off from seeing them. By *limiting* her time with some research participants, she could extend these relationships well beyond the three-month window. Though she did not spend as much time as possible with many of her participants, choosing key moments to drop in on them or touch base with them allowed her to gather insightful data and also maintain a level of trust with them. These kinds of tactics suggest that being "sufficiently close" or "close enough" to participants can produce just as illuminating data as being "as close as possible."

To the extent that intimacy is part of ethnographic research, we need to focus on maintaining boundaries at the same time. Our participants with applied training as counselors or social workers noted that even as they valued vulnerability and intimacy as research tools, their professional training was useful in helping to maintain professional boundaries in the field. Janet, a black sociologist, was one of the few participants who felt her graduate adviser had taught her about establishing good boundaries while in the field (and even then, she learned this by observing her adviser rather than something she explicitly said). Fieldwork is "emotionally terrifying," she said, and, as a result, establishing good boundaries and a sense of personal safety become paramount.

> Yes, it's good to get in the field and have them respect and trust you, but I think it's equally as important to put limits, even when you are in the field. You don't have to interview every single person in the neighborhood, you don't have to go to every single meeting. . . . There are times when you need to recharge so you can be your complete self. . . . I feel like you are under a microscope when you are in the field and it's hard to live all the time like that. So I think it's important as ethnographers [to] not give all of ourselves to it and have borders and saying no, . . . having time to recharge by yourself when you are not under the microscope.

The feeling of not being able to be one's full self in the field affects most field researchers, of course. However, many of our women participants spoke of a gendered split in their sense of self that was especially debilitating (see chap. 4), indicating a particular need to address limits and boundaries in methods instruction.

Recognizing All Research as Embodied

To deny multiplicity is to deny the body as constitutive of knowledge production. And we expect little change to occur until researchers embrace the multiple ways that gender, race, sexuality, and other aspects of embodiment shape the research process and understand that all research is embodied. If we take seriously the idea that our bodies are part of the research process, shaping the data we collect, it makes little sense to talk about ethnographic studies being fully replicable. This standard only holds if we assume that bodies engaged in research are the same, an assumption we have dismantled over the course of this book. The unease with which researchers' bodies "fit" into the homogenous narratives we have critiqued in this book suggests that the diversification of people who have access to do ethnography can disrupt these narratives and the fixations that demand them. Though reflecting on urban studies, Rios's call for "ethnography that is more embracive of multiple perspectives, that is comfortable with a cadre of ethnographers that persistently questions our intentions and our role as researchers," is applicable to all research.[20] Indeed, as Rios notes, in order to bring out the human complexity in the populations we study, ethnographers must demand more diversity and complexity within our ranks.

To recognize multiple perspectives in methods courses, we suggest the following questions as initial steps. First, as methods professors design their syllabi, they should ask themselves the following: Does my syllabus take into account perspectives different from my own? Who wrote the ethnographies and other qualitative studies I have assigned? Are the authors largely (or only) men? Are most of the authors white and from the Global North? Whose perspectives and field experiences am I using to train future researchers? How can I incorporate a range of embodied experiences and challenges faced by different researchers through the materials and activities I assign? Apart from authorship, we must also consider the content of the studies and methodological texts we assign. Teachers and mentors must ask themselves: Do the readings I assign or recommend to my students encourage ethnographic fixations? Do these readings assume that a "neutral" body is conducting research? Are they blind to the power dynamics that structure different field experiences?

Finally, beyond encouraging students to consider their positionality and embodiment in the field, experienced professors must consistently consider how their embodiment and social location might limit their vision and effectiveness as mentors and teachers and what they can do to expand their understandings to provide better support to students and peers. Thus the "zealous reflexivity" that Rios calls for during research should also be applied to our relationships within academia.

Both inside and outside the classroom, mentors and peers need to reflect on how they speak about research relationships and how they respond to others' experiences with sexual harassment and discrimination. Our women participants pointed out that this study is important to men as well as women, because we are all embodied, and also because women ethnographers need men to be allies. This is also true for LGBTQIA+ people and people of color who are subject to harassment in the field. Too often our participants described advisers and graduate school colleagues who dismissed their experiences, attributed the blame to them as researchers, or mansplained their experiences to them. In other words, they were shamed for being transparent about what occurred during their fieldwork. If sexuality, gender, intersectionality, and embodiment seem more relevant when discussing women's research, it is only because women remain an other in many of the settings we study (whether in the United States or abroad) and in our academic disciplines. As we discuss below, we must question—not only as individuals but also as members of an intellectual community—why responses to experiences with harassment—on the basis of gender, sexual identity, or race—often involve shaming, doubt and disbelief, or an expectation that the objects of harassment "suck it up" if they are to succeed in their careers. Mentors and teachers must recognize that their own positionalities contribute to inequalities within academia and may restrict the conversations students—and colleagues—are willing to have with them. While critique at the individual level, as we discuss below, will never be sufficient, it is in the content of everyday interactions that we either reinforce or challenge broader cultural norms.

INSTITUTIONAL CHANGE IN THE DISCIPLINES

Ethnographers, like other academics, make choices as members of broader communities in which disciplinary norms shape individuals' behavior and understandings of their experiences.[21] In this section, we suggest ways to transform disciplinary norms and the evaluative practices that we engage in as an academic community in order to move beyond ethnographic fixations and overcome the silence surrounding sexual harassment and violence in the disciplines.

Those in less dominant positions in the academic field tend to bear the burden of theorizing positionality and reflexivity, at least in part because they are more likely to be called on to justify why their positionalities do not invalidate their research. As Lena, an Asian American participant, pointed out, people of color undergo additional scrutiny when "studying their own." Ethnographic methods, as Rios writes, still assume that researchers are "all homogenous (white) and that we are all studying an 'other.'"[22] This scrutiny, Rios writes, occurs less often with white researchers studying white and nonwhite groups and individuals; indeed, white men built the Chicago school by conducting ethnographic studies of communities of color. The invasion of people of color's personal spaces, an "exotic interlude from normativity," is a hallmark of ethnography.[23] The privilege of entering these spaces without having to account for it remains rampant in ethnography. In contrast, scholars who are not white are frequently asked to account for how their positionality influenced their work, particularly if they are racial or cultural "insiders."[24]

Reflexivity cannot remain an individual practice, however. It is not sufficient for individual researchers to contemplate privilege and power, reflecting alone in their field sites or offices on how their presence and positionality shape the fieldwork they conduct. In order to move toward meaningful systematic change, we must be reflexive as a community of scholars, recognizing that norms and standards in academic fields are the result of power distributions. As Joey Sprague has written, disciplines are not an "it," not an "external force," but rather "systems of relations among scholars, maintained by the interrelated practices that each of us as individual scholars engages in with an eye to the standards and expectations of our peers."[25] Collective reflexivity as a community of scholars is essential if we are address the ways our disciplinary practices may reinforce systemic inequalities.[26]

To shift this burden, ethnographic training should prepare researchers— particularly those in socially dominant positions but all of us, too—to be more attuned to race, gender, class, and other systems of oppression. By recognizing that *all* research is embodied, we are also recognizing that *all* bodies are the product of systems of domination, which necessitates change at the level of the system and the institutions that uphold it. Berry and her colleagues have forcefully rejected the sexist and racist implications of the epistemic structure of our disciplines, writing, "We refuse the emblematic racially privileged male anthropologist and the . . . assumptive logics of *doing* ethnographic fieldwork, both of which undergird the discipline's implicit masculinist 'shut up and take it' mentality in reference to gendered violence in the field."[27] Researchers should be empowered to reject these logics and open up spaces to discuss and expose gender / intersectional violence, in the field and in our disciplines. Because all researchers enter academic institutions that work to socialize us into gender- and race-neutral ideologies, even scholars from groups that have historically been marginalized need exposure to these ideas; reflexivity does not come "naturally," even for scholars who are members of groups that are othered within the social order.

Beyond training, this shift requires that throughout the evaluation process scholarship from different perspectives must be recognized and legitimized. Those in positions of power within organizations—the "gatekeepers" of academia—must be held accountable to new standards. Journal editors and reviewers, committee members, and others with evaluative power must reconceptualize how they respond when scholars write about embodied experiences—particularly negative ones—in accounts of the field. As Sprague has written, "If we want to change how we do our own research without incurring serious economic and professional costs in our careers, we need to change the standards we employ in evaluating one another's work."[28]

Alternative evaluative standards should require that scholars engage with their bodies as constituting research sites and data and hold researchers accountable when they do not do this. Rather than see bodies as barriers, drawbacks, or potential points of critique that are best buried in methodological appendixes or briefly mentioned in introductions, these standards would expect scholars to take seriously how emotions and bodies "clue us in to" what is going on in the field.[29] In contrast to standards that expect intimacy built on full integration, alternative standards would appreciate how the presence of a researcher in a field site dominated by participants who identify with a gender different from the researcher's might "destabilize" that site, leading to new insights about the social relations within it.

It is time to shake off the expectation that all ethnographers become full participants in their field sites. Instead, as a discipline, we must value uneven integration in research sites as data. The notion of full integration in research settings presents research relationships as either fixed and static or awkward, conditions that we eventually overcome. However, ethnographic relationships and researcher identities are "shifting social relationships that have constantly to be negotiated."[30] Thinking about them in this way allows researchers to be more honest about the awkward and uncomfortable relationships that many of us depend on to do research. In addition, this perspective allows us to value these changes and shifts as data, reflecting on what they reveal about their participants and field sites.

If norms and standards are to change, the white (cis, straight) androcentric perspective must be challenged and decentered from its hegemonic position in our disciplines, where it informs us what we should expect fieldwork to look like before the fact and how to evaluate our findings after the fact.[31] As Elizabeth Armstrong, Miriam Gleckman-Krut, and Lanora Johnson write, "Rectifying epistemic exclusion will require changes in our practices. Continuing to diversify our graduate programs and departments to remedy the historical exclusion of marginalized voices is a first step."[32] We should also continue to increase the numbers of gatekeeper positions—including but not limited to journal editors and reviewers, search committees, association presidents, and section chairs—filled by those who have historically been locked out of them.

Of course, representation is necessary but not sufficient to change academic culture, and we must explicitly debate and work toward changing norms and standards that serve those marginalized by our disciplines, and the construction of knowledge, poorly. Moreover, not all scholars (ethnographers or otherwise) will be swayed by our arguments, and we do not expect that all (or perhaps even most) gatekeepers will change their beliefs about how "good" qualitative research is done. Thus we must also consider ways in which to circumvent the gatekeepers altogether—by taking over leadership positions, starting new academic journals or demanding control of existing ones, putting together panels at conferences that challenge ethnographic fixations, organizing conferences apart from those dominated by intransigent gatekeepers, or even starting our own organizations. In other words, feminist, antiracist scholars need to take control of the means of intellectual production.[33]

This brings us back to the question about institutional reflexivity: What do we value—explicitly or implicitly—as a discipline? Whose voices and perspectives are affirmed by how we teach methods, review manuscripts, and mentor students? Our findings suggest that our disciplines continue to value "disembodied and neutral" observations and understandings of social worlds that are in reality anything but. As a community of scholars we must consider how to upend these values and hold those who continue to champion them accountable. We must reflect on why the common response to accusations of harassment in field sites and academic fields is to doubt or to consider these experiences as just another part of life as a qualitative researcher. When we doubt the accounts of those who are harassed or tell them to "suck it up," we must ask whose voices these responses prioritize and whose they silence. And although we have spent much of this conclusion calling for individual and collective change, we also recognize that those with power are often loath to give it up. Thus those of us who care about these issues should not wait for someone else to respond to our concerns (even as we invite them to). Instead, we should make the change we want to see.

We began this project before the #MeToo movement became a national phenomenon.[34] As we completed the book, the national conversation that has begun to take place on issues of sexual harassment in the workplace made it clear to us that nothing short of systemic change in the academic workplace will suffice. If the way in which we teach methods is ever going to change— and if that change is going to have any meaningful impact—we must demand transformation beyond the classroom. Nothing short of the restructuring of academic culture will do.

In his book *Interrogating Ethnography,* the law professor Steven Lubet criticizes ethnographers for failing to verify and substantiate their data, specifically, the things research participants tell them in the field.[35] If ethnography suffers from an "accuracy problem," as Lubet has alleged, we would argue that this problem is less about failing to "verify" our data and more about the lack of honesty and transparency about how our data are collected. Embodied ethnography is a call for more transparent, valid, and ethical approaches to knowledge production. Recognizing that all research is embodied dispels the long-held myth of neutral research, resituating conversations about validity and reliability. Instead of avoiding and obscuring the actual ways in which research is carried out, embodied ethnography demands honest and transparent engagement with the essential instrument with which we conduct qualitative research: our bodies. In other words, it increases validity by providing critical details and information about our inquiry and discovery process. If rigor in qualitative research means having access to the decisions made throughout the research process and the rationales for these decisions, then research that incorporates embodied experiences is undoubtedly more rigorous. As we have seen throughout this book, ethnographers make various decisions based on embodied experiences, such as sexual harassment, racial harassment, and assault. Current ethnographic standards discourage researchers from including information about these aspects of the research process. Our data show that experiences of harassment and sexualization in the field are shoved aside, marked as unimportant and irrelevant to the construction of knowledge. However, acknowledging and analyzing these experiences are part of a more fully developed understanding of ethnographic research itself. To the degree that ethnographic research is replicable, embodied ethnography allows future researchers to more fully understand how researchers had access to and collected their data. As Burawoy has written, the social world is not a laboratory experiment that can be replicated over and over again,[36] but we can repeat previous studies to understand how field sites change, or remain the same, over time. If we take replicability to mean repeatability—an extension of previous studies rather than a replication of them—the degree to which we can connect our data and findings to those of previous researchers requires understanding their process of knowledge production, a process that cannot be separated from embodied experiences in the field.

Rather than tips and strategies for dealing with harassment in the field, our central concern in this book has been what the obfuscation of gender, sexuality, and embodiment (recognizing that each of these is also constituted by other structures of inequality, including race, age, and nationality) in fieldwork means for the construction of ethnographic knowledge. As we have shown, this obfuscation encourages researchers to relegate their bodies to awkward surplus and perpetuates the notion that the identities that set the researcher apart from those they study must be shed at the beginning of any worthwhile project.

The embodied ethnographic approach we have advocated for here, however, is not *the* solution to the problems we have identified in this book. Rather, we ask readers to think of it as one of multiple (and imperfect) projects that seek to alter how academics produce and evaluate knowledge, building on the progress made by feminist, critical race, queer, and other theoretical traditions. For example, in response to their fieldwork experiences with gendered, sexualized, and racialized violence, Berry and colleagues have called for a "fugitive anthropology," which, among other things, pursues epistemological decolonization, rejecting the racist, colonialist, and sexist standards that have had such negative effects on the lives of research participants as well as ethnographers who are women of color.[37] Rios has called for a decolonial reflexivity, a "consistent, overzealous reflexivity. One where we constantly ask ourselves about research design, our relationship with our research participants, the labels we give them, and the way we write about them."[38] We would further suggest, as we detail above, consistent collective reflection, which requires sharing research design, analysis, and writing with other scholars (particularly scholars with different perspectives and social locations). This collective reflexivity must also involve thinking about and working to dismantle the many ways in which our disciplines and institutions foster a culture of silence surrounding issues of gender, sexuality, and race that can perpetuate harassment in the field as well as in the halls of academia. Beyond reflexivity, researchers must implement a system of checks and balances that requires that we question how our social locations, or our support for systems of oppression, might compromise the knowledge production process.[39] Furthermore, decolonizing ethnographic methods requires empowering those who have historically been excluded from knowledge production to generate knowledge in ways that more accurately represent their lived social worlds.[40] Embodied ethnography must be part of these practices and contribute to a broader series of changes that include breaking silences in other ways and transforming the structure of power in our disciplines more generally.

Some might argue that the kind of reflexivity we advocate for here—focused largely on the integration of our bodies into ethnographic work—is not feasible in an academic world that is increasingly focused on articles and journal placement. There is, they might argue, no space to incorporate "additional" information in ethnographic articles. However, there are ethical and practical justifications for embodied ethnography. Including our bodies in our writing (without falling prey to solipsism) can be one form of resisting the political economy of academic journal publishing, which forces authors to cut context, detail, and positionality from our work to make room for the "real" data. Although ethnography emerged from colonialist and naturalist endeavors, it can also be used to challenge social inequality and injustice. If a goal of ethnography is to reduce the violence and injustices done to the human beings we research, we should also demand that ethnographic methods contribute to reducing violence and injustices done to those conducting research. Finally, as Adjepong has written, examining how our bodies fit, or fail to fit, into field sites destabilizes the researcher as a "non-disruptive, merely innocent observer, by interrupting the ethnographic narrative with the ethnographer's disorientations."[41] All writing and analysis requires reduction. However, the case of sexual harassment in ethnographic research shows that our bodies—like the situations, events, and contexts that we are expected to detail—can speak to the social processes we are studying and, thus, warrant a place in our analysis and writing. The friction, destabilization, and disorientation created by researchers' bodies can lead to rich analytic insight. Rather than ask if we have space for our bodies in our writing, we should consider what is lost—what insights and knowledge we push aside—when we do not include them.

This book sheds light on the experience of sexual harassment in the field to demonstrate its implications for the construction of ethnographic knowledge. Recognizing that the power relationships in which bodies are situated shape research and knowledge production, we hope, will redistribute the burden of explaining and justifying positionalities, which is most often carried by scholars whose bodies challenge the standards that have been set by white cis men. Finally, embodied ethnography is a call for more ethical research, with the lives, dignity, and rights of our participants, as well as ourselves, in mind.

We hope this book serves to ignite discussions in classrooms on the ideological forms that structure ethnographic knowledge. Specifically, we call for ethnographers to stop fixating on danger, the solitary researcher, and intimacy. But more broadly, we hope this book reveals the power dynamics within academic institutions and structures that articulate with those in our field sites and reproduce methodological silence on harassment and sexualization. Indeed, a recent crowd-sourced survey asking about sexual harassment within academia received almost two thousand entries (mostly from women) over a two-month period, detailing violence and threats they had faced from colleagues and mentors.[42] If we are to make any progress toward reducing sexual harassment of researchers, we cannot separate out the violence we experience within the academic field from the violence we experience in our field sites.

This book is a case study of sexual harassment in one (albeit amorphous) workplace: academic fieldwork. We have shown that if we want to address sexual harassment in the field, we must first turn to the academic norms that elevate standards based on a presumed "neutral researcher" that in fact does not exist. We must transform our understanding of what makes "good" ethnography and leave behind the androcentric, colonialist, positivist assumptions of the past once and for all. The fact that the writing of this book has coincided with a time when sexual harassment is being discussed nationally in a range of settings and occupations drives home the extent to which the changes we are calling for transcend the norms surrounding qualitative fieldwork to challenge the broader culture of silence and legitimation surrounding sexual and other forms of harassment in our disciplines. We hope this book will contribute to lifting that silence and working toward institutional change.

NOTES

INTRODUCTION

1. Gary Alan Fine, "Ten Lies of Ethnography: Moral Dilemmas of Field Research," *Journal of Contemporary Ethnography* 22, no. 3 (1993): 283.

2. Jeannine A. Gailey and Ariane Prohaska, "Power and Gender Negotiations during Interviews with Men about Sex and Sexually Degrading Practices," *Qualitative Research* 11, no. 4 (2011): 365–80; Liz Grauerholz, Mandi Barringer, Timothy Colyer, Nicholas Guittar, Jaime Hecht, Rachel L. Rayburn, and Elizabeth Swart, "Attraction in the Field: What We Need to Acknowledge and Implications for Research and Teaching," *Qualitative Inquiry* 19, no. 3 (2013): 167–78; Gill Green, Rosaline S. Barbour, Marina Barnard, and Jenny Kizinger, "'Who Wears the Trousers?' Sexual Harassment in Research Settings," *Women's Studies International Forum* 16, no. 6 (1993): 627–37; Jennifer Huff, "The Sexual Harassment of Researchers by Research Subjects: Lessons from the Field," in *Researching Sexual Violence against Women,* edited by Martin D. Schwartz (Thousand Oaks, CA: Sage, 1997), 115–27; Deborah Lee, "Interviewing Men: Vulnerabilities and Dilemmas," *Women's Studies International Forum* 20, no. 4 (1997): 553–64; Lisa M. Mugge, "Sexually Harassed by Gatekeepers: Reflections on Fieldwork in Surinam and Turkey," *International Journal of Social Research Methodology* 16, no. 6 (2013): 541–46; Gwen Sharp and Emily Kremer, "The Safety Dance: Confronting Harassment, Intimidation, and Violence in the Field," *Sociological Methodology* 36, no. 1 (2006): 317–27; Bianca C. Williams, "'Don't Ride the Bus!' and Other Warnings Women Anthropologists Are Given during Fieldwork," *Transforming Anthropology* 17, no. 2 (2009): 155–58; Dalit Yassour-Borochowitz, "'Only If She Is Sexy': An Autoethnography of Female Researcher–Male Participants Relations," *Equality, Diversity & Inclusion* 31, no. 5–6 (2012): 402–17.

3. For work that goes beyond individual reflections, see Amy Pollard, "Field of Screams: Difficulty and Ethnographic Fieldwork," *Anthropology Matters* 11, no. 2 (2009): 1–24; and Fran Markowitz and Michael Ashkenazi, eds., *Sex, Sexuality, and the Anthropologist* (Champaign: University of Illinois Press, 1999). In addition,

in his handbook on dangerous research, Raymond Lee briefly discusses specific dangers faced by women ethnographers, focusing especially on sexual violence: *Dangerous Fieldwork* (Thousand Oaks, CA: Sage, 1995). Some contributors to Diane Bell, Pat Caplan, and Wazir Jahan Karim, eds., *Gendered Fields: Women, Men and Ethnography* (New York: Routledge, 1993), also make brief mention of potential dangers surrounding sex and gender in the field.

4. Markowitz and Ashkenazi, *Sex*, 1.

5. Joan H. Fujimura, "Sex Genes: A Critical Sociomaterial Approach to the Politics and Molecular Genetics of Sex Determination," *Signs* 32, no. 1 (2006): 49–82.

6. See E. J. Langer, *Mindfulness* (New York: Addison-Wesley, 1989).

7. Carolyn Ellis, "Fighting Back or Moving On: An Authoethnographic Response to Critics," *International Review of Qualitative Research* 3, no. 2 (2009): 371–78; Sandra Harding, *Whose Science? Whose Knowledge?* (Ithaca, NY: Cornell University Press, 1991); Chandra Talpade Mohanty, "Under Western Eyes: Feminist Scholarship and Colonial Discourses," in *Third World Women and the Politics of Feminism,* edited by Chandra Talpade Mohanty, Ann Russo, and Lourdes Torres (Bloomington: Indiana University Press, 1991). Maurice Punch also writes about the importance of recognizing that the white male perspective in research is not objective but rather privileged. "Politics and Ethics in Qualitative Research," in *Handbook of Qualitative Research,* edited by Norman K. Denzin and Yvonna S. Lincoln (Thousand Oaks, CA: Sage, 1994).

8. Some of the findings in this book were originally presented in our 2017 article in *Sociological Forum*. Rebecca Hanson and Patricia Richards, "Sexual Harassment and the Construction of Ethnographic Knowledge," *Sociological Forum* 32, no. 3 (2017): 587–609.

9. Kathryn B. H. Clancy, Robin G. Nelson, Julienne N. Rutherford, and Katie Hinde, "Survey of Academic Field Experiences: Trainees Report Harassment and Assault," *PLOS One* 9, no. 7 (2014). The survey conducted by Clancy et al. focuses on biological anthropology and other sciences and found that 64 percent of female field scientists experienced sexual harassment and 20 percent had been victims of sexual assault. It is likely that this figure is similar for ethnographers, although a survey focusing on the social sciences has yet to be carried out.

10. Begoña Aretxaga, *Shattering Silence: Women, Nationalism, and Political Subjectivity in Northern Ireland* (Princeton, NJ: Princeton University Press, 1997).

11. Ibid.

12. Barbara Sutton, *Bodies in Crisis: Culture, Violence, and Women's Resistance in Neoliberal Argentina* (New Brunswick, NJ: Rutgers University Press, 2010).

13. Joan Scott, "The Evidence of Experience," *Critical Inquiry* 17, no. 4 (1991): 773–97.

14. Ibid., 777.

15. Dorothy E. Smith, "Women's Perspective as a Radical Critique of Sociology," *Sociological Inquiry* 44, no. 1 (1974): 7–13; reprinted in *The Feminist Standpoint Theory Reader: Intellectual and Political Controversies,* edited by Sandra Harding (New York: Routledge, 2004).

16. See, e.g., Colleen Flaherty, "'Holding Space' for Victims of Harassment," *Inside Higher Ed* (December 8, 2017), www.insidehighered.com/news/2017/12/08/what-can-crowdsourced-survey-sexual-harassment-academia-tell-us-about-problem; Carolina Fredrickson, "When Will the 'Harvey Effect' Reach Academia?," *The Atlantic* (October 30, 2017), www.theatlantic.com/education/archive/2017/10/when-will-the-harvey-effect-reach-academia/544388/; Nell Gluckman, "What Happens When Sex Harassment Disrupts Victims' Academic Careers," *Chronicle of Higher Education* (December 28, 2017), www-chronicle-com.lp.hscl.ufl.edu/article/What-Happens-When-Sex/241994; Stephanie Singer, "I Spoke Up against My Harasser—And Paid a Steep Price," *Chronicle of Higher Education* (December 6, 2017), www-chronicle-com.lp.hscl.ufl.edu/article/I-Spoke-Up-Against-My-Harasser/241991; Linda Wang and Andrea Widener, "Confronting Sexual Harassment in Chemistry," *Chemical and Engineering News* 95, no. 37 (2017): 28–37.

17. John Van Maanen, *Tales of the Field: On Writing Ethnography,* 2nd ed. (Chicago: University of Chicago Press, 2011).

18. Michel Foucault, *The Order of Things* (New York: Vintage, [1966] 1994), 168.

19. Antonio Gramsci, *Selections from the Prison Notebooks of Antonio Gramsci,* edited by Quintin Hoare and Geoffrey Nowell-Smith (New York: International Publishers, 1971).

20. Nancy Scheper-Hughes, "Introduction: The Problem of Bias in Androcentric and Feminist Anthropology," *Women's Studies: An Interdisciplinary Journal* 10, no. 2 (1983): 115.

21. Michael Burawoy, "Critical Sociology: A Dialogue between Two Sciences," *Contemporary Sociology* 27, no. 1 (1998): 12–20.

22. Sandra Harding, "After the Neutrality Ideal: Science, Politics, and Strong Objectivity," *Social Research* 59, no. 3 (1992): 585.

23. Norman K. Denzin, *Symbolic Interactionism and Cultural Studies: The Politics of Interpretation* (Cambridge, MA: Blackwell, 2008).

24. Mary Jo Deegan, *Jane Addams and the Men of the Chicago School* (New Brunswick, NJ: Transaction Press, 1988); Joey Sprague, *Feminist Methodologies for Critical Researchers: Bridging Differences,* 2nd ed. (New York: Rowman & Littlefield, 2016).

25. Aldon D. Morris, *The Scholar Denied: W. E. B. Du Bois and the Birth of Modern Sociology* (Berkeley: University of California Press, 2015).

26. Earl Wright II and Thomas Calhoun, "W. E. B. Du Bois and the Atlanta Sociological Laboratory," *Berkeley Journal of Sociology* (February 2016), http://berkeleyjournal.org/2016/02/w-e-b-du-bois-and-the-atlanta-sociological-laboratory/.

27. See Ronald R. Giere, "The Feminism Question in the Philosophy of Science," in *Feminism, Science, and the Philosophy of Science,* edited by Lynn Hankinson Nelson and Jack Nelson (London: Kluwer Academic, 1997), 3–16, for a taxonomy.

28. Ruth Milkman, "Redefining 'Women's Work': The Sexual Division of Labor in the Auto Industry during World War II," *Feminist Studies* 8 (1982): 337–72; Rosabeth Moss Kanter, *Men and Women of the Corporation* (New York: Basic Books, 1977).

29. Harding, "After the Neutrality Ideal."

30. Dorothy E. Smith, "An Analysis of Ideological Structures and How Women Are Excluded: Considerations for Academic Women," *Canadian Review of Sociology* 12, no. 4 (1975): 353–69. For more on feminist methodologies written by sociologists, see Nancy A. Naples, *Feminism and Method: Ethnography, Discourse Analysis, and Activist Research* (New York: Routledge, 2003); Sprague, *Feminist Methodologies*.

31. Harding, *Whose Science?*

32. Jill A. McCorkel and Kristen Meyers, "What Difference Does Difference Make? Position and Privilege in the Field," *Qualitative Sociology* 26, no. 2 (2003): 203.

33. E.g., Herbert Blumer, *Symbolic Interactionism* (Berkeley: University of California Press, 1969).

34. Sharlene Nagy Hesse-Biber and Patrica Leavy, *The Practice of Qualitative Research,* 2nd ed. (Los Angeles: Sage, 2011).

35. In chapter 2, we use Rebecca's data to show how adding a paragraph and some additional detail to a vignette can position the researcher and their body without taking it over.

36. Andrea Doucet and Natasha S. Mauthner, "Feminist Methodologies and Epistemology," in *21st Century Sociology,* edited by Clifton D. Bryant and Dennis L. Peck (New York: Sage, 2006), 42.

37. David Swartz, *Culture and Power: The Sociology of Pierre Bourdieu* (Chicago: University of Chicago Press, 2012), 273.

38. Barbara Risman, "Gender as a Social Structure: Theory Wrestling with Activism," *Gender & Society* 18, no. 4 (2004): 446.

39. Leslie Salzinger, *Genders in Production: Making Workers in Mexico's Global Factories* (Berkeley: University of California Press, 2003), 153.

40. Candace West and Don H. Zimmerman, " Doing Gender," *Gender & Society* 1, no. 2 (1987): 125–51.

41. Judith Butler, "Performative Acts and Gender Constitution: An Essay in Phenomenology and Feminist Theory," in *Writing on the Body: Female Embodiment and Feminist Theory,* edited by Katie Conboy, Nadia Medina, and Sarah Stanbury (New York: Columbia University Press, 1997), 402.

42. Ibid.

43. West and Zimmerman, " Doing Gender."

44. Butler, "Performative acts and Gender Constitution."

45. Markowitz and Ashkenazi, *Sex,* 2.

46. Kimberle Crenshaw, "Mapping the Margins: Intersectionality, Identity Politics, and Violence against Women of Color," *Stanford Law Review* 43 no. 6 (1991): 1241–99; Patricia Hill Collins, *Black Feminist Thought* (New York: Routledge, 1990).

47. María Lugones, "The Coloniality of Gender," *Worlds and Knowledges Otherwise* (2008), https://globalstudies.trinity.duke.edu/wp-content/themes/cgsh/materials/WKO/v2d2_Lugones.pdf; Mohanty, "Under Western Eyes"; Uma Narayan, *Dislocating Cultures: Identities, Traditions, and Third World Feminism* (New York: Routledge, 1997).

48. Maya Berry, Claudia Cháves Argüelles, Shanya Cordis, Sarah Ihmoud, and Elizabeth Velásquez Estrada, "Toward a Fugitive Anthropology: Gender, Race, and Violence in the Field," *Cultural Anthropology* 32, no. 4 (2017): 537–65; Bianca C. Williams, "#MeToo: A Crescendo in the Discourse about Sexual Harassment, Fieldwork, and the Academy (Parts 1 & 2)," *Savage Minds: Notes and Queries in Anthropology,* October 28, 2017, https://savageminds.org/2017/10/28/metoo-a-crescendo-in-the-discourse-about-sexual-harassment-fieldwork-and-the-academy-part-1/; https://savageminds.org/2017/10/28/metoo-a-crescendo-in-the-discourse-about-sexual-harassment-fieldwork-and-the-academy-part-2/.

49. Judith Butler, *Gender Trouble* (New York: Routledge, 1990); bell hooks, *Feminist Theory: From Margin to Center* (Boston: South End Press, 1984).

50. Sinah Theres Kloß, "Sexual(ized) Harassment and Ethnographic Fieldwork: A Silenced Aspect of Social Research," *Ethnography* 18, no. 3 (2017): 396–414.

51. Our Bodies Our Selves, "Rape and Sexual Assault," last modified October 15, 2011, www.ourbodiesourselves.org/health-info/rape-and-sexual-assault/.

52. Ibid.

53. Sandy Welsh, Jacquie Carr, Barbara MacQuarrie, and Audrey Huntley, "I'm Not Thinking of It as Sexual Harassment: Understanding Harassment across Race and Citizenship," *Gender & Society* 20, no. 1 (2006): 87–107.

54. Annmarie Cano, "The Credibility Gap in Academe," *Chronicle of Higher Education,* December 6, 2017, www.chronicle.com/article/The-Credibility-Gap-in-Academe/241980?cid=at&utm_source=at&utm_medium=en&elqTrackId=48953 22c04c54eb9beea73b1ce1f4edb&elq=a6753c5c75c04d9a88608d92625f3f5a&elqaid =17027&elqat=1&elqCampaignId=7382.

55. Joan Acker, "Hierarchies, Jobs, Bodies: A Theory of Gendered Organizations," *Gender and Society* 4, no. 2 (1990): 139–58; Salzinger, *Genders in Production;* Patti A. Giuffre and Christine L. Williams, "Boundary Lines: Labeling Sexual Harassment in Restaurants," *Gender & Society* 8, no. 3 (1994): 378–401; Kirsten Dellinger and Christine Williams, "The Locker Room and the Dorm Room: Workplace Norms and the Boundaries of Sexual Harassment in Magazine Editing," *Social Problems* 49, no. 2 (2002): 242–57; Christine L. Williams, "The Unintended Consequences of Feminist Legal Reform: Commentary on *The Sanitized Workplace,*" *Thomas Jefferson Law Review* 29 (2006): 101–10.

56. John A. Clausen, ed., *Socialization and Society* (Boston: Little, Brown, 1968). See also Elizabeth Hordge-Freeman, Sarah Mayorga, and Eduardo Bonilla-Silva, "Exposing Whiteness Because We Are Free: Emancipation Methodological Practice in Becoming Empowered Sociologists of Color," in *Rethinking Race and Objectivity in Research Methods,* edited by John Stanfield (New York: Left Coast Press, 2011), 95–121.

57. Sexual harassment is an exercise of power that both men and women can engage in, and some allegations against women professors have recently come to light. Although men are more likely to engage in sexual harassment, this is because of the positions of power they hold, not due to biological drives or other essentialist explanations.

58. Smith, "Women's Perspective as a Radical Critique of Sociology."

59. Frances Beale, "Double Jeopardy: To Be Black and Female," in *The Black Woman,* edited by Toni Cade (New York: Signet, 1970), 90–110; Hill Collins, *Black Feminist Thought;* Angela Davis, *Women, Race, and Class* (New York: Random House, 1981).

60. Patricia Hill Collins, "Learning from the Outsider Within: The Sociological Significance of Black Feminist Thought," *Social Problems* 33, no. 6 (1986): 14–32.

61. Hordge-Freeman, Mayorga, and Bonilla-Silva, "Exposing Whiteness Because We Are Free," 105.

62. Michel Foucault, *Discipline and Punish: The Birth of the Prison* (New York: Random House, [1977] 1995).

63. Among the many feminist scholars who have written on this issue, see Sandra Lee Bartky, "Foucault, Femininity, and the Modernization of Patriarchal Power," in *Feminism and Foucault,* edited by Irene Diamond and Lee Quinby (Boston: Northeastern University Press, 1988), 61–86; Susan R. Bordo, "The Body and the Reproduction of Femininity," in Conboy, Medina, and Stanbury, *Writing on the Body,* 90–110; Jill A. McCorkel, "Embodied Surveillance and the Gendering of Punishment," *Journal of Contemporary Ethnography* 32, no. 1 (2003): 41–76.

64. Thomas Csordas, "Introduction: The Body as Representation and Being-in-the-World," in *Embodiment and Experience: The Existential Ground of Culture and Self,* edited by Thomas Csordas (Cambridge: Cambridge University Press, 1997), 10.

65. Kathleen Stewart, *Ordinary Affects* (Durham, NC: Duke University Press, 2007).

66. Pierre Bourdieu and Loïc Wacquant, *An Invitation to Reflexive Sociology* (Chicago: University of Chicago Press, 1992); Donna Haraway, "Situated Knowledges: The Science Question in Feminism as a Site of Discourse on the Privilege of Partial Perspective," *Feminist Studies* 14 (1988): 575–99; Sandra Harding, "Feminism, Science and the Anti-Enlightenment Critiques," in *Feminism / Postmodernism,* edited by Linda Nicholson (New York: Routledge, 1990), 83–106.

67. Mary Steedly, *Hanging without a Rope* (Princeton, NJ: Princeton University Press, 1993), 25.

68. Naples, *Feminism and Method,* 197.

69. Aretxaga, *Shattering Silence;* Sutton, *Bodies in Crisis.*

70. All categories are self-identifications.

71. Also see Berry et al., "Toward a Fugitive Anthropology"; Leanne Johansson, "Dangerous Liaisons: Risk, Positionality and Power in Women's Anthropological Fieldwork," *Journal of the Anthropological Society of Oxford* 7, no. 1 (2015): 55–63.

72. Also see Hale C. Bolak, "Studying One's Own in the Middle East: Negotiating Gender and Self-Other Dynamics in the Field," in *Reflexivity and Voice,* edited by Rosanna Hertz (Thousand Oaks, CA: Sage, 1997), 95–118; Kathrin Zippel also reports that the scientists she interviewed felt they were not subject to the same norms as other women in the countries where they participated in international collaborations. *Women in Global Science: Advancing Academic Careers through International Collaboration* (Stanford, CA: Stanford University Press, 2017).

73. See Anima Adjepong, "Invading Ethnography: A Queer of Color Reflexive Practice," *Ethnography* (2017), https://doi.org/10.1177/1466138117741502.

CHAPTER ONE. ETHNOGRAPHIC FIXATIONS

1. Clancy et al., "Survey."
2. Pierre Bourdieu used the term "disinterested" to refer to experts' ostensible neutrality on and detachment from their areas of specialization, which allows them to appear objective while at the same time furthering their own interests and increasing their symbolic capital. Pierre Bourdieu, "The Forms of Capital," in *Handbook of Theory and Research for the Sociology of Education,* edited by J. Richardson (New York: Greenwood, 1986), 241–58.
3. Smith, "Analysis of Ideological Structures."
4. See Michel Anteby, *Manufacturing Morals: The Values of Silence in Business School Education* (Chicago: University of Chicago Press, 2013).
5. Ibid.
6. Kimberly Kay Hoang, *Dealing in Desire: Asian Ascendancy, Western Decline, and the Hidden Currencies of Global Sex Work* (Berkeley: University of California Press, 2015); Mignon R. Moore, "Women of Color in the Academy: Navigating Multiple Intersections and Multiple Hierarchies," *Social Problems* 64, no. 2 (2017): 200–205; Morris, *The Scholar Denied;* Victor Rios, "Beyond Power-Blind Ethnography," *Sociological Focus* 50, no. 1 (2017): 99–101.
7. Berry et al., "Toward a Fugitive Anthropology"; Williams, "#MeToo." In addition, as NiCole Buchanan and Alayne Ormerod show in their study of black women's experiences with harassment in the academy, white women are frequently perpetrators of racialized sexual harassment. "Racialized Sexual Harassment in the Lives of African American Women," *Women & Therapy* 25, no. 3–4 (2002): 107–24.
8. Smith, "Analysis of Ideological Structures."
9. Lisa Wedeen, "Ethnography as Interpretive Enterprise," in *Political Ethnography: What Immersion Contributes to the Study of Power,* edited by Edward Schatz (Cambridge: Cambridge University Press, 2009), 75.
10. Jeffrey H. Cohen, "Problems in the Field: Participant Observation and the Assumption of Neutrality," *Field Methods* 12, no. 4 (2000): 318.
11. Bina Bhardwa, "Alone, Asian, and Female: The Unspoken Challenges of Conducting Fieldwork in Dance Settings," *Journal of Electronic Dance Music Culture* 5, no. 1 (2013): 43.
12. Sarah Gilmore and Kate Kenny, "Work-Worlds Colliding: Self-Reflexivity, Power and Emotion in Organizational Ethnography," *Human Relations* 68, no. 1 (2015): 55–78.
13. E.g., Gianpaolo Baiocchi et al., *The Civic Imagination: Making a Difference in American Political Life* (New York: Paradigm, 2014).
14. Pauline Greenhill, "Epistemological Reflections on Sex and Fieldwork," *Resources for Feminist Research* 32, no. 3–4 (2007): 87–99; Weeden, "Ethnography."

15. Helen Sampson and Michelle Thompson, "Risk and Responsibility," *Qualitative Research* 3, no. 2 (2003): 184.

16. Scheper-Hughes, "Problem of Bias."

17. Kimberly Theidon, "How Was Your Trip? Self-Care for Researchers Working and Writing On Violence," 2015, Working Paper No. 2, Drugs, Security, and Democracy Program, 5; also see Adam Baird, "Dancing with Danger: Ethnographic Safety, Male Bravado and Gang Research in Colombia," *Qualitative Research* 18, no. 3 (2018): 342–60.

18. See also Ingrid L. Nelson, "The Allure and Privileging of Danger over Everyday Practice in Field Research," *Area* 45, no. 4 (2013): 419–25.

19. See also Randol Contreras, *The Stickup Kids: Race, Drugs, Violence, and the American Dream* (Berkeley: University of California Press, 2012); Victor Rios, *Punished: Policing and the Lives of Black and Latino Boys* (New York: New York University Press, 2011).

20. Norman K. Denzin, "On Understanding Emotion: The Interpretive-Cultural Agenda," in *Research Agendas in the Sociology of Emotion,* edited by Theodor Kemper, 85–116 (Albany: State University of New York Press, 1990), 106.

21. Martha Knisely Huggins and Marie-Louise Glebbeek, *Women Fielding Danger: Negotiating Ethnographic Identities in Field Research* (Lanham, MD: Rowman & Littlefield, 2009); Raymond M. Lee, *Dangerous Fieldwork* (Thousand Oaks, CA: Sage, 1995); Icarbord Tshabangu, "The Challenge of Researching Violent Societies: Navigating Complexities in Ethnography," *Issues in Educational Research* 19, no. 2 (2009): 162–74.

22. Nelson, "Allure and Privileging of Danger."

23. Rios, *Punished.*

24. See, respectively, Arjun Appadurai, "Discussion: Fieldwork in the Era of Globalization," *Anthropology and Humanism* 22, no. 1 (1997): 115–18; and Joseph C. Hermanowicz, "The Great Interview: 25 Strategies for Studying People in Bed," *Qualitative Sociology* 25, no. 4 (2002): 479–99.

25. Loïc Wacquant, "For a Sociology of Flesh and Blood," *Qualitative Sociology* 38, no. 1 (2015): 1–11; Jeff Ferrell and Mark S. Hamm, *Ethnography at the Edge: Crime, Deviance, and Field Research* (Boston: Northeastern University Press, 1998).

26. Wacquant, "Flesh and Blood," 4–5.

27. Ann Oakley, "Interviewing Women: A Contradiction in Terms," in *Doing Feminist Research,* edited by Helen Roberts (London: Routledge, 1981), 30–62; Diane L. Wolf, *Feminist Dilemmas in Fieldwork* (Boulder, CO: Westview Press, 1996); Liz Stanley and Sue Wise, "Method, Methodology and Epistemology in Feminist Research Processes," in *Feminist Praxis,* edited by Liz Stanley (London: Routledge, 1990), 20–60.

28. Johansson also faced harassment from gatekeepers during her fieldwork in Central Africa. She observes that rather than concern about intimacy, she was paralyzed by the expectation that a good ethnographer engages in reflexive self-critique about power, ethnocentric assumptions, and so forth. Insofar as this notion, too, implicitly takes a gender-neutral ethnographer as its starting point, it in essence

encouraged her to put the interests of her harassers above her own. Johansson, "Dangerous Liaisons."

29. Greenhill, "Epistemological Reflections."

30. Baird, "Dancing with Danger."

31. Judith Stacey, "Can There Be a Feminist Ethnography?," *Women's Studies International Forum* 11 (1988): 21–27.

32. Katherine Irwin, "Into the Dark Heart of Ethnography: The Lived Ethics and Inequality of Intimate Field Relationships." *Qualitative Sociology* 29 (2006): 157.

33. Gailey and Prohaska, "Power and Gender Negotiations"; Caroline Gatrell, "Interviewing Fathers: Feminist Dilemmas in Fieldwork," *Journal of Gender Studies* 15, no. 3 (2006): 237–51; Laura A. Orrico, "'Doing Intimacy' in a Public Market: How the Gendered Experience of Ethnography Reveals Situated Social Dynamics," *Qualitative Research* 15, no. 4 (2015): 473–88; Stacey, "Feminist Ethnography."

34. Kloß, "Sexual(ized) Harassment"; Orrico, "'Doing Intimacy.'"

35. Men, too, may face sexual risks in the field. Moreover, as Jane Ward has argued, sexual acts between white men are often not labeled sexual. *Not Gay: Sex between Straight White Men* (New York: New York University Press, 2015). Nevertheless, "adult women remain the most frequent targets of classic sexual harassment markers"; see Heather McLaughlin, Christopher Uggen, and Amy Blackstone, "The Economic and Career Effects of Sexual Harassment on Working Women," *Gender & Society* 31, no. 3 (2017): 88.

36. See Marshall and Rossman, *Designing Qualitative Research.*

37. Don Kulick and Margaret Willson, eds., *Taboo: Sex, Identity and Erotic Subjectivity in Anthropological Fieldwork* (New York: Routledge, 1995).

38. Jo Reger, "Emotions, Objectivity, and Voice: An Analysis of a 'Failed' Participant Observation," *Women's Studies International Forum* 24, no. 5 (2001): 612.

39. Mary Romero notes the racial components of these standards of validity in "Reflections on 'The Department Is Very Male, Very White, Very Old, and Very Conservative': The Functioning of the Hidden Curriculum in Graduate Sociology Departments," *Social Problems* 64, no. 2 (2017): 212–18.

40. Kari Lerum, "Subjects of Desire: Academic Armor, Intimate Ethnography, and the Production of Critical Knowledge," *Qualitative Inquiry* 7, no. 4 (2001): 466–83.

41. Erving Goffman, "On Fieldwork," *Journal of Contemporary Ethnography* 18 (1989): 129.

42. Orrico, "'Doing Intimacy.'"

43. See, e.g., Anselm L. Strauss and Juliet M. Corbin, *Basics of Qualitative Research: Techniques and Procedures for Developing Grounded Theory* (Thousand Oaks, CA: Sage, 1998).

44. Kristen Schilt and Christine Williams, "Access Denied," *Men and Masculinities* 11, no. 2 (2008): 222.

45. Yvonna S. Lincoln, Susan A. Lynham, and Egon G. Guba, "Contractions, and Emerging Confluences, Revisited," in *The Sage Handbook of Qualitative*

Research, 4th ed., edited by Norman K. Denzin and Yvonna S. Lincoln (Thousand Oaks, CA: Sage, 2011), 97–128.

46. Bourdieu and Wacquant, *An Invitation to Reflexive Sociology.*

47. Harding, "After the Neutrality Ideal."

48. Hermanowicz, "The Great Interview," 481.

49. Markowitz and Ashkenazi, *Sex,* 2.

50. Ibid.

51. Smith, "Women's Perspective as a Radical Critique of Sociology."

52. Eva Moreno, "Rape in the Field: Reflections from a Survivor," in Kulick and Willson, *Taboo,* 256.

53. On this point, see Elizabeth A. Armstrong, Miriam Gleckman-Krut, and Lanora Johnson, "Silence, Power, and Inequality: An Intersectional Approach to Sexual Violence," *Annual Review of Sociology* 44 (2018): 99–122.

54. The association of women and pollution is of course a much broader theme. Scholars in a range of disciplines have addressed the capacity of women's bodies to pollute across a variety of cultural contexts and in relation to multiple subjects: menstruation, medicine, promiscuity, pregnancy, breastfeeding, sorcery, and more. For a few examples, see Alison Bashford, *Purity and Pollution: Gender, Embodiment and Victorian Medicine* (New York: Springer, 1998); Shirley Lindenbaum, "Sorcerers, Ghosts, and Polluting Women: An Analysis of Religious Belief and Population Control," *Ethnology* 11, no. 3 (1972): 241–53; Kevin P. Siena, "Pollution, Promiscuity, and the Pox: English Venereology and the Early Modern Medical Discourse on Social and Sexual Danger," *Journal of the History of Sexuality* 8, no. 4 (1998): 553–74. And, of course, women historically have been associated with nature and the body rather than the mind, calling into question their role as knowers in the first place. Susan R. Bordo, *Unbearable Weight: Feminism, Western Culture, and the Body* (Berkeley: University of California, 1993); Evelyn Fox Keller, *Reflections on Gender and Science* (New Haven, CT: Yale University Press, 1985); Sandra Harding, *The Science Question in Feminism* (Ithaca, NY: Cornell University Press, 1986).

55. This is part and parcel, of course, of the ongoing marginalization of women within academia. Danica Savonick and Cathy Davidson, "Gender Bias in Academe: An Annotated Bibliography of Important Recent Studies," HASTAC.org, January 26, 2015, www.hastac.org/blogs/superadmin/2015/01/26/gender-bias-academe-annotated-bibliography-important-recent-studies; Imogen Clark and Andrea Grant, "Sexuality and Danger in the Field: Starting an Uncomfortable Conversation," *Journal of the Anthropological Society of Oxford* 7, no. 1 (2015): 1–14; Moreno, "Rape in the Field."

56. Of course, this also can happen to men studying women-dominated settings. The men whose research Schilt and Williams review tended to blame the site or their subjects for problems with access rather than grappling with the fact that "getting in always requires negotiation, rapport, and persistence." "Access Denied," 222. In contrast, our participants recognized that such efforts were required, but experienced self-doubt and self-blame when those efforts took on a gendered or sexualized undercurrent. For similar findings, see Clark and Grant, "Sexuality and Danger."

57. Esther Newton, "My Best Informant's Dress: The Erotic Equation in Field-work," *Cultural Anthropology* 8, no. 1 (1993): 3–23; Orrico, "'Doing Intimacy.'"

58. Anteby, *Manufacturing Morals.*

59. Moreno, "Rape in the Field."

60. Orrico, "'Doing Intimacy,'" 475; see also Moreno, "Rape in the Field"; Newton, "My Best Informant's Dress."

61. Fujimura, "Sex Genes."

62. Anteby, *Manufacturing Morals.*

CHAPTER TWO. GENDERED BODIES
AND FIELD RESEARCH

1. See Wacquant, "For a Sociology of Flesh and Blood."

2. Maree Burns, "Interviewing: Embodied Communication." *Feminism & Psychology* 13, no. 2 (2003): 1643.

3. Denise Riley, *Am I That Name? Feminism and the Category of "Women" in History* (New York: Springer, 1988), 99; see also Scott, "Evidence of Experience."

4. Sutton, *Bodies in Crisis,* 194.

5. For a slightly different take on the idea of the academic other, see Diane Bell, "Introduction 1: The Context," in *Gendered Fields: Women, Men, and Ethnography,* edited by Diane Bell, Pat Caplan, and Wazir Jahan Karim (New York: Routledge, 1993), 1–18.

6. Pierre Bourdieu, *Distinction: A Social Critique of the Judgment of Taste* (Cambridge, MA: Harvard University Press, 1984).

7. Hordge-Freeman, Mayorga, and Bonilla-Silva, "Exposing Whiteness Because We Are Free."

8. Tukufu Zuberi and Eduardo Bonilla-Silva, *White Logic, White Methods: Racism and Methodology* (Lanham, MD: Rowman & Littlefield, 2008), 17.

9. W. E. B. Du Bois, *The Souls of Black Folk* (Chicago: A. C. McGlurg & Co., 1903).

10. Reger, "Emotions, Objectivity, and Voice," 612.

11. Zuberi and Bonilla-Silva, *White Logic, White Methods,* 17.

12. Dorothy Smith, "A Sociology for Women," in *The Prism of Sex,* edited by Julia A. Sherman (Madison: University of Wisconsin Press, 1979), 138.

13. Bell, "Introduction 1."

14. Researchers in general are discouraged from divulging emotion in their research (see Denzin, "On Understanding Emotion"). However, the reasons that divulging emotion might seem inappropriate depend on the researcher's positionality. For example, while a woman might be labeled irrational or hysterical, a man might be characterized as weak or timid.

15. On this topic, also see Gladys L. Mitchell-Walthour and Elizabeth Hordge-Freeman, *Race and the Politics of Knowledge Production: Diaspora and Black Transnational Scholarship in the United States and Brazil* (London: Palgrave Macmillan, 2016).

16. Smith, "Analysis of Ideological Structures."

17. Ibid., 366.

18. We use the word *girl* here because it evokes youth, innocence, and naïveté, expressing the ways in which research participants viewed women ethnographers' bodies and interacted with them.

19. Women's adherence to social expectations of beauty can also be useful in research with other women. See Burns, "Interviewing: Embodied Communication."

20. Linley Walker, "Chivalrous Masculinity among Juvenile Offenders in Western Sydney: A New Perspective on Young Working Class Men and Crime," *Current Issues in Criminal Justice* 9, no. 3 (1998): 283; see also Karen Lumsden, "'Don't Ask a Woman to Do Another Woman's Job': Gendered Interactions and the Emotional Ethnographer," *Sociology* 43, no. 3 (2009): 497–513.

21. Ruth Milkman, *Farewell to the Factory* (Berkeley: University of California Press, 1997).

22. It is important to keep in mind that in certain contexts, rather than "play up" feminine stereotypes, women must try to "neutralize" their feminine characteristics or risk losing access. For example, some women may wear more gender-neutral clothing to downplay gender and sexuality and appear more professional. See C. J. Pascoe, *Dude You're a Fag: Masculinity and Sexuality in High School* (Berkeley: University of California Press, 2011); Green et al., "'Who Wears the Trousers?'"

23. See Lumsden, "'Don't Ask a Woman.'"

24. At Michelle's request, for the sake of anonymity and confidentiality, we have omitted all identifying characteristics and categories.

25. In cross-cultural research, assumptions associated with women's friendliness can make access extremely difficult to navigate. Bev, a white woman, described not wanting to be too friendly with the immigrant group she was working with because "there are already stereotypes about white women being loose."

26. Janet Foster, "The Dynamics of Gender in Ethnographic Research: A Personal View," *Studies in Qualitative Methodology* 4 (1994): 81–106.

27. Sabine Grenz, "Intersections of Sex and Power in Research on Prostitution: A Female Researcher Interviewing Male Heterosexual Clients," *Signs* 30, no. 4 (2005): 2091–2113.

28. Wacquant, "For a Sociology of Flesh and Blood," 6.

29. Baird, "Dancing with Danger."

30. As Green et al., "Who Wears the Trousers?," found, our participants reported that most inappropriate behavior was instigated by cis men.

31. Shamus R. Khan, *Privilege: The Making of an Adolescent Elite at St. Paul's School* (Princeton, NJ: Princeton University Press, 2011), 116.

32. See Grauerholz et al., "Attraction in the Field."

33. For researchers who have addressed this issue in other disciplines, see Julie Cupples, "The Field as a Landscape of Desire: Sex and Sexuality in Geographical Fieldwork," *Area* 34, no. 4 (2002): 382–90; contributors to Kulick and Willson, *Taboo;* contributors to Markowitz and Ashkenazi, *Sex;* John Osburg, "Meeting the 'Godfather': Fieldwork and Ethnographic Seduction in a Chinese Nightclub," *PoLAR: Political and Legal Anthropology Review* 36, no. 2 (2013): 298–303.

34. Michael Connors Jackman, "The Trouble with Fieldwork: Queering Methodologies," in *Queer Methods and Methodologies: Intersecting Queer Theories and Social Science Research,* edited by Kath Browne and Catherine J. Nash (Burlington, VT: Ashgate, 2010), 124.

35. Grauerholz et al., "Attraction in the Field," 169.

36. E.g., Allen Abramson, "Between Autobiography and Method: Being Male, Seeing Myth and the Analysis of Structures of Gender and Sexuality in the Eastern Interior of Fiji," in Bell, Caplan, and Karim, *Gendered Fields,* 63–77; Paul Rabinow, *Reflections on Fieldwork in Morocco* (Berkeley: University of California Press, 1977); Peter Wade, "Sexuality and Masculinity in Fieldwork among Colombian Blacks," in Bell, Caplan, and Karim, *Gendered Fields,* 199–214.

37. Kathleen M. DeWalt and Billie R. DeWalt, *Participant Observation: A Guide for Fieldworkers* (Lanham, MD: Rowman & Littlefield, 2001).

38. Black women in academia are perhaps most penalized for even the slightest suggestion of sexuality, given that the white gaze has made black women's bodies "synonymous with accessibility, availability" and sexual deviance, as bell hooks has emphasized: "Selling Hot Pussy: Representations of Black Female Sexuality in the Cultural Marketplace," in *Writing on the Body,* edited by Katie Conboy, Nadia Medina, and Sarah Stanbury (New York: Colombia University Press, 1997), 117; also see Berry et al., "Toward a Fugitive Anthropology."

39. H. L. Busier, K. A. Clark, R. A. Esch, C. Glesne, Y. Pigeon, and J. M. Tarule, "Intimacy in Research," *Qualitative Studies in Education* 10, no. 2 (1997): 165–70; Orrico, "'Doing Intimacy.'"

40. Aaron Turner, "Embodied Ethnography: Doing Culture," *Social Anthropology* 8, no. 1 (2000): 53. Turner uses the concept of embodied ethnography to discuss the ways in which researchers are involved in the social processes we study and to advocate for the incorporation of researchers' sensory experiences in our work. While our work overlaps with his, our conceptualization of embodied ethnography uses an intersectional lens to analyze the different ways researchers become a part of, or are locked out of, these social processes.

41. Victor Rios, "Comment on 'Contexts Editors on the Magazine's Ethnography Forum,'" Speak for Sociology (American Sociological Association blog), April 6, 2016.

CHAPTER THREE. SEXUAL HARASSMENT IN THE FIELD

1. Also see Ashleigh E. McKinzie, "Scared to Death: Reflections on Panic and Anxiety in the Field," *Symbolic Interaction* 40, no. 4 (2017): 483–97.

2. We do not go into great detail in describing all cases of harassment or other unwelcome sexual contact in this chapter because many are discussed in other chapters.

3. At Michelle's request, we have left out all identifying characteristics and categories whenever she is mentioned in the book.

4. For powerful accounts of this dynamic, see Berry et al., "Toward a Fugitive Anthropology"; Williams, "#MeToo."

5. Also see Williams, "#MeToo."

6. See Kaitlin M. Boyle and Ashleigh E. McKinzie, "Resolving Negative Affect and Restoring Meaning: Responses to Deflection Produced by Unwanted Sexual Experiences," *Social Psychology Quarterly* 78, no. 2 (2015): 151–72; Justine Tinkler, Sarah Becker, and Kristen A. Clayton, "Kind of Natural, Kind of Wrong: Young People's Beliefs about the Morality, Legality, and Normalcy of Sexual Aggression in Public Drinking Settings," *Law & Social Inquiry* 43, no. 1 (2018): 28–57.

7. Melanie S. Harned, "Understanding Women's Labeling of Unwanted Sexual Experiences," *Violence Against Women* 11, no. 3 (2005): 374–413.

8. Littleton et al., for example, have argued that "unacknowledged" victims may be at greater risk of revictimization than "acknowledged" victims. Heather L. Littleton, Danny Axsom, and Amie Grills-Taquechel, "Sexual Assault Victims' Acknowledgment Status and Revictimization Risk," *Psychology of Women Quarterly* 33, no. 1 (2009): 34–42.

9. Sarah Deer, *The Beginning and End of Rape: Confronting Sexual Violence in Native America* (Minneapolis: University of Minnesota Press, 2015): xvi–xvii.

10. Among others, see Gailey and Prohaska, "Power and Gender Negotiations"; Green et al., "Who Wears the Trousers?"; Barbara Paterson, David Gregory, and Sally Thorne, "A Protocol for Researcher Safety," *Qualitative Health Research* 9, no. 2 (1999): 259–69.

11. Moreno, "Rape in the Field."

CHAPTER FOUR. THE COSTS

1. Heather R. Hlavka, "Normalizing Sexual Violence: Young Women Account for Harassment and Abuse," *Gender & Society* 28, no. 3 (2014): 337–58; see also Elizabeth Stanko, *Intimate Intrusions: Women's Experience of Male Violence* (London: Routledge, 1985).

2. For a review of the literature, see Sara Bastomski and Philip Smith, "Gender, Fear, and Public Places: How Negative Encounters with Strangers Harm Women," *Sex Roles* 76, no. 1–2 (2017): 73–88.

3. Sherryl Kleinman and Martha A. Copp, *Emotions and Fieldwork* (Newbury Park, CA: Sage, 1993), vii.

4. Hlavka, "Normalizing Sexual Violence"; Moreno, "Rape in the Field"; D. L. Tolman, "Doing Desire: Adolescent Girls' Struggles for / with Sexuality," *Gender & Society* 8 (1994): 324–42.

5. Butler, *Doing Gender;* Fine, "Ten Lies of Ethnography"; Tolman, "Doing Desire."

6. On this point, also see Hlavka, "Normalizing Sexual Violence."

7. In this case, woman's "place" is to assume responsibility for harassment, to take the place of the culpable party.

8. Dana Britton, "Beyond the Chilly Climate: The Salience of Gender in Women's Academic Careers," *Gender & Society* 31, no. 1 (2017): 10. Women downplay gendered experiences in other workplaces as well. See, for one example, Deborah A. Harris and Patti Giuffre, *Taking the Heat: Women Chefs and Gender Inequality in the Professional Kitchen* (New Brunswick, NJ: Rutgers University Press, 2015).

9. See also Armstrong, Gleckman-Krut, and Johnson, "Silence, Power, and Inequality."

10. Wacquant, "For a Sociology of Flesh and Blood."

11. As in other chapters, we do not include specific information about Michelle or the site where she worked, which she requested in the interest of anonymity.

12. See also Antonio C. La Pastina, "The Implications of an Ethnographer's Sexuality," *Qualitative Inquiry* 12, no. 4 (2006): 724–35.

13. Jason N. Houle, Jeremy Staff, Jeylan T. Mortimer, Christopher Uggan, and Amy Blackstone, "The Impact of Sexual Harassment on Depressive Symptoms during the Early Occupational Career," *Society and Mental Health* 1, no. 2 (2011): 89–105.

14. La Pastina, "Implications of an Ethnographer's Sexuality."

15. Ibid., 729.

16. Ibid., 727.

17. Ibid., 726.

18. Hoang, *Dealing in Desire,* 192.

19. See also Williams, "#Metoo."

20. Johansson, "Dangerous Liaisons."

21. Britton, "Beyond the Chilly Climate," 7.

22. Richard Tewksbury and Patricia Gagné, "Transgenderists: Products of Non-Normative Intersections of Sex, Gender, and Sexuality," *Journal of Men's Studies* 5, no. 2 (1996): 105–29.

23. Reuben A. Buford May, "When the Methodological Shoe Is on the Other Foot: African American Interviewer and White Interviewees," *Qualitative Sociology* 37 no. 1 (2014): 117–36.

24. Kathleen Blee, "White on White: Interviewing Women in US White Supremacist Groups," in *Racing Research, Researching Race,* edited by France W. Twine and Jonathan W. Warren (New York: New York University Press, 2000), 93–110.

25. Bernadette Barton, "My Auto/Ethnographic Dilemma: Who Owns the Story?," *Qualitative Sociology* 34, no. 3 (2011): 431–45.

26. Aretxaga, *Shattering Silence.*

27. La Pastina, "Implications of an Ethnographer's Sexuality."

28. Wacquant, "For a Sociology of Flesh and Blood."

29. See, e.g., several contributors to Imogen Clark and Andrea Grant, eds., special issue of *Journal of the Anthropological Society of Oxford* 7, no. 1 (2015); Gailey and Prohaska, "Power and Gender Negotiations"; Grauerholz et al., "Attraction in the Field"; Green et al., "Who Wears the Trousers?"; Huff, "The Sexual Harassment of Researchers"; Kloß, "Sexual(ized) Harassment"; Mugge, "Sexually Harassed by

Gatekeepers"; Sharp and Kremer, "The Safety Dance"; Williams, "'Don't Ride the Bus!'"; Yassour-Borochowitz, "'Only If She Is Sexy.'"

30. E.g., those cited in note 29 above as well as Johansson, "Dangerous Liaisons"; Moreno, "Rape in the Field"; Orrico, "'Doing Intimacy'"; Pollard, "Field of Screams."

31. E.g., Dellinger and Williams, "The Locker Room"; Giuffre and Williams, "Boundary Lines"; McLaughlin, Uggen, and Blackstone, "The Economic and Career Effects of Sexual Harassment on Working Women"; Christopher Uggen and Amy Blackstone, "Sexual Harassment as a Gendered Expression of Power," *American Sociological Review* 69, no. 1 (2004): 64–92; Christine L. Williams, Patti A. Giuffre, and Kirsten Dellinger, "Sexuality in the Workplace: Organizational Control, Sexual Harassment, and the Pursuit of Pleasure," *Annual Review of Sociology* 25, no. 1 (1999): 73–93; La Pastina, "Implications of an Ethnographer's Sexuality."

32. E.g., Bolak, "Studying One's Own"; Hoang, *Dealing in Desire;* Elizabeth Hordge-Freeman, "Out of Bounds? Negotiating Researcher Positionality in Brazil," in *Bridging Scholarship and Activism: Reflections from the Frontlines of Collaborative Research,* edited by Bernd Reiter and Ulrich Oslender (East Lansing: Michigan State University Press, 2015); McKinzie, "Scared to Death."

33. Elizabeth A. Hoffman, "Open-Ended Interviews, Power, and Emotional Labor," *Journal of Contemporary Ethnography* 36, no. 3 (2007): 318–46; Paul Atkinson and Martin Hammersley, "Ethnography and Participant Observation," in Denzin and Lincoln, *Handbook of Qualitative Research,* 248–61; James Davies and Dimitrina Spencer, *Emotions in the Field: The Psychology and Anthropology of Fieldwork Experience* (Stanford, CA: Stanford University Press, 2010).

34. Kleinman and Copp, *Emotions and Fieldwork,* vii.

CHAPTER FIVE. CONSTRUCTING KNOWLEDGE

1. Laura L. Ellingson, "Embodied Knowledge: Writing Researchers' Bodies into Qualitative Health Research," *Qualitative Health Research* 16, no. 16 (2006): 298–310.

2. Smith, "Women's Perspective"; Dorothy E. Smith, *The Everyday World as Problematic: A Feminist Sociology* (Toronto: University of Toronto Press, 1987); Harding, *The Science Question;* Hill Collins, *Black Feminist Thought;* Susan R. Bordo, *The Flight to Objectivity: Essays on Cartesianism and Culture* (Albany: State University of New York Press, 1987); Haraway, "Situated Knowledges"; Genevieve Lloyd, "Maleness, Metaphor, and the 'Crisis' of Reason," in *Feminist Social Thought: A Reader,* edited by Diana Tietjens Meyers (New York: Routledge, 2014), 286–300; Genevieve Lloyd, *The Man of Reason: "Male" and "Female" in Western Philosophy* (Minneapolis: University of Minnesota Press, 1993); Linda Martín Alcoff, "On Judging Epistemic Credibility: Is Social Identity Relevant," in *Engendering Rationalities,* edited by Nancy Tuana and Sandra Morgen (Albany: State University of New York Press, 2001), 53–80; Nancy Tuana, Introduction to Tuana and Morgen,

Engendering Rationalities, 1–20. See also Pierre Bourdieu, *The Logic of Practice* (Stanford, CA: Stanford University Press, 1990).

3. Fujimura, "Sex Genes."

4. Ibid., 51.

5. Ibid.

6. There is a long tradition of these associations within philosophy and the social sciences that is too extensive to engage here. For discussions and critiques of these traditions, see Harding, *The Science Question;* Elizabeth A. Grosz, *Volatile Bodies: Toward a Corporeal Feminism* (Bloomington: Indiana University Press, 1994); Sue Curry Jansen, "Is Science a Man? New Feminist Epistemologies and Reconstructions of Knowledge," *Theory and Society* 19, no. 2 (1990): 235–46; Raia Prokhovnik, *Rational Woman: A Feminist Critique of Dichotomy* (Manchester: Manchester University Press, 1999).

7. Vrushali Patil, "The Heterosexual Matrix as Imperial Effect," *Sociological Theory* 36, no. 1 (2018): 1–26.

8. Berry et al., "Toward a Fugitive Anthropology," 567.

9. Johannson, "Dangerous Liaisons," 58, 60.

10. Ibid., 60; James Clifford and George E. Marcus, *Writing Culture: The Poetics and Politics of Ethnography (*Berkeley: University of California Press, 1986).

11. Henrika Kuklick, "After Ishmael: The Fieldwork Tradition and Its Future," in *Anthropological Locations: Boundaries and Grounds of a Field Science,* edited by Akhil Gupta and James Ferguson (Berkeley: University of California Press, 1997), 47–65; Wedeen, "Ethnography as Interpretive Enterprise."

12. www.chronicle.com/article/Vulnerable-Observers-Notes-on/238042.

13. Nancy Chi Cantalupo and William C. Kidder, "A Systematic Look at a Serial Problem: Sexual Harassment of Students by University Faculty" *Utah Law Review* 2018, no. 3 (2018): 671–786.

14. Fredrickson, "When Will the 'Harvey Effect' Reach Academia?"

15. Ibid.

16. Moreno, "Rape in the Field."

17. The exception was for some participants whose advisers were feminists.

18. As noted in previous chapters, Michelle's identifying characteristics have been withheld at her request.

19. Not wanting to make a scene is likely also related to the women's sensitivity to the postcolonial, reflexive critiques discussed above.

20. Victor Rios, *Punished: Policing and the Lives of Black and Latino Boys* (New York: New York University Press, 2011); Rios, "Beyond Power-Blind Ethnography."

21. Rios, "Beyond Power-Blind Ethnography," 99.

22. Mitchell-Walthour and Hordge-Freeman, *Race and the Politics of Knowledge Production;* Rios, "Comment."

23. Kristine Kilanski, "Trust, Intimacy, and Sexual Harassment: What Doing 'Good' Qualitative Research Means for Women in the Field," Panel, Sociologists for Women in Society, Washington, DC, February 2015.

24. E.g., Strauss and Corbin, *Basics of Qualitative Research.*

25. Schilt and Williams, "Access Denied," 222.

26. Williams, "#MeToo."

27. Sonya Sharma, Sheryl Reimer-Kirkham, and Marie Cochrane, "Practicing the Awareness of Embodiment in Qualitative Health Research: Methodological Reflections," *Qualitative Health Research* 19, no. 11 (2009): 1647.

28. Ibid., 1648.

29. Smith, "Women's Perspective," 7. As we note in the introduction, the effects of this system of knowledge are intersectional, meaning here that people who are disadvantaged by this system in some contexts (such as white women) may derive benefits from it in others.

30. Sutton, *Bodies in Crisis*.

31. Scheper-Hughes, "Introduction."

32. Ruth Behar, *The Vulnerable Observer* (Boston: Beacon Press, 1996).

33. Ibid., 5–6.

34. Sharma, Reimer-Kirkham, and Cochrane, "Practicing the Awareness," 1648.

35. Hordge-Freeman, "Out of Bounds?"

36. Ibid., 131.

37. Ibid., 123.

38. Mitchell-Walthour and Hordge-Freeman, *Race and the Politics of Knowledge Production*.

39. Karen Throsby and Debra Gimlin, "Critiquing Thinness and Wanting to Be Thin," in *Secrecy and Silence in the Research Process: Feminist Reflections,* edited by Róisín Ryan-Flood and Rosalind Gill (New York: Routledge, 2010), 114; original emphasis.

40. Jennifer Randles, "Pregnant Embodiment and Field Research," in *The Oxford Handbook of the Sociology of Bodies and Embodiment,* edited by Natalie Boero and Kate Mason (Oxford: Oxford University Press, 2018).

41. Also see Sutton, *Bodies in Crisis,* 14, for a discussion of how her pregnancy shaped her research and the data she gathered.

42. Randles, "Pregnant Embodiment."

43. Burns, "Interviewing."

44. Ibid., 232.

45. Fujimura, "Sex Genes," 67.

CHAPTER SIX. MOVING FORWARD

1. Because we provide recommendations for moving away from solitary research in chapters 3 and 4, here we focus primarily on teaching and writing about intimacy and danger. However, we would like to reiterate the need to move away from "lone wolf" research by envisioning, valuing, and funding ethnographic projects in ways that do not isolate or individualize the research experience. For further reading on collaborative research projects, see Javier Auyero, ed., *Invisible in Austin: Life and Labor in an American City* (Austin: University of Texas Press, 2015); Baiocchi

et al., *The Civic Imagination;* Victor Rios, *Human Targets: Schools, Police, and the Criminalization of Latino Youth* (Chicago: University of Chicago Press, 2017).

2. Orrico, "'Doing Intimacy,'" 475; see also Moreno, "Rape in Field"; Newton, "My Best Informant's Dress."

3. Syed Ali and Philip Cohen, eds., "How to Do Ethnography Right," *Contexts* 15, no. 2 (2016): 10–19. In this collection, Kimberly Kay Hoang and Rhacel Salazar Parreñas write about researching women sex workers but focus on sampling strategies. Both authors do reflect on gender and sexuality in the field in other published work.

4. Rios, "Beyond Power-Blind Ethnography."

5. Rios, *Punished.*

6. Gloria González-López, "Mindful Ethics: Comments on Informant-Centered Practices in Sociological Research," *Qualitative Sociology* 34 (2011): 447–61; Valerie Malhotra Bentz and Jeremy J. Shapiro, *Mindful Inquiry in Social Research* (Thousand Oaks, CA: Sage, 1998); Adjepong, "Invading Ethnography"; Behar, *The Vulnerable Observer;* Harding, "Whose Science?"; Haraway, "Situated Knowledges"; Pierre Bourdieu, *Science of Science and Reflexivity* (Cambridge: Polity Press, 2004); Michael Burawoy, "The Extended Case Method," *Sociological Theory* 16, no. 1 (1998): 1–33.

7. Johansson, "Dangerous Liaisons," 62.

8. See Kenneth F. Ferraro, "Women's Fear of Victimization: Shadow of Sexual Assault?" *Social Forces* 75 1996): 667–90; Jocelyn A. Hollander, "Vulnerability and Dangerousness: The Construction of Gender through Conversation about Violence," *Gender & Society* 15 (2001): 83–109.

9. Hollander, "Vulnerability and Dangerousness," 84.

10. Kristine Kilanski, "A Boom for Whom? Gender, Labor, and Community in a Modern Day Oil Boomtown" (PhD dissertation, University of Texas–Austin, 2015). See also Stephanie Riger and Margaret T. Gordon "The Fear of Rape: A Study in Social Control," *Journal of Social Issues* 37 (1981): 71–92; Gill Valentine, "The Geography of Women's Fear," *Area* 21 (1989): 385–90.

11. Ferraro, "Women's Fear of Victimization."

12. Elizabeth Kenyon and Sheila Hawker, "'Once Would Be Enough': Some Reflections on the Issue of Safety for Lone Researchers," *International Journal of Social Research Methodology* 2, no. 4 (1999): 313–27.

13. Stephanie Bonnes, "The Bureaucratic Harassment of U.S. Servicewomen," *Gender & Society* 31, no. 6 (2017): 804–29. Bonnes finds that organizational and bureaucratic features in the military, such as discretion, hierarchy, and the blending of work and personal life, allow for the manipulation of administrative rules and regulations in ways that negatively influence women's personal lives and careers.

14. Berry et al., "Toward a Fugitive Anthropology," 560.

15. See Robin G. Nelson, Julienne N. Rutherford, Katie Hinde, and Kathryn B. H. Clancy. "Signaling Safety: Characterizing Fieldwork Experiences and Their Implications for Career Trajectories." *American Anthropologist* 119, no. 4 (2017): 710–22.

16. Wacquant, "For a Sociology of Flesh and Blood," 5.

17. Putting oneself in harm's way for research may garner accolades and respect within academia. However, our research suggests that gender and race can mitigate the praise a scholar receives for conducting dangerous research. The fact that not all researchers accrue academic capital by adhering to the ethnographic fixations demonstrates the androcentric and racialized systems on which such evaluation is based.

18. Stacey, "Can There Be a Feminist Ethnography?"

19. Berry et al., "Toward a Fugitive Anthropology," 539.

20. Rios, *Human Targets,* 176.

21. See Anteby, *Manufacturing Morals.*

22. Rios, *Punished,* 176.

23. Adjepong, "Invading Ethnography."

24. Contreras, *The Stickup Kids;* Hoang, *Dealing in Desire.*

25. Sprague, *Feminist Methodologies,* 236.

26. Bourdieu, of course, was a champion of such collective reflexivity. See Bourdieu and Wacquant, *An Invitation to Reflexive Sociology.*

27. Berry et al., "Toward a Fugitive Anthropology," 538; original emphasis.

28. Sprague, *Feminist Methodologies,* 236.

29. Contreras, *The Stickup Kids;* Sutton, *Bodies in Crisis.*

30. Turner, "Embodied Ethnography," 53.

31. Also see Berry et al., "Toward a Fugitive Anthropology."

32. Armstrong, Gleckman-Krut, and Johnson, "Silence, Power, and Inequality."

33. We thank Christine Williams for this point.

34. It is important to recognize that Tarana Burke started the grassroots #MeToo movement in 2006, long before numerous allegations against Harvey Weinstein in 2017 catalyzed the movement and corresponding hashtag national headlines.

35. Steven Lubet, *Interrogating Ethnography* (Oxford: Oxford University Press, 2017).

36. Burawoy, "The Extended Case Method."

37. Berry et al., "Toward a Fugitive Ethnography."

38. Rios, *Human Targets,* 187.

39. Rios, *Human Targets.*

40. Linda Tuhiwai Smith, *Decolonizing Methodologies: Research and Indigenous Peoples* (London: Zed Books, 1999).

41. Adjepong, "Invading Ethnography."

42. Karen Kelsky, "A Crowdsourced Survey of Sexual Harassment in the Academy" The Professor Is In, December 1, 2017, https://theprofessorisin .com/2017/12/01/a-crowdsourced-survey-of-sexual-harassment-in-the-academy/.

REFERENCES

Abramson, Allen. "Between Autobiography and Method: Being Male, Seeing Myth and the Analysis of Structures of Gender and Sexuality in the Eastern Interior of Fiji." In *Gendered Fields: Women, Men and Ethnography,* edited by Diane Bell, Pat Caplan, and Wazir Jahan Karim, 63–77. New York: Routledge, 1993.

Acker, Joan. "Hierarchies, Jobs, Bodies: A Theory of Gendered Organizations." *Gender and Society* 4, no. 2 (1990): 139–58.

Adjepong, Anima. "Invading Ethnography: A Queer of Color Reflexive Practice." *Ethnography* (2017), https://doi.org/10.1177/1466138117741502.

Ali, Syed, and Philip Cohen, eds. "How to Do Ethnography Right." *Contexts* 15, no. 2 (2016): 10–19.

Anteby, Michel. *Manufacturing Morals: The Values of Silence in Business School Education.* Chicago: University of Chicago Press, 2013.

Appadurai, Arjun. "Discussion: Fieldwork in the Era of Globalization." *Anthropology and Humanism* 22, no. 1 (2008): 115–18.

Aretxaga, Begoña. *Shattering Silence: Women, Nationalism, and Political Subjectivity in Northern Ireland.* Princeton, NJ: Princeton University Press, 1997.

Armstrong, Elizabeth A., Miriam Gleckman-Krut, and Lanora Johnson. "Silence, Power, and Inequality: An Intersectional Approach to Sexual Violence." *Annual Review of Sociology* 4 (2018): 99–122.

Atkinson, Paul, and Martin Hammersley. "Ethnography and Participant Observation." In *Handbook of Qualitative Research,* edited by Norman K. Denzin and Yvonna S. Lincoln, 248–61. Thousand Oaks, CA: Sage, 1994.

Auyero, Javier, ed. *Invisible in Austin: Life and Labor in an American City* Austin: University of Texas Press, 2015.

Baiocchi, Gianpaolo, et al. *The Civic Imagination: Making a Difference in American Political Life.* New York: Paradigm, 2014.

Baird, Adam. "Dancing with Danger: Ethnographic Safety, Male Bravado and Gang Research in Colombia." *Qualitative Research* 18, no. 3 (2018): 342–60.

Bartky, Sandra Lee. "Foucault, Femininity, and the Modernization of Patriarchal Power." In *Feminism and Foucault,* edited by Irene Diamond and Lee Quinby, 61–86. Boston: Northeastern University Press, 1988.

Barton, Bernadette. "My Auto/Ethnographic Dilemma: Who Owns the Story?" *Qualitative Sociology* 34, no. 3 (2011): 431–45.

Bashford, Alison. *Purity and Pollution: Gender, Embodiment and Victorian Medicine.* New York: Springer, 1998.

Bastomski, Sara, and Philip Smith. "Gender, Fear, and Public Places: How Negative Encounters with Strangers Harm Women." *Sex Roles* 76, no. 1–2 (2017): 73–88.

Beale, Frances. "Double Jeopardy: To Be Black and Female." In *The Black Woman,* edited by Toni Cade, 90–110. New York: Signet, 1970.

Behar, Ruth. *The Vulnerable Observer.* Boston: Beacon Press, 1996.

Bell, Diane. "Introduction 1: The Context." In *Gendered Fields: Women, Men, and Ethnography,* edited by Diane Bell, Pat Caplan, and Wazir Jahan Karim, 1–18. New York: Routledge, 1993.

Bell, Diane, Pat Caplan, and Wazir Jahan Karim, eds. *Gendered Fields: Women, Men and Ethnography.* New York: Routledge, 1993.

Berry, Maya J., Claudia Cháves Argüelles, Shanya Cordis, Sarah Ihmoud, and Elizabeth Velásquez Estrada. "Toward a Fugitive Anthropology: Gender, Race, and Violence in the Field." *Cultural Anthropology* 32, no. 4 (2017): 537–65.

Bhardwa, Bina. "Alone, Asian, and Female: The Unspoken Challenges of Conducting Fieldwork in Dance Settings." *Journal of Electronic Dance Music Culture* 5, no. 1 (2013): 39–60.

Blee, Kathleen. "White on White: Interviewing Women in US White Supremacist Groups." In *Racing Research, Researching Race,* edited by France W. Twine and Jonathan W. Warren, 93–110. New York: New York University Press, 2000.

Blumer, Herbert. *Symbolic Interactionism.* Berkeley: University of California Press, 1969.

Bolak, Hale C. "Studying One's Own in the Middle East: Negotiating Gender and Self-Other Dynamics in the Field." In *Reflexivity and Voice,* edited by Rosanna Hertz, 95–118. Thousand Oaks, CA: Sage, 1997.

Bordo, Susan R. "The Body and the Reproduction of Femininity." In *Writing on the Body,* edited by Katie Conboy, Nadia Medina, and Sarah Stanbury, 90–110. New York: Colombia University Press, 1997.

———. *The Flight to Objectivity: Essays on Cartesianism and Culture.* Albany: State University of New York Press, 1987.

———. *Unbearable Weight: Feminism, Western Culture, and the Body.* Berkeley: University of California, 1993.

Bonnes, Stephanie. "The Bureaucratic Harassment of U.S. Servicewomen." *Gender & Society* 31, no. 6 (2017): 804–29.

Bourdieu, Pierre. *Distinction: A Social Critique of the Judgment of Taste.* Cambridge, MA: Harvard University Press, 1984.

———. "The Forms of Capital." In *Handbook of Theory and Research for the Sociology of Education,* edited by John G. Richardson, 241–58. New York: Greenwood Press, 1986.

———. *The Logic of Practice.* Stanford, CA: Stanford University Press, 1990.

———. *Science of Science and Reflexivity.* Cambridge: Polity Press, 2004.

Bourdieu, Pierre, and Loïc Wacquant. *An Invitation to Reflexive Sociology.* Chicago: University of Chicago Press, 1992.

Boyle, Kaitlin M., and Ashleigh E. McKinzie. "Resolving Negative Affect and Restoring Meaning: Responses to Deflection Produced by Unwanted Sexual Experiences." *Social Psychology Quarterly* 78, no. 2 (2015): 151–72.

Britton, Dana. "Beyond the Chilly Climate: The Salience of Gender in Women's Academic Careers." *Gender & Society* 31, no. 1 (2017): 5–27.

Buchanan, NiCole T., and Alayne J. Ormerod. 2002. "Racialized Sexual Harassment in the Lives of African American Women." *Women & Therapy* 25, no. 3–4 (2002): 107–24.

Burawoy, Michael. "Critical Sociology: A Dialogue between Two Sciences." *Contemporary Sociology* 27, no. 1 (1998): 12–20.

———. "The Extended Case Method." *Sociological Theory* 16, no. 1 (1998): 1–33.

Burns, Maree. "Interviewing: Embodied Communication." *Feminism & Psychology* 13, no. 2 (2003): 229–36.

Busier, H. L., K. A. Clark, R. A. Esch, C. Glesne, Y. Pigeon, and J. M. Tarule. "Intimacy in Research." *Qualitative Studies in Education* 10, no. 2 (1997): 165–70.

Butler, Judith. *Gender Trouble.* New York: Routledge, 1990.

———. "Performative Acts and Gender Constitution: An Essay in Phenomenology and Feminist Theory." In *Writing on the Body: Female Embodiment and Feminist Theory,* edited by Katie Conboy, Nadia Medina, and Sarah Stanbury, 401–18. New York: Columbia University Press, 1997.

Cano, Annmarie. "The Credibility Gap in Academe." *Chronicle of Higher Education,* December 6, 2017. www.chronicle.com/article/The-Credibility-Gap-in-Academe/241980?cid=at&utm_source=at&utm_medium=en&elqTrackId=4895322c04c54eb9beea73b1ce1f4edb&elq=a6753c5c75c04d9a88608d92625f3f5a&elqaid=17027&elqat=1&elqCampaignId=7382.

Cantalupo, Nancy Chi, and William C. Kidder. "A Systematic Look at a Serial Problem: Sexual Harassment of Students by University Faculty." *Utah Law Review* no. 3 (2017): 671–786.

Clancy, Kathryn B. H., Robin G. Nelson, Julienne N. Rutherford, and Katie Hinde. "Survey of Academic Field Experiences: Trainees Report Harassment and Assault." *PLOS One* 9, no. 7 (2014), https://doi.org/10.1371/journal.pone.0102172.

Clark, Imogen, and Andrea Grant. "Sexuality and Danger in the Field: Starting an Uncomfortable Conversation." *Journal of the Anthropological Society of Oxford* 7, no. 1 (2015): 1–14.

Clausen, John A., ed. *Socialization and Society.* Boston: Little, Brown, 1968.

Clifford, James, and George E. Marcus. *Writing Culture: The Poetics and Politics of Ethnography.* Berkeley: University of California Press, 1986.

Cohen, Jeffrey H. 2000. "Problems in the Field: Participant Observation and the Assumption of Neutrality." *Field Methods* 12, no. 4 (2000): 316–33.

Contreras, Randol. *The Stickup Kids: Race, Drugs, Violence, and the American Dream.* Berkeley: University of California Press, 2012.

Crenshaw, Kimberle. "Mapping the Margins: Intersectionality, Identity Politics, and Violence against Women of Color." *Stanford Law Review* 43 no. 6 (1991): 1241–99.

Csordas, Thomas. "Introduction: The Body as Representation and Being-in-the-World." In *Embodiment and Experience: The Existential Ground of Culture and Self,* edited by Thomas Csordas, 1–26. Cambridge: Cambridge University Press, 1997.

Cupples, Julie. "The Field as a Landscape of Desire: Sex and Sexuality in Geographical Fieldwork." *Area* 34, no. 4 (2002): 382–90.

Davies, James, and Dimitrina Spencer. *Emotions in the Field: The Psychology and Anthropology of Fieldwork Experience.* Stanford, CA: Stanford University Press, 2010.

Davis, Angela. *Women, Race, and Class.* New York: Random House, 1981.

Deegan, Mary Jo. *Jane Addams and the Men of the Chicago School.* New Brunswick, NJ: Transaction Press, 1988.

Deer, Sarah. *The Beginning and End of Rape: Confronting Sexual Violence in Native America.* Minneapolis: University of Minnesota Press, 2015.

Dellinger, Kirsten, and Christine Williams. "The Locker Room and the Dorm Room: Workplace Norms and the Boundaries of Sexual Harassment in Magazine Editing." *Social Problems* 49, no. 2 (2002): 242–57.

Denzin, Norman K. "On Understanding Emotion: The Interpretive-Cultural Agenda." In *Research Agendas in the Sociology of Emotion,* edited by Theodor Kemper, 85–116. Albany: State University of New York Press, 1990.

———. *Symbolic Interactionism and Cultural Studies: The Politics of Interpretation.* Cambridge, MA: Blackwell, 2008.

DeWalt, Kathleen M., and Billie R. DeWalt. *Participant Observation: A Guide for Fieldworkers.* Lanham, MD: Rowman & Littlefield, 2001.

Doucet, Andrea, and Natasha S. Mauthner. "Feminist Methodologies and Epistemology." In *21st Century Sociology,* edited by Clifton D. Bryant and Dennis L. Peck., 11–36. New York: Sage, 2006.

Du Bois, W. E. B. *The Souls of Black Folk.* Chicago: A. C. McGlurg & Co., 1903.

Ellingson, Laura L. "Embodied Knowledge: Writing Researchers' Bodies into Qualitative Health Research." *Qualitative Health Research* 16 (2006): 298–310.

Ellis, Carolyn. 2009. "Fighting Back or Moving On: An Authoethnographic Response to Critics." *International Review of Qualitative Research* 3, no. 2 (2009): 371–78.

Ellmann, Mary. *Thinking about Women.* New York: Harcourt Brace Jovanovich, 1968.

Ferraro, Kenneth F. "Women's Fear of Victimization: Shadow of Sexual Assault?" *Social Forces* 75 (1996): 667–90.

Ferrell, Jeff, and Mark S. Hamm. *Ethnography at the Edge: Crime, Deviance, and Field Research.* Boston: Northeastern University Press, 1998.

Fine, Gary Alan. "Ten Lies of Ethnography: Moral Dilemmas of Field Research." *Journal of Contemporary Ethnography* 22, no. 3 (1993): 267–94.

Flaherty, Colleen. "'Holding Space' for Victims of Harassment." *Inside Higher Ed,* December 8, 2017, www.insidehighered.com/news/2017/12/08/what-can-crowdsourced-survey-sexual-harassment-academia-tell-us-about-problem.

Foster, Janet. "The Dynamics of Gender in Ethnographic Research: A Personal View." *Studies in Qualitative Methodology* 4 (1994): 81–106.

Foucault, Michel. *Discipline and Punish: The Birth of the Prison.* New York: Random House, [1977] 1995.

———. *The Order of Things.* New York: Vintage, [1966] 1994.

Fredrickson, Carolina. "When Will the 'Harvey Effect' Reach Academia?" *The Atlantic,* October 30, 2017, www.theatlantic.com/education/archive/2017/10/when-will-the-harvey-effect-reach-academia/544388/.

Fujimura, Joan H. "Sex Genes: A Critical Sociomaterial Approach to the Politics and Molecular Genetics of Sex Determination." *Signs* 32, no. 1 (2006): 49–82.

Gailey, Jeannine A., and Ariane Prohaska. "Power and Gender Negotiations during Interviews with Men about Sex and Sexually Degrading Practices." *Qualitative Research* 11, no. 4 (2011): 365–80.

Gatrell, Caroline. "Interviewing Fathers: Feminist Dilemmas in Fieldwork." *Journal of Gender Studies* 15, no. 3 (2006): 237–51.

Giere, Ronald R. "The Feminism Question in the Philosophy of Science." In *Feminism, Science, and the Philosophy of Science,* edited by Lynn Hankinson Nelson and Jack Nelson, 3–16. London: Kluwer Academic, 1997.

Gill, Fiona, and Catherine Maclean. "Knowing Your Place: Gender and Reflexivity in Two Ethnographies." *Sociological Research Online* 7, no. 2 (2002): 1–11.

Gilmore, Sarah, and Kate Kenny. "Work-Worlds Colliding: Self-Reflexivity, Power and Emotion in Organizational Ethnography." *Human Relations* 68, no. 1 (2015): 55–78.

Giuffre, Patti A., and Christine L. Williams. "Boundary Lines: Labeling Sexual Harassment in Restaurants." *Gender & Society* 8, no. 3 (1994): 378–401.

Glebbeek, Marie-Louise. *In the Crossfire of Democracy: Police Reform and Police Practice in Post–Civil War Guatemala.* West Lafayette, IN: Purdue University Press, 2004.

Gluckman, Nell. "What Happens When Sex Harassment Disrupts Victims' Academic Careers." *Chronicle of Higher Education,* December 28, 2017, www-chronicle-com.lp.hscl.ufl.edu/article/What-Happens-When-Sex/241994.

Goffman, Alice. *On the Run: Fugitive Life in an American City.* Chicago: University of Chicago Press, 2015.

Goffman, Erving. "On Fieldwork." *Journal of Contemporary Ethnography* 18 (1989): 123–32.

González-López, Gloria. "Mindful Ethics: Comments on Informant-Centered Practices in Sociological Research." *Qualitative Sociology* 34 (2011): 447–61.

Gramsci, Antonio. *Selections from the Prison Notebooks of Antonio Gramsci*. Edited by Quintin Hoare and Geoffrey Nowell-Smith. New York: International Publishers, 1971.

Grauerholz, Liz, Mandi Barringer, Timothy Colyer, Nicholas Guittar, Jaime Hecht, Rachel L. Rayburn, and Elizabeth Swart. "Attraction in the Field: What We Need to Acknowledge and Implications for Research and Teaching." *Qualitative Inquiry* 19, no. 3 (2013): 167–78.

Green, Gill, Rosaline S. Barbour, Marina Barnard, and Jenny Kizinger. "Who Wears the Trousers? Sexual Harassment in Research Settings." *Women's Studies International Forum* 16, no. 6 (1993): 627–37.

Greenhill, Pauline. "Epistemological Reflections on Sex and Fieldwork." *Resources for Feminist Research* 32, no. 3–4 (2007): 87–99.

Grenz, Sabine. "Intersections of Sex and Power in Research on Prostitution: A Female Researcher Interviewing Male Heterosexual Clients." *Signs* 30, no. 4 (2005): 2091–2113.

Grosz, Elizabeth A. *Volatile Bodies: Toward a Corporeal Feminism*. Bloomington: Indiana University Press, 1994.

Gurney, Joan N. "Not One of the Guys: The Female Researcher in a Male-Dominated Setting." *Qualitative Sociology* 8, no. 1 (1985): 42–62.

Hanson, Rebecca, and Patricia Richards. "Sexual Harassment and the Construction of Ethnographic Knowledge." *Sociological Forum* 32, no. 3 (2017): 587–609.

Haraway, Donna. "Situated Knowledges: The Science Question in Feminism as a Site of Discourse on the Privilege of Partial Perspective." *Feminist Studies* 14 (1988): 575–99.

Harding, Sandra. "After the Neutrality Ideal: Science, Politics, and Strong Objectivity." *Social Research* 59, no. 3 (1992): 567–87.

———. "Feminism, Science and the Anti-Enlightenment Critiques." In *Feminism/Postmodernism*, edited by Linda J. Nicholson, 83–106. New York: Routledge, 1990.

———. *The Science Question in Feminism*. Ithaca, NY: Cornell University Press, 1986.

———. 1991. *Whose Science? Whose Knowledge?* Ithaca, NY: Cornell University Press, 1991.

Harned, Melanie S. "Understanding Women's Labeling of Unwanted Sexual Experiences." *Violence Against Women* 11, no. 3 (2005): 374–413.

Harris, Deborah A., and Patti Giuffre. *Taking the Heat: Women Chefs and Gender Inequality in the Professional Kitchen*. New Brunswick, NJ: Rutgers University Press, 2015.

Hermanowicz, Joseph C. "The Great Interview: 25 Strategies for Studying People in Bed." *Qualitative Sociology* 25, no. 4 (2002): 479–99.

Hesse-Biber, Sharlene Nagy, and Patricia Leavy. *The Practice of Qualitative Research*. 2nd ed. Los Angeles: Sage, 2011.

Hill Collins, Patricia. 1990. *Black Feminist Thought*. New York: Routledge.

———. 1986. "Learning from the Outsider Within: The Sociological Significance of Black Feminist Thought." *Social Problems* 33, no. 6 (1986): 14–32.

Hlavka, Heather R. "Normalizing Sexual Violence: Young Women Account for Harassment and Abuse." *Gender & Society* 28, no. 3 (2014): 337–58.

Hoang, Kimberly Kay. *Dealing in Desire: Asian Ascendancy, Western Decline, and the Hidden Currencies of Global Sex Work.* Berkeley: University of California Press, 2015.

Hoffmann, Elizabeth A. "Open-Ended Interviews, Power, and Emotional Labor." *Journal of Contemporary Ethnography* 36, no. 3 (2007): 318–46.

Hollander, Jocelyn A. "Vulnerability and Dangerousness: The Construction of Gender through Conversation about Violence." *Gender & Society* 15 (2001): 83–109.

hooks, bell. *Feminist Theory: From Margin to Center.* Boston: South End Press, 1984.

———. "Selling Hot Pussy: Representations of Black Female Sexuality in the Cultural Marketplace." In *Writing on the Body,* edited by Katie Conboy, Nadia Medina, and Sarah Stanbury, 113–28. New York: Colombia University Press, 1997.

Hordge-Freeman, Elizabeth. "Out of Bounds? Negotiating Researcher Positionality in Brazil." In *Bridging Scholarship and Activism: Reflections from the Frontlines of Collaborative Research,* edited by Bernd Reiter and Ulrich Oslender, 123–33. East Lansing: Michigan State University Press, 2015.

Hordge-Freeman, Elizabeth, Sarah Mayorga, and Eduardo Bonilla-Silva. "Exposing Whiteness Because We Are Free: Emancipation Methodological Practice in Becoming Empowered Sociologists of Color." In *Rethinking Race and Objectivity in Research Methods,* edited by John Stanfield, 95–121. New York: Left Coast Press, 2011.

Houle, Jason N., Jeremy Staff, Jeylan T. Mortimer, Christopher Uggen, and Amy Blackstone. "The Impact of Sexual Harassment on Depressive Symptoms during the Early Occupational Career." *Society and Mental Health* 1, no. 2 (2011): 89–105.

Huang, Mingwei. "Vulnerable Observers: Notes on Fieldwork and Rape." *Chronicle of Higher Education,* October 12, 2016, www.chronicle.com/article/Vulnerable-Observers-Notes-on/238042.

Huff, Jennifer. "The Sexual Harassment of Researchers by Research Subjects: Lessons from the Field." In *Researching Sexual Violence against Women,* edited by Martin D. Schwartz, 115–27. Thousand Oaks, CA: Sage, 1997.

Huggins, Martha Knisely, and Marie-Louise Glebbeek. *Women Fielding Danger: Negotiating Ethnographic Identities in Field Research.* Lanham, MD: Rowman & Littlefield, 2009.

Irwin, Katherine. "Into the Dark Heart of Ethnography: The Lived Ethics and Inequality of Intimate Field Relationships." *Qualitative Sociology* 29 (2006): 155–75.

Jackman, Michael Connors. "The Trouble with Fieldwork: Queering Methodologies." In *Queer Methods and Methodologies: Intersecting Queer Theories and Social Science Research,* edited by Kath Browne and Catherine J. Nash, 112–28. Burlington, VT: Ashgate, 2010.

Jansen, Sue Curry. "Is Science a Man? New Feminist Epistemologies and Reconstructions of Knowledge." *Theory and Society* 19, no. 2 (1990): 235–46.

Johansson, Leanne. "Dangerous Liaisons: Risk, Positionality and Power in Women's Anthropological Fieldwork." *Journal of the Anthropological Society of Oxford* 7, no. 1 (2015): 55–63.

Kanter, Rosabeth Moss. *Men and Women of the Corporation.* New York: Basic Books, 1977.

Keller, Evelyn Fox. *Reflections on Gender and Science.* New Haven, CT: Yale University Press, 1985.

Kelsky, Karen. "A Crowdsourced Survey of Sexual Harassment in the Academy," The Professor Is In, December 1, 2017, https://theprofessorisin.com/2017/12/01/a-crowdsourced-survey-of-sexual-harassment-in-the-academy/.

Kenyon, Elizabeth, and Sheila Hawker. 1999. "'Once Would Be Enough': Some Reflections on the Issue of Safety for Lone Researchers." *International Journal Social Research Methodology* 2, no. 4 (1999): 313–27.

Khan, Shamus R. *Privilege: The Making of an Adolescent Elite at St. Paul's School.* Princeton, NJ: Princeton University Press, 2011.

Kilanski, Kristine. "A Boom for Whom? Gender, Labor, and Community in a Modern Day Oil Boomtown." PhD dissertation, University of Texas at Austin, 2015.

———. "Trust, Intimacy, and Sexual Harassment: What Doing 'Good' Qualitative Research Means for Women in the Field." Paper presented at the winter meeting of Sociologists for Women in Society, Washington, DC, February 2015.

Kleinman, Sherryl, and Martha A. Copp. *Emotions and Fieldwork.* Newbury Park, CA: Sage, 1993.

Kloß, Sinah Theres. "Sexual(ized) Harassment and Ethnographic Fieldwork: A Silenced Aspect of Social Research." *Ethnography* 18, no. 3 (2017): 396–414.

Kosygina, Larisa V. "Doing Gender in Research: Reflection on Experience in Field." *Qualitative Report* 10, no. 1 (2005): 87–95.

Kuklick, Henrika. "After Ishmael: The Fieldwork Tradition and Its Future." In *Anthropological Locations: Boundaries and Grounds of a Field Science,* edited by Akhil Gupta and James Ferguson, 47–65. Berkeley: University of California Press, 1997.

Kulick, Don, and Margaret Willson, eds. *Taboo: Sex, Identity and Erotic Subjectivity in Anthropological Fieldwork.* New York: Routledge, 1995.

Langer, E. J. *Mindfulness.* New York: Addison-Wesley, 1989.

La Pastina, Antonio C. "The Implications of an Ethnographer's Sexuality." *Qualitative Inquiry* 12, no. 4 (2006): 724–35.

Lee, Deborah. "Interviewing Men: Vulnerabilities and Dilemmas." *Women's Studies International Forum* 20, no. 4 (1997): 553–64.

Lee, Raymond M. *Dangerous Fieldwork.* Thousand Oaks, CA: Sage, 1995.

Lerum, Kari. "Subjects of Desire: Academic Armor, Intimate Ethnography, and the Production of Critical Knowledge." *Qualitative Inquiry* 7, no. 4 (2001): 466–83.

Lincoln, Yvonna S., Susan A. Lynham, and Egon G. Guba. "Contractions, and Emerging Confluences, Revisited." In *The Sage Handbook of Qualitative Research,* 4th ed., edited by Norman K. Denzin and Yvonna S. Lincoln, 97–128. Thousand Oaks, CA: Sage, 2011.

Lindenbaum, Shirley. "Sorcerers, Ghosts, and Polluting Women: An Analysis of Religious Belief and Population Control." *Ethnology* 11, no. 3 (1972): 241–53.

Littleton, Heather L., Danny Axsom, and Amie Grills-Taquechel. 2009. "Sexual Assault Victims' Acknowledgment Status and Revictimization Risk." *Psychology of Women Quarterly* 33, no. 1 (2009): 34–42.

Lloyd, Genevieve. "Maleness, Metaphor, and the 'Crisis' of Reason." In *Feminist Social Thought: A Reader,* edited by Diana Tietjens Meyers, 286–300. New York: Routledge, 2014.

———. *The Man of Reason: "Male" and "Female" in Western Philosophy.* Minneapolis: University of Minnesota Press, 1993.

Lubet, Steven. *Interrogating Ethnography.* Oxford: Oxford University Press, 2017.

Lugones, María. 2008. "The Coloniality of Gender." *Worlds and Knowledges Otherwise,* https://globalstudies.trinity.duke.edu/wp-content/themes/cgsh/materials/WKO/v2d2_Lugones.pdf.

Lumsden, Karen. "'Don't Ask a Woman to Do Another Woman's Job': Gendered Interactions and the Emotional Ethnographer." *Sociology* 43, no. 3 (2009): 497–513.

Malhotra Bentz, Valerie, and Jeremy J. Shapiro. *Mindful Inquiry in Social Research.* Thousand Oaks, CA: Sage, 1998.

Markowitz, Fran, and Michael Ashkenazi, eds. *Sex, Sexuality, and the Anthropologist.* Champaign: University of Illinois Press, 1999.

Marshall, Catherine, and Gretchen Rossman. *Designing Qualitative Research.* Thousand Oaks, CA: Sage, 2010.

Martín Alcoff, Linda. "On Judging Epistemic Credibility: Is Social Identity Relevant?" In *Engendering Rationalities,* edited by Nancy Tuana and Sandra Morgen, 53–80. Albany: State University of New York Press, 2001.

May, Reuben A. Buford. "When the Methodological Shoe Is on the Other Foot: African American Interviewer and White Interviewees." *Qualitative Sociology* 37, no. 1 (2014): 117–36.

McCorkel, Jill A. "Embodied Surveillance and the Gendering of Punishment." *Journal of Contemporary Ethnography* 32, no. 1 (2003): 41–76.

McCorkel, Jill A., and Kristen Myers. 2003. "What Difference Does Difference Make? Position and Privilege in the Field." *Qualitative Sociology* 26, no. 2 (2003): 199–231.

McKinzie, Ashleigh E. "Scared to Death: Reflections on Panic and Anxiety in the Field." *Symbolic Interaction* 40, no. 4 (2017): 483–97.

McLaughlin, Heather, Christopher Uggen, and Amy Blackstone. 2017. "The Economic and Career Effects of Sexual Harassment on Working Women." *Gender & Society* 31, no. 3 (2017): 333–58.

Milkman, Ruth. *Farewell to the Factory.* Berkeley: University of California Press, 1997.

———. "Redefining 'Women's Work': The Sexual Division of Labor in the Auto Industry during World War II." *Feminist Studies* 8 (1982): 337–72.

Mitchell-Walthour, Gladys L., and Elizabeth Hordge-Freeman, eds. *Race and the Politics of Knowledge Production: Diaspora and Black Transnational Scholarship in the United States and Brazil.* London: Palgrave Macmillan, 2016.

Mohanty, Chandra Talpade. "Under Western Eyes: Feminist Scholarship and Colonial Discourses." In *Third World Women and the Politics of Feminism,* edited by Chandra T. Mohanty, Ann Russo, and Lourdes Torres, 51–80. Bloomington: Indiana University Press, 1991.

Moore, Mignon R. "Women of Color in the Academy: Navigating Multiple Intersections and Multiple Hierarchies." *Social Problems* 64, no. 2 (2017): 200–205.

Moreno, Eva. "Rape in the Field: Reflections from a Survivor." In *Taboo: Sex, Identity and Erotic Subjectivity in Anthropological Fieldwork,* edited by Don Kulick and Margaret Willson, 166–89. New York: Routledge, 1995.

Morris, Aldon D. *The Scholar Denied: W. E. B. Du Bois and the Birth of Modern Sociology.* Berkeley: University of California Press, 2015.

Mugge, Liza M. 2013. "Sexually Harassed by Gatekeepers: Reflections on Fieldwork in Surinam and Turkey." *International Journal of Social Research Methodology* 16, no. 6 (2013): 541–46.

Naples, Nancy A. *Feminism and Method: Ethnography, Discourse Analysis, and Activist Research.* New York: Routledge, 2003.

Narayan, Uma. *Dislocating Cultures: Identities, Traditions, and Third World Feminism.* New York: Routledge, 1997.

Nelson, Ingrid L. "The Allure and Privileging of Danger over Everyday Practice in Field Research." *Area* 45, no. 4 (2013): 419–25.

Nelson, Robin G., Julienne N. Rutherford, Katie Hinde, and Kathryn B. H. Clancy. "Signaling Safety: Characterizing Fieldwork Experiences and Their Implications for Career Trajectories." *American Anthropologist* 119, no. 4 (2017): 710–22.

Newton, Esther. "My Best Informant's Dress: The Erotic Equation in Fieldwork." *Cultural Anthropology* 8, no. 1 (1993): 3–23.

Oakley, Ann. "Interviewing Women: A Contradiction in Terms." In *Doing Feminist Research,* edited by Helen Roberts, 30–62. New York: Routledge, 1981.

Orrico, Laura A. "'Doing Intimacy' in a Public Market: How the Gendered Experience of Ethnography Reveals Situated Social Dynamics." *Qualitative Research* 15, no. 4 (2015): 473–88.

Osburg, John. "Meeting the 'Godfather': Fieldwork and Ethnographic Seduction in a Chinese Nightclub." *PoLAR: Political and Legal Anthropology Review* 36, no. 2 (2013): 298–303.

Our Bodies Our Selves. "Rape and Sexual Assault." www.ourbodiesourselves.org /health-info/rape-and-sexual-assault/. Last modified October 15, 2011.

Pascoe, C. J. *Dude You're a Fag: Masculinity and Sexuality in High School.* Berkeley: University of California Press, 2011.

Paterson, Barbara, David Gregory, and Sally Thorne. 1999. "A Protocol for Researcher Safety." *Qualitative Health Research* 9, no. 2 (1999): 259–69.

Patil, Vrushali. "The Heterosexual Matrix as Imperial Effect." *Sociological Theory* 36, no. 1 (2018): 1–26.

Perrone, Dina. "Gender and Sexuality in the Field: A Female Ethnographer's Experience Researching Drug Use in Dance Clubs." *Substance Use and Misuse* 45, no. 5 (2010): 717–35.

Pollard, Amy. "Field of Screams: Difficulty and Ethnographic Fieldwork." *Anthropology Matters* 11, no. 2 (2009): 1–24.

Prokhovnik, Raia. *Rational Woman: A Feminist Critique of Dichotomy.* Manchester: Manchester University Press, 1999.

Punch, Maurice. 1994. "Politics and Ethics in Qualitative Research." In *Handbook of Qualitative Research,* edited by Norman K. Denzin and Yvonna S. Lincoln, 83–97. Thousand Oaks, CA: Sage, 1994.

Rabinow, Paul. 1977. *Reflections on Fieldwork in Morocco.* Berkeley: University of California Press, 1977.

Randles, Jennifer. "Pregnant Embodiment and Field Research." In *The Oxford Handbook of the Sociology of Bodies and Embodiment,* edited by Natalie Boero and Kate Mason. New York: Oxford University Press, 2018.

Reger, Jo. "Emotions, Objectivity, and Voice: An Analysis of a 'Failed' Participant Observation." *Women's Studies International Forum* 24, no. 5 (2001): 605–16.

Riger, Stephanie, and Margaret T. Gordon. "The Fear of Rape: A Study In Social Control." *Journal of Social Issues* 37 (1981): 71–92.

Riley, Denise. *Am I That Name? Feminism and the Category of "Women" in History.* New York: Springer, 1988.

Risman, Barbara. "Gender as a Social Structure: Theory Wrestling with Activism." *Gender & Society* 18, no. 4 (2004): 429–50.

Rios, Victor. "Beyond Power-Blind Ethnography." *Sociological Focus* 50, no. 1 (2017): 99–101.

———. "Comment on 'Contexts Editors on the Magazine's Ethnography Forum.'" Speak for Sociology (American Sociological Association blog). April 6, 2016. http://speak4sociology.org/2016/04/04/contexts-editors-on-the-magazines-ethnography-forum/.

———. *Human Targets: Schools, Police, and the Criminalization of Latino Youth.* Chicago: University of Chicago Press, 2017.

———. *Punished: Policing and the Lives of Black and Latino Boys.* New York: New York University Press, 2011.

Romero, Mary. "Reflections on 'The Department Is Very Male, Very White, Very Old, and Very Conservative': The Functioning of the Hidden Curriculum in Graduate Sociology Departments." *Social Problems* 64, no. 2 (2017): 212–18.

Salzinger, Leslie. *Genders in Production: Making Workers in Mexico's Global Factories.* Berkeley: University of California Press, 2003.

Sampson, Helen, and Michelle Thompson. "Risk and Responsibility." *Qualitative Research* 3, no. 2 (2003): 165–89.

Savonick, Danica, and Cathy Davidson. "Gender Bias in Academe: An Annotated Bibliography of Important Recent Studies." HASTAC.org, January 26, 2015, www.hastac.org/blogs/superadmin/2015/01/26/gender-bias-academe-annotated-bibliography-important-recent-studies.

Scheper-Hughes, Nancy. "Introduction: The Problem of Bias in Androcentric and Feminist Anthropology." *Women's Studies: An Interdisciplinary Journal* 10, no. 2 (1983): 109–16.

Schilt, Kristen, and Christine Williams. "Access Denied." *Men and Masculinities* 11, no. 2 (2008): 219–26.

Scott, Joan. "The Evidence of Experience." *Critical Inquiry* 17, no. 4 (1991): 773–97.

Sharma, Sonya, Sheryl Reimer-Kirkham, and Marie Cochrane. "Practicing the Awareness of Embodiment in Qualitative Health Research: Methodological Reflections." *Qualitative Health Research* 19, no. 11 (2009): 1642–50.

Sharp, Gwen, and Emily Kremer. "The Safety Dance: Confronting Harassment, Intimidation, and Violence in the Field." *Sociological Methodology* 36, no. 1 (2006): 317–27.

Siena, Kevin P. "Pollution, Promiscuity, and the Pox: English Venereology and the Early Modern Medical Discourse on Social and Sexual Danger." *Journal of the History of Sexuality* 8, no. 4 (1998): 553–74.

Singer, Stephanie. "I Spoke Up against My Harasser—And Paid a Steep Price." *Chronicle of Higher Education,* December 6, 2017, www-chronicle-com.lp.hscl .ufl.edu/article/I-Spoke-Up-Against-My-Harasser/241991.

Smith, Dorothy E. "An Analysis of Ideological Structures and How Women Are Excluded: Considerations for Academic Women." *Canadian Review of Sociology* 12, no. 4 (1975): 353–69.

———. *The Everyday World as Problematic: A Feminist Sociology.* Toronto: University of Toronto Press, 1987.

———. "A Sociology for Women." In *The Prism of Sex,* edited by Julia A. Sherman, 135–87. Madison: University of Wisconsin Press, 1979.

———. "Women's Perspective as a Radical Critique of Sociology." *Sociological Inquiry* 44, no. 1 (1974): 7–13. Reprinted in *The Feminist Standpoint Theory Reader: Intellectual and Political Controversies,* edited by Sandra Harding, 21–33. New York: Routledge, 2004.

Smith, Linda Tuhiwai. *Decolonizing Methodologies: Research and Indigenous Peoples.* London: Zed Books, 1999.

Sprague, Joey. *Feminist Methodologies for Critical Researchers: Bridging Differences.* New York: Rowman & Littlefield, 2016.

Stacey, Judith. "Can There Be a Feminist Ethnography?" *Women's Studies International Forum* 11 (1988): 21–27.

Stanko, Elizabeth. *Intimate Intrusions: Women's Experience of Male Violence.* London: Routledge, 1985.

Stanley, Liz, and Sue Wise. "Method, Methodology and Epistemology in Feminist Research Processes." In *Feminist Praxis,* edited by Liz Stanley, 20–60. London: Routledge, 1990.

Steedly, Mary. *Hanging without a Rope.* Princeton, NJ: Princeton University Press, 1993.

Stewart, Kathleen. *Ordinary Affects.* Durham, NC: Duke University Press, 2007.

Strauss, Anselm L., and Juliet M. Corbin. *Basics of Qualitative Research: Techniques and Procedures for Developing Grounded Theory.* Thousand Oaks, CA: Sage, 1998.

Sutton, Barbara. *Bodies in Crisis: Culture, Violence, and Women's Resistance in Neoliberal Argentina.* New Brunswick, NJ: Rutgers University Press, 2010.

Swartz, David. *Culture and Power: The Sociology of Pierre Bourdieu.* Chicago: University of Chicago Press, 2012.

Tewksbury, Richard, and Patricia Gagné. 1996. "Transgenderists: Products of Non-Normative Intersections of Sex, Gender, and Sexuality." *Journal of Men's Studies* 5, no. 2 (1996): 105–29.

Thiedon, Kimberly. "How Was Your Trip? Self-Care for Researchers Working and Writing On Violence." Working Paper No. 2, Drugs, Security, and Democracy Program, November 18, 2015, https://kimberlytheidon.com/2015/11/18/how-was-your-trip-self-care-for-researchers-working-and-writing-in-violence/.

Throsby, Karen, and Debra Gimlin. "Critiquing Thinness and Wanting to Be Thin." In *Secrecy and Silence in the Research Process: Feminist Reflections,* edited by Róisín Ryan-Flood and Rosalind Gill, 105–16. New York: Routledge, 2010.

Tinkler, Justine E., Sarah Becker, and Kristen A. Clayton. "Kind of Natural, Kind of Wrong: Young People's Beliefs about the Morality, Legality, and Normalcy of Sexual Aggression in Public Drinking Settings." *Law & Social Inquiry* 43, no. 1 (2018): 28–57.

Tolman, D. L. "Doing Desire: Adolescent Girls' Struggles for/with Sexuality." *Gender & Society* 8 (1994): 324–42.

Tshabangu, Icarbord. "The Challenge of Researching Violent Societies: Navigating Complexities in Ethnography." *Issues in Educational Research* 19, no. 2 (2009): 162–74.

Tuana, Nancy. Introduction to *Engendering Rationalities,* edited by Nancy Tuana and Sandra Morgen, 1–20. Albany: State University of New York Press, 2001.

Turner, Aaron. "Embodied Ethnography: Doing Culture." *Social Anthropology* 8, no. 1 (2000): 51–60.

Uggen, Christopher, and Amy Blackstone. "Sexual Harassment as a Gendered Expression of Power." *American Sociological Review* 69, no. 1 (2004): 64–92.

Valentine, Gill. "The Geography of Women's Fear." *Area* 21 (1989): 385–90.

Van Maanen, John. *Tales of the Field: On Writing Ethnography.* 2nd ed. Chicago: University of Chicago Press, 2011.

Wacquant, Loïc. "For a Sociology of Flesh and Blood." *Qualitative Sociology* 38, no. 1 (2015): 1–11.

Wade, Peter. "Sexuality and Masculinity in Fieldwork among Colombian Blacks." In *Gendered Fields: Women, Men and Ethnography,* edited by Diane Bell, Pat Caplan, and Wazir Jahan Karim, 199–214. New York: Routledge, 1993.

Walker, Linley. "Chivalrous Masculinity among Juvenile Offenders in Western Sydney: A New Perspective on Young Working Class Men and Crime." *Current Issues in Criminal Justice* 9, no. 3 (1998): 279–93.

Wang, Linda, and Andrea Widener. "Confronting Sexual Harassment in Chemistry." *Chemical and Engineering News* 95, no. 37 (2017): 28–37.

Ward, Jane. *Not Gay: Sex between Straight White Men.* New York: New York University Press, 2015.

Wedeen, Lisa. "Ethnography as Interpretive Enterprise." In *Political Ethnography: What Immersion Contributes to the Study of Power,* edited by Edward Schatz, 75–94. Cambridge: Cambridge University Press, 2009.

Welsh, Sandy, Jacquie Carr, Barbara MacQuarrie, and Audrey Huntley. "I'm Not Thinking of It as Sexual Harassment: Understanding Harassment across Race and Citizenship." *Gender & Society* 20, no. 1 (2006): 87–107.

West, Candace, and Don H. Zimmerman. "Doing Gender." *Gender & Society* 1, no. 2 (1987): 125–51.

Williams, Bianca C. "'Don't Ride the Bus!' and Other Warnings Women Anthropologists Are Given during Fieldwork." *Transforming Anthropology* 17, no. 2 (2009): 155–58.

———. "#MeToo: A Crescendo in the Discourse about Sexual Harassment, Fieldwork, and the Academy (Parts 1 & 2)." Savage Minds: Notes and Queries in Anthropology, October 18, 2017, https://savageminds.org/2017/10/28/metoo-a-crescendo-in-the-discourse-about-sexual-harassment-fieldwork-and-the-academy-part-1/; https://savageminds.org/2017/10/28/metoo-a-crescendo-in-the-discourse-about-sexual-harassment-fieldwork-and-the-academy-part-2/.

Williams, Christine L. "The Unintended Consequences of Feminist Legal Reform: Commentary on *The Sanitized Workplace.*" *Thomas Jefferson Law Review* 29 (2006): 101–10.

Williams, Christine L., Patti A. Giuffre, and Kirsten Dellinger. "Sexuality in the Workplace: Organizational Control, Sexual Harassment, and the Pursuit of Pleasure." *Annual Review of Sociology* 25, no. 1 (1999): 73–93.

Wolf, Diane L. *Feminist Dilemmas in Fieldwork.* Boulder, CO: Westview Press, 1996.

Wright II, Earl. "W. E. B. Du Bois and the Atlanta Sociological Laboratory." *Berkeley Journal of Sociology* (February 2016). http://berkeleyjournal.org/2016/02/w-e-b-du-bois-and-the-atlanta-sociological-laboratory/.

Wright II, Earl, and Thomas C. Calhoun. "Jim Crow Sociology: Toward an Understanding of the Origin and Principles of Black Sociology via the Atlanta Sociological Laboratory." *Sociological Focus* 39, no. 1 (2006): 1–18.

Yassour-Borochowitz, Dalit. "'Only If She Is Sexy': An Autoethnography of Female Researcher–Male Participants Relations." *Equality, Diversity & Inclusion* 31, no. 5–6 (2012): 402–17.

Zippel, Kathrin. *Women in Global Science: Advancing Academic Careers through International Collaboration.* Stanford, CA: Stanford University Press, 2017.

Zuberi, Tukufu, and Eduardo Bonilla-Silva. *White Logic, White Methods: Racism and Methodology.* Lanham, MD: Rowman & Littlefield, 2008.

INDEX

academic capital, 54, 137, 141

access, 9, 22, 28, 37, 39, 41, 43, 47, 50,
52–53, 58–78, 80–81, 83–84, 86–88,
91, 95, 97, 99, 100, 103–4, 113, 115,
117–21, 123, 126, 134, 139, 141, 142, 144,
147–50, 161–62, 166–67, 170–71, 177,
183–85, 191

adviser, 29, 31–32, 34, 37, 43, 48–49,
55, 83, 92–93, 99, 104, 106, 122,
129, 140, 157–58, 160–61, 163,
168–69, 179, 182, 184, 186. *See also*
mentors

androcentric, 4, 7–8, 16–17, 21–22, 26, 28,
35, 40, 42, 155–56, 180, 194

androcentrism, 40, 51

assault, 1, 13, 19–21, 23, 29, 32, 36, 38, 48,
55, 80, 92, 94, 98, 103–4, 107, 119, 121,
123, 125–27, 129–30, 132–33, 138, 141,
145, 151, 159, 160–61, 177, 180, 182,
191

awkward surplus, 2–3, 23, 52, 85, 94, 120,
154–55, 157–61, 165, 173, 192

boundaries, 6, 14, 39, 60, 77, 82, 115–17, 135,
157, 180, 184–85

Bourdieu, Pierre, 10, 41, 176

carnal ethnography, 35–36, 135

Chicago School, 7, 8, 43, 187

colonialism, 1, 4, 16, 17, 21, 83, 109, 132, 146,
155, 159, 178, 180, 182, 192–94; postcolonial, 8, 9, 12, 21

coping, 22, 36, 92, 110, 113, 115, 119, 123–25,
179. *See also* self-care

cultural context, 14, 62, 65, 73, 81, 108–9

danger, 2, 4–6, 17, 22–25, 28–29, 31–35,
37–39, 45, 49–50, 60, 75, 82, 91, 93–94,
99–100, 105–6, 110, 114, 118, 120–24,
130, 135–37, 143, 145–46, 151, 153–54, 157,
159, 161.62, 164–65, 167–69, 175–78,
180–81, 194

embodied ethnography, 3, 16–17, 21, 87, 163,
191–93

ethnographic fixations, 2, 4, 19, 22–23, 25, 28

feminine, 11, 35, 46–47, 59, 64, 138–39, 173

femininity, 7, 11, 55, 57–58, 60, 177

flirtation, 13, 19, 22, 23, 31, 38, 50, 53, 56, 59,
62, 67, 76–84, 86–87, 90, 92, 94–96,
107, 141, 155, 167

Foucault, Michel, 7, 16, 76, 197

Fujimura, Joan, 2, 23, 120, 154–55, 196

gender performance, 10, 11, 57, 66, 92

gender role, 39, 69, 73, 83, 181

Harding, Sandra, 8, 41, 154, 176

hegemonic masculinity, 2, 35, 37, 102, 162,
177–78

heteronormativity, 2, 28, 62, 112, 127, 143,
180

homophobia, 28, 37, 99–100, 114, 142, 146

intersectionality, 10, 12, 16, 28, 186, 188

intimacy, 2, 4, 22, 24–25, 28, 32, 35–39,
41–42, 60, 67, 75, 79, 84, 86–88, 91,
94–95, 98, 129, 135, 154, 158, 164, 175–76,
181–84

IRB, 18, 117, 128

masculine, 35, 37, 43, 67, 158, 162–63, 181

masculinity, 7, 11, 40, 64, 68, 72, 99, 114,
122–23, 167, 169

mentors, 2–4, 14–15, 24, 27, 29–30, 41–42,
45, 47, 50–51, 55, 57, 106, 120, 124,
127–30, 132, 134, 141, 143, 151, 153, 161,
172, 175–79, 186–87, 194

misogyny, 81, 99–101, 115, 124, 142, 147–48

objectification, 19, 68, 108, 126–27, 139–40,
148–49

objectivity, 7–9, 15–16, 26, 34, 38, 40–42,
46–47, 55, 156, 170

positivism, 4, 7–8, 15, 21–22, 25, 40–43,
46–47, 51, 155, 162, 194

preliminary research, 48, 98, 103, 106, 108,
121–22, 177, 179

racism, 16, 25, 27–28, 40, 43, 99–100, 104,
125, 133, 142–47, 155–56, 180, 188, 190,
192

rape, 13, 20, 23, 70, 92, 98, 103, 107–8, 119,
132–33, 147, 160, 167, 177

reflexivity, 3, 8–10, 17, 23, 41, 43–44, 76,
82–83, 88, 140, 155, 159, 163–64, 166,
170–71, 174, 176, 186–88, 190,
192–93

Rios, Victor, 27, 88, 164, 170, 176, 185–87,
192

self-blame, 23, 126, 128–31, 135–36, 150, 153

self-care, 106, 178–79

self-doubt, 126, 128, 134–36, 150

sexism, 1–2, 16, 37, 40, 99–101, 125, 147, 188,
192

sexualization, 13–15, 19, 21, 25–27, 34, 37, 41,
43, 46–47, 49, 51–52, 55, 63, 65, 67–69,
71, 76, 81, 86, 89, 92–93, 95, 99–100,
104, 107–8, 112–13, 115, 120, 124, 128, 135,
140, 143, 146–47, 150–51, 153, 158–62,
165, 173, 176, 180, 191–92

sexual abuse, 13, 124

sexual identity, 19, 72, 92, 139, 146, 187

sexual relationships, 84–86

sexual violence, 45, 64, 83, 98, 113, 135–37,
151, 168, 175

shame, 86, 120, 124–25, 128, 133, 135, 149,
179–80, 186

Smith, Dorothy, 5, 15–16, 25–28, 55, 57, 154,
157, 166

solitude, 2, 4, 22, 24–25, 28–32, 45, 94, 117,
135, 152, 154, 164, 175, 194

trust, 20, 22, 28, 33, 39, 53, 56, 63–64,
66–67, 70–72, 74–75, 84, 86–87, 91,
106, 108, 117, 130, 140, 147, 156, 165,
167–68, 184–85

validity, 4, 7–8, 15, 22, 24–25, 40–41,
46–47, 49–52, 56, 77, 80, 87, 94, 123,
162, 164–66, 169–70, 187, 191

venting journal, 3, 171

violence, 1–3, 14–15, 17, 36–38, 51, 53, 63, 67,
70, 74, 85, 93, 96, 107, 114–15, 117–18,
123–27, 134, 137, 167, 177–79, 182, 187–
88, 192–94

vocal silence, 27, 51–52

www.ingramcontent.com/pod-product-compliance
Lightning Source LLC
Chambersburg PA
CBHW020857270326
41928CB00006B/753